From Kosovo to Kabul and Beyond

From reviews of the first edition:

'Chandler makes an invaluable contribution in spelling out how the human rights activists have rationalised an abandonment of the rule of law and return to a system in which "might makes right". That the human rights rationale for interventionism is a genuine menace to human rights and to democracy is convincingly demonstrated in this fine book,' Edward S. Herman

'Chandler deftly unpicks the hypocrisy and double standards behind our "ethical" bombing in the Balkans and Asia.' Boyd Tonkin, *Independent*

'David Chandler has emerged in recent years as one of Britain's foremost critics of the hypocrisy of human rights.' John Laughland, *Spectator*

'This is an important and well-documented book, which should be on every list.' *The Political Quarterly*

'This outstanding book shows how British and US governments use the anti-democratic human rights ideology to boost their image and support foreign interventions. Chandler proves that attacks on states' sovereignty are also attacks on democracy.' *Morning Star*

'This is a thought provoking book, which fairly states an important question. It is for the reader to decide whether it gives the right answer.' *New World*

'Chandler has written a searing attack on the rhetoric and justification of the post-1989 "New World Order", the "humanitarian intervention", the "just war", and the international agency-based state-building that has characterised much of our foreign news coverage in the past decade ... there are a lot of assumptions questioned, and matters to ponder, in this important book.' *Green Socialist*

'This book is helpful for all readers interested in a critical and solid view of the debates on humanitarian action since the beginning of the 1990s.' *Political Studies Review*

'This is a compelling read, regardless of whether or not you share the author's worldview.' *Journal of Commonwealth Lawyers Association*

Also by David Chandler:

Bosnia: Faking Democracy After Dayton, Second edition
Constructing Global Civil Society: Morality and Power in International Relations
Rethinking Human Rights: Critical Approaches to International Politics (editor)
Peace Without Politics?: Ten Years of International State-Building in Bosnia (editor)
Global Civil Society: Contested Futures

From Kosovo to Kabul and Beyond

Human Rights and International Intervention

New Edition

David Chandler

Pluto  Press

LONDON • ANN ARBOR, MI

First published 2002 as
From Kosovo to Kabul: Human Rights and International Intervention
New edition published 2006 by Pluto Press
345 Archway Road, London N6 5AA
and 839 Greene Street, Ann Arbor, MI 48106

www.plutobooks.com

British Library Cataloguing in Publication Data
A catalogue record for this book is available from the British Library

ISBN 0 7453 2504 1 paperback

Library of Congress Cataloging in Publication Data applied for

10   9   8   7   6   5   4   3   2   1

Designed and produced for Pluto Press by
Chase Publishing Services Ltd, Fortescue, Sidmouth EX10 9QG, England
Typeset from disk by Stanford DTP Services, Northampton, England
Printed and bound in the European Union by
Antony Rowe, Chippenham and Eastbourne, England

Contents

List of Abbreviations

AFP	Agence France-Presse
CGG	Commission on Global Governance
CNRT	National Council for Timorese Resistance
ECHO	European Community Humanitarian Office
EU	European Union
ICC	International Criminal Court
ICFY	International Conference on the Former Yugoslavia
ICJ	International Court of Justice
ICRC	International Committee of the Red Cross
ICTY	International Criminal Tribunal for the former Yugoslavia
IICK	Independent International Commission on Kosovo
IMF	International Monetary Fund
MSF	Médecins sans Frontières
Nato	North Atlantic Treaty Organisation
NGO	non-governmental organisations
OSCE	Organisation for Security and Co-operation in Europe
RFE/RL	Radio Free Europe/Radio Liberty
RUF	Revolutionary United Front of Sierra Leone
UKFAC	United Kingdom House of Commons Foreign Affairs Committee
UKSCD	United Kingdom House of Commons Select Committee on Defence
UNAMIR	United Nations Assistance Mission for Rwanda
UNHCR	United Nations High Commissioner for Refugees
UNICEF	United Nations International Children's Emergency Fund
UNITAF	Unified Task Force
UNMIK	United Nations Mission in Kosovo

Acknowledgements

I would like to thank the Policy Research Institute, Leeds Metropolitan University, for the grant of a Post-Doctoral Research Fellowship which provided me with the time and resources to complete this work, and for the support of staff at the Institute, especially the assistance of the Information Officer, Ben Mitchell.

This work would not have been possible without the support of my wife Bonnie, and the final product would certainly have been a lesser one without the help of friends and associates who commented on drafts or shared work in progress, in particular Noam Chomsky, Edward Herman, Michael Savage, Philip Hammond, David Peterson, Mick Hume, John Laughland, Vanessa Pupavac, Alan Bullion, Jon Holbrook, Philip Cunliffe, Christopher Bickerton and James Heartfield. I would also like to express my gratitude for the support and assistance of Anne Beech and the editorial, production and marketing teams at Pluto Press. It goes without saying that the responsibility for the material and arguments presented in the following chapters is mine alone.

An earlier version of Chapter 2 was published under the title 'The Road to Military Humanitarianism: How the Human Rights NGOs Shaped a New Humanitarian Agenda' in the *Human Rights Quarterly*, Vol. 23, No. 3, 2001, pp. 678–700. An amended version of Chapter 3 was published as 'Rhetoric without Responsibility: The Attraction of "Ethical" Foreign Policy' in the *British Journal of Politics & International Relations*, Vol. 5, No. 3, 2003, pp. 295–316. A revised version of Chapter 4 was published under the title 'Universal Ethics and Elite Politics: The Limits of Normative Human Rights Theory' in the *International Journal of Human Rights*, Vol. 5, No. 4, 2001, pp. 72–89. Parts of Chapters 5 and 6 were published as 'International Justice' in the *New Left Review*, Vol. 2, No. 6, 2000, pp. 55–66. Parts of Chapters 6 and 7 appeared as 'The People-Centred Approach to Peace Operations: The New UN Agenda' in *International Peacekeeping*, Vol. 8, No. 1, 2001, pp. 1–19.

For my wife Bonnie, Harvey (known as bump at the time of the first edition), and his baby brother Oliver.

1   Introduction: 'The Idea of our Time'

Human rights is the idea of our time, the only political-moral idea that has received universal acceptance' – Louis Henkin, *The Age of Rights* (1990), p. ix.

The terrorist attacks on Manhattan and Washington on 11 September 2001 set in process a chain of responses that have made human rights intervention the leitmotif of a new ethical order in international affairs. The bombing of Afghanistan, launched on 7 October, was announced by President Bush to be an action of 'generosity of America and our allies' in the aid of the 'oppressed people of Afghanistan' (2001b). The US Defense Secretary, Donald Rumsfeld, argued that the military action was in line with previous US-led interventions in Kuwait, Northern Iraq, Somalia, Bosnia and Kosovo 'for the purpose of denying hostile regimes the opportunity to oppress their own people and other people', adding that: 'We stand with those Afghans who are being repressed by a regime that abuses the very people it purports to lead.' (2001)

Far from stressing US national interests in responding to an attack on its major symbols of economic and military dominance, the US establishment and the coalition of supporting states stressed the ethical and humanitarian nature of the military response, which included the dropping of food and medical provisions. On the first night of the military campaign a leading US senator noted on *Larry King Live*:

> This is the first time in contemporary military history where a military operation is being conducted against the government of a country, and simultaneously, with the troops carrying out the mission, other troops are trying to take care of the innocent victims who all too often are caught in harm's way. (Solomon, 2001)

As Senator Warner remarked, the dropping of humanitarian aid at the same time as cruise missiles marked a turning point in the presentation of international intervention. American military planners also firmly rejected the Powell doctrine of the use of overwhelming military force to carry out a clear and limited political objective. The assault on Afghanistan had no clearly limited political objective and no exit strategy (M.R. Gordon, 2001). Western leaders stressed that they were going to be committed for the long term and would secure a post-war 'government of stability' in the interests of the people of Afghanistan and the region (Wintour and White, 2001). For many commentators, the Bush Republican administration's response to the attacks in the United States symbolises the transformation of international politics since the Cold War, highlighting the consensus of support for a new ethical and morally-committed world order, established on the basis of protecting and promoting human rights.

Today, it would appear that the idea of human rights is universally accepted. Governments and international institutions claim human rights as one of the essential pillars of the international system, and they are proclaimed in the same breath as peace, democracy and the rule of law as a universal value of the highest order. But the concept of human rights is not merely accepted by policy-makers and governments, it is also seen to denote a radical and transformative approach to international society. The discourse of human rights appears to go beyond the liberal democratic framework and aspire to a broader normative project of human progress, which celebrates the universal nature of humanity. This radical aspiration is reflected through the development of a human-centred approach to global questions, putting the value of human dignity above the search for economic gain or the narrow interests of particular national governments. This approach is seen as a progressive development from the divisions of the Cold War period, in which geo-political competition between the West and the Soviet bloc led to the downplaying of questions of individual and group rights.

This chapter seeks to establish the radical attraction and claims of the human rights approach and briefly considers the transformations of the international order, since 1990, which substantiate the view that the discourse of human rights has shaped, and to a large extent transformed, the international sphere. The consensus in favour of the process of prioritising a human rights approach is highlighted as well as the limited nature of critical appraisals of this shift in international policy focus. Following this, there is a consideration of the reasons for this transition in international relations and the consequences of displacing previous mechanisms of international regulation. Finally, the framework of the material to be considered in the following chapters is set out.

ETHICAL ASPIRATIONS

The concept of human rights is seen by many commentators as establishing a radical framework for progressive change in international relations because it contains within it three powerful and interrelated ideas. First, there is the idea of universality, on the basis that in an increasingly globalised world promoting human rights concerns is in the interests of us all. Second, the idea of empowerment, because unlike politics, which is often seen to legitimise the power of a government or elected elite, human rights are seen to redress the balance and provide support for the claims of individuals, oppressed minorities or socially excluded groups. Third, the idea of a human-centred approach, based on ethics and morality rather than an adherence to grand political schemas connected to the politics of Left or Right.

The popular use of the concept of human rights has coincided with a growing belief that we are living in a global community, where our interests are closely connected to those of others who may not live in the same state or even on the same continent as us. As the British Prime Minister, Tony Blair, stated, after the terrorist attacks on the Twin Towers and the Pentagon:

> Round the world, September 11 is bringing governments and people to reflect, consider and change ... There is a coming together. The power of community is asserting itself. We are realising how fragile are our frontiers in the face of the world's new challenges. Today conflicts rarely stay within national boundaries. Today a tremor in one financial market is repeated in the markets of the world. Today confidence is global – either its presence or its absence ... [T]his interdependence defines the new world we live in. (2001b)

International responses to the attacks have highlighted the developments analysed in the report by the United Nations Commission on Global Governance (CGG), *Our Global Neighbourhood*, which suggested that international policy-making is increasingly posed in relation to global concerns of war, poverty, the rights of children, women and minorities, and the environment (CGG, 1995). The concept of universality, inherent in the human rights approach, reflects the shift in political focus towards global concerns and away from the constrictions of the territorially-bound nation-state.

Human rights are considered to be universal in two respects. First, and most importantly, because the subject of human rights is the universal citizen not the political citizen defined by the nation-state. The discourse of human rights 'inaugurates a new kind of citizenship, the citizenship of humanity' (Pieterse, 1997:72). For Michael Ignatieff, the lesson of 11 September was that in a globalised world, the global rich and powerful have a duty to assist the poor and disempowered, not just out of altruism but also self-interest. The events of 11 September, therefore, 'collapsed the justification for keeping national interests safe from infestation of talk of values' (2001). As Nicholas Wheeler writes: 'The notion of common humanity/human solidarity is diametrically opposed to the statist paradigm which is predicated on the contention that state leaders and citizens do not have moral responsibilities or obligations to aid those beyond their borders.' (1997:10) The prioritisation of universal concerns over the national is sustained by the claim that the globalised nature of central issues, from international terrorism and drug trafficking to ozone depletion and HIV/AIDS, means that we should be concerned with the needs of others no matter how far away they are or how different their lives.

Second, the idea of universality is a very powerful one because support for human rights is, in fact, universal. The Universal Declaration of Human Rights, adopted by the UN General Assembly in 1948, has been approved by virtually all governments representing all societies. As Louis Henkin states:

> Human rights are enshrined in the constitutions of virtually every one of today's 170 states – old states and new; religious, secular, and atheist; Western and Eastern; democratic, authoritarian, and totalitarian; market economy, socialist, and mixed; rich and poor, developed, developing, and less developed. (1990:ix)

This international acceptance of human rights supports the position that they do, in fact, constitute a moral community of humankind, not confined to any political system, democratic or not. Therefore commentators argue that, because human rights cannot be bound territorially or to any social system, in any hierarchy of rights, human rights are at the top and in this sense 'trump' all other claims (Evans, 1997:125).

The idea of empowerment has also been a very forceful focus for the human rights concept. Human rights are seen as a protection against inequality and the domination of the powerful over the weak. David Forsythe asserts: 'It cannot be stressed too much that … the idea of human rights is a defense against abuse of power everywhere.' (2000:219) As Mary Kaldor argues, 'many non-Western states are sources of stark oppression and denial of democracy' and the non-state orientated approach of the human rights movement can 'facilitate the representation of the weak and powerless in the non-West' (1999a:223). For Jack Donnelly: 'Human rights is the language of victims and the dispossessed.' (1998b:20) Helena Kennedy QC argues:

> The time has come to uncouple the law from the state and give people the sense that the law is theirs. Human rights are the privileged ground where we can bring the law back to the common conversation of humankind. (2000:xv)

The idea of human-centred rights putting people first, regardless of the sectional interests of big businesses or political parties, derives more from the spheres of morality and ethics than that of politics. For many commentators, the moral aspirations behind human rights claims gives them a legitimacy which cannot be gained merely through the institutional practices of state-based politics. In fact, some advocates would argue that campaigning on the basis of human rights is the opposite of a political approach, because it is about principles, not about making compromises, and about protecting minorities, as opposed to enforcing the power of majorities. Where politics is seen to be about the expression of self-interest and the competition of views, human rights is regarded as an expression of altruism and the collective values of a moral community, the articulation of 'an underlying moral consensus' (Kennedy, 2000:xiv). Putting people before profits and politics has been a powerful idea and is widely seen as a refreshingly positive view of human potential and human progress. In the view of Zbigniew Brzezinski, former US national security adviser, 'human rights is the single most magnetic political idea of the contemporary time' (cited in Forsythe, 2000:33). For the *New York Times*, the 'great flowering of the idea of universal human rights … is among the most important political legacies of this century' (1999). Mary Robinson, the UN High Commissioner for Human Rights, speaks for many in her belief 'that the growth in the human rights movement is one of the most hopeful, optimistic developments of our time' (1999).

CHANGE SINCE 1990

Since 1990, these aspirations appear to have been guiding the reshaping of the international order. World leaders, like former US president Bill Clinton and the UK Prime Minister, Tony Blair, greeted this shift away from the Cold War domination of political and ideological competition with enthusiasm. Bill Clinton claimed that under his administration the United States 'has made human rights a cornerstone of our foreign policy', while Tony Blair argues that the prioritisation of human rights has lead to 'a new internationalism based on values' (Apodaca and Stohl, 1999:186; Blair, 1999d). The development of a new ethical and moral foreign policy has also been welcomed by government critics in the media, by international relations academics on both sides of the Atlantic, and by leading non-governmental organisations (NGOs) campaigning on human rights issues, like Oxfam, Amnesty International and Human Rights Watch.

For many commentators, this shift in approach, already well underway before the events of 11 September 2001, reflects an adherence to the original aims of the UN, established at the end of the Second World War, to ensure that the international community would stand up to governments or political groupings who sought to oppress minorities or to deny the rights of their citizens. They assert that during the Cold War human rights were deprioritised, as the geo-political divide between the West and the Soviet bloc led to the ideologically-driven protection of brutal client regimes. With the end of superpower rivalry there appeared to be no reason why the international community could not once again focus collectively on the prevention of abuses by governments. This shift in approach to the international order, therefore, questioned the institutions and practices that had developed during the 50 years of the Cold War.

There is a general consensus today that the old basis of international policy-making and the institutions of its enforcement are outmoded and unwieldy. For example, the UN Security Council seems to be emasculated by its mechanisms which rely on political unanimity between its members, ensuring that the five big powers in 1945, the United States, Russia, the United Kingdom, France and China, have a veto on policy even today, which they are willing to manipulate for their own ends. Even more importantly, for many commentators, the UN appears to be held back by its antiquated historical focus on nation-states as the main actors in the international order. Leading human rights advocates regularly suggest that 'the [UN] Charter's bias towards sovereign independence is anachronistic when the real evils are civil war and state-sponsored terrorism' (G. Robertson, 1999:382).

The speed with which the Cold War framework has been brought into question and recast since 1990 is startling. Every international conference on human rights seems to break new ground, focusing on new issues which, it is agreed, should no longer be seen purely within the purview of the nation-state, advocating the establishment of new institutions to monitor rights concerns, or giving support to new mechanisms of policy enforcement. Similarly, every international crisis since the early 1990s has appeared to set key international precedents for the developing framework of human rights enforcement. International institutions, such as the UN, the Organisation for Security and Co-operation in Europe (OSCE) and Nato, were granted new powers and the old rules governing the relations between international institutions, nation-states and citizens have been adjusted to take human rights concerns into account. These changes will be briefly illustrated using the central interrelated ideas of the human rights concept, those of universality, empowerment and the human-centred approach.

Universality

Protections for the human rights of the 'global citizen' have been developed through the extension of 'universal justice'. The planned establishment of the International Criminal Court (ICC), *ad hoc* tribunals for war crimes in former Yugoslavia and Rwanda, and UN and Nato actions in Somalia, Bosnia, Kosovo and East Timor, in the 1990s, highlighted new developments in international law and the granting of new powers of intervention awarded to international institutions and states active in human rights promotion. The radical nature of this shift is demonstrated by the fact that the teachings of the civil rights leader Reverend Martin Luther King are today held up by the US State Department as a guide to international action. His declaration that 'injustice anywhere is a threat to justice everywhere' is used to confirm the moral and political need for an activist foreign policy in the interests of all (Wagenseil, 1999:13). The shift towards the universality of rights by the world's sole remaining superpower is evident in the US State Department's annual Country

Reports on Human Rights Practices. The first report, in 1977, ran to 137 pages, the last report of the twentieth century, the largest ever, covered 194 countries, totalling 6,000 pages (USDoS, 2000).

The prioritisation of human rights issues has transformed the language and institutional practices of international relations. International bodies, from the UN and Nato to the International Monetary Fund (IMF) and World Bank, whose mandates may seem to be unrelated to human rights, have integrated these concerns and acted on them in ways unthinkable ten years ago (Bradlow and Grossman, 1995). Today the language of human rights infiltrates every discussion on international themes. For example, discussions about economic development, in UN committees, take the form of human rights debates over the priority of 'economic or developmental rights' in relation to civil and political rights. As one experienced commentator remarks: 'Today, practically no state can afford not to participate in some form of human rights diplomacy.' (Müllerson, 1997:5) Even the states at the critical end of many human rights resolutions, such as Russia, China, Cuba, Syria and Libya, argue that they are upholding human rights principles and are supportive of international action on the issue. They in turn raise human rights criticisms of the United States and other Western states regarding responses to poverty, institutionalised racism, prison conditions and aggressive militarism (see, for example, UN, 1996; 1999b).

In the field of international human rights interventionism, the shift in policy practices has been institutionalised in an *ad hoc* manner through the UN Security Council, which, since 1990, has empowered itself to consider humanitarian emergencies as a threat to international peace and security (Weller, 1999a). In 1991, the Gulf War to defend Kuwait was followed by the international community's attempt to protect the human rights of the Kurds and Marsh Arabs through a 'safe haven' policy. With the UN Security Council's support, the US-led coalition established aerial exclusion zones in northern and southern Iraq, denying the government control over its own territory. Iraqi aircraft entering the zones, formally within Iraqi airspace, were considered hostile and shot down (Weller, 1999b:94–5). Iraqi sovereignty was also undermined by UN sanctions preventing Iraq from developing 'weapons of mass destruction' as well as from trading freely with other states. The international regulation of Iraq, in which sovereignty was subordinated to human rights concerns, was subsequently seen as a legal precedent for universal human rights-based intervention. This was acted upon the following year when the UN authorised unilateral United States intervention in Somalia to protect humanitarian food convoys. In Bosnia in 1993, the UN authorised a multilateral military intervention to protect humanitarian aid and, in 1995, a Nato force, in its first combat action since it was founded, was mandated to impose a peace settlement. The international military action against Yugoslavia over the Kosovo crisis in 1999 was widely greeted as the first international military intervention against a sovereign state for purely human rights purposes (Klug, 2000b:2). As Tony Blair asserted, this was a war fought 'not for territory but for values' (1999b).

As the role and remit of international institutions has been strengthened, international action under human rights mandates has been reactive as well as of a long-term nature. This was demonstrated with international institutions acquiring powers of long-term administration over Bosnia in the Dayton peace settlement. These administrative powers were later extended on an indefinite basis and, in 1999, the UN acquired formal powers of administrative regulation in Kosovo and East Timor. Through this process, the role of the UN Security Council has been fundamentally transformed from being a policeman of international security, concerned with the welfare of states, to a supranational 'government and administration body' supporting the human rights of citizens in complex political emergencies (Thurer, 1999).

Empowerment

The new focus on human rights has been held to have a radical and empowering impact. For many commentators the shift in policy perspectives is seen to represent the influence of grass-roots civil society movements on the international agenda. At the 1993 UN World Conference on Human Rights in Vienna, some 3,000 representatives of over 500 international NGOs attended, virtually outnumbering the representatives of states (K. Boyle, 1995). At the UN World Conference on Women's Rights in Beijing, in 1995, there were around 35,000 participants mainly from NGOs (Korey, 1999:166). Many human rights advocates have also suggested that the reason for this transition has been the influence of ordinary people, creating a 'people's politics' in which 'a campaigning mass movement is putting pressure on democratic governments to practise what they preach' (G. Robertson, 1999:115).

It is often argued that one of the main achievements of the human rights movement has been the new legal protections put in place to protect minorities from persecution or oppression. International justice was once more on the agenda, and 'a start was at last made to capitalise on the Nuremberg legacy', through The Hague and Arusha tribunals for war crimes in the early 1990s (G. Robertson, 1999:xv). For many commentators, the tribunals marked an important change in international relations, as 'the seeds of a new resistance to evil have been planted' (Urquhart, 2000). In September 1998, the Rwandan tribunal sentenced Jean Kambanda, former prime minister and head of the Rwandan government, to life imprisonment for crimes against humanity. This precedent was in turn used by the UK House of Lords which, in March 1999, ruled that General Pinochet had no sovereign immunity and could be extradited to be tried for crimes against humanity. This was the first time a former head of state had faced criminal proceedings for breaches of international law while in office, in a foreign court (Bianchi, 1999:255). A few months later, the indictment of a sitting head of state, Slobodan Milosevic, for crimes against humanity was greeted as confirmation that there had been 'a revolution in international law' (Moghalu, 1999).

Today, it appears that both international and national courts can indict presidents and elected leaders if they are held to have abused their citizens' human rights. The empowerment of the vulnerable individual or group against government repression is seen as a major transformation in power relations. International institutions and new treaty bodies now have the power to prevent or punish abuses which, during the Cold War, would have been protected by sovereign immunity. As Michael Ignatieff notes: 'Taken together, these changes amount to a revolution: they enfranchise the individual against the state for the first time in international law.' (2000b:201)

The Human-Centred Approach

The human rights approach to international policy-making has struck a chord with many commentators, academics and activists because of its radical rejection of the ideology and politics of the Cold War era. The focus on protecting individuals, rather than operating on the basis of the needs of governments, challenges the international framework developed since 1945. At the 1993 UN international conference in Vienna the UN Charter was widely construed to mean that human rights should take precedence over sovereignty. By the end of the 1990s, with UN protectorates established in Kosovo and East Timor and the indictment of Yugoslav President Slobodan Milosevic for war crimes, international relations were no longer seen to be dominated by the need for interstate consensus. Although human rights had been a concept of international agreements since the Second World War, before the 1990s the promise of concerted action on the issue had never been fulfilled. At its September 2000 Millennium Summit the UN confirmed the need for people-centred reforms of the institution and affirmed the rejection of its previous 'state-centred' framework (UN, 2000b). The change in approach on behalf of the international community has been greeted by human rights advocates as marking a new historical period for human rights: 'the age of enforcement' (G. Robertson, 1999:xvi).

This new consensus behind international policy shifts in the 1990s suggests that international activism in support of human rights is likely to shape the international political framework of the new century. For many commentators, this radical shift at the end of the 1990s meant that a century marked by world war and genocide ended on a positive and hopeful note. This optimism is based on the belief that international policy based on human rights can make the twenty-first century safer and more just than the preceding one. As Bernard Kouchner declared:

> Can we dream of a 21st Century where the horrors of the 20th will not be repeated? Where Auschwitz or the mass exterminations that took place in Cambodia under the Khmer Rouge, and later in Rwanda, and the killings in Kosovo, cannot happen again? The answer is a hopeful yes. (1999)

This optimism appeared to be fully justified in the international response to the World Trade Center and Pentagon attacks, where finally international society seemed willing to take on the 'moral responsibility' for tackling human rights abuses wherever they might occur (Blair, 2001b; Woollacott, 2001). This brave new world of human rights regulation has been hailed as an era of 'post-international politics' where states and fixed boundaries will no longer dictate whose rights will be protected and whose will not (James Rosenau, cited in Mills, 1997:289).

LIMITED CRITIQUE

The application of human rights aspirations, in the policy practice of NGOs, the foreign policy of states and regional institutions, from the European Union to Nato, and in the activities of the UN, has not been without its detractors. Commentators across the board, from academics to journalists, state officials and NGO practitioners, have raised a large body of criticism.

This criticism has originated largely within the human rights discourse itself. The policy-makers and institutional actors have been criticised for failing to act on behalf of human rights in some areas of the world, or when they have acted, have been criticised for being too slow to respond or for merely taking half measures. Much of this criticism has also been focused on the low level of institutional change in the international sphere, for example: the UN Security Council composition and power of veto; UN Charter restrictions on international intervention; the slow development of the International Criminal Court; the lack of institutional integration of NGOs in international decision-making; and the remaining outdated privileges of state sovereignty.

As Alex de Waal has noted, 'to date most sociological study of humanitarian action implicitly accepts the axioms of the humanitarian international'. Statements by human rights NGOs, states and international institutions acting in the name of human rights are often taken at face value as if the nobility of aim confers immunity from sociological analysis or political critique. Waal sums up the strength of consensus by analogy: 'It is as though the sociological study of the church were undertaken by committed Christians only: criticism would be solely within the context of advancing the faith itself.' (1997a:65)

No Questioning

Despite the rapid nature of the transformation of the language and powers of international institutions, there has been little critical consideration of this change. The radical challenge of human rights to the post-war international framework has been accepted in essence, with discussion focusing on the nature of the required institutional changes and the speed with which they are possible.

It is becoming increasingly clear that the human rights discourse is rewriting the international law books and policy-making procedures from the starting point of ethics and universal values, and in so doing, is challenging the previous frameworks of legal and political rights at both international and domestic levels. As Jack Donnelly notes, the discourse of human rights implicitly recognises 'a new kind of accountability' (2000:128). The shift away from forms of accountability linked to the nation-state opens up a series of theoretical and practical alternatives that did not appear possible during the Cold War period. Where the nation-state was previously seen to be solely responsible for the protection of the rights of its citizens, and state sovereignty upheld as the first principle of international society, today the global citizen is seen to require a more global or cosmopolitan political framework of rights protection. As the International Criminal Tribunal for the former Yugoslavia (ICTY), at The Hague, held in the *Tadić* case: '[it] would be a travesty of law and a betrayal of the universal need for justice, should the concept of State sovereignty be allowed to be raised successfully against human rights' (cited in Bianchi, 1999:261).

There has been little discussion of the new forms of international law, which would need to be developed and legitimised once the former political equality of sovereign states is replaced by a legal framework that prioritises individual rights in the international arena. Another area, which has received little discussion, is the impact of these changes on the domestic political framework of states, particularly those subject to international regulation, once the political framework is determined by the universal ethics of human rights priorities. Just as the recasting of international law assumes a different starting point, so do domestic forms of human rights-based regulation: 'Democracy and human rights have very different, and often competing, theoretical and moral foundations.' (Donnelly, 2000:154) The challenge of the human rights discourse to the existing framework of international law and political decision-making is clearly a fundamental one, yet the broader consequences seem rarely to be considered. Most critical discussion is focused on particular crisis situations, and the response made to them, and tends to assume that the wider long-term consequences of a shift to a human rights-orientated world must be entirely positive.

The lack of a critical consideration of the broader consequences of the prioritisation of the human rights framework may be because the arguments have already been played out and the old political framework consciously rejected. It may be that this was justified because of its failure to meet the new demands of universality, or inability to protect or empower minorities, or to provide a human-centred and progressive framework of social relations. Yet, a study of the academic literature on human rights seems to bear little evidence of such a conscious level of consideration. For many commentators, the human rights framework appears to be justified as a *fait accompli* because governments and international institutions have already accepted it. Richard Rorty, for example, argues that human rights are so well established that 'the question whether human beings really have the rights enumerated in the [1975 OSCE] Helsinki Declaration is not worth raising' (1993:116). Jerome Shestack puts the issue more forcefully, arguing that theoretical debate is now redundant because the arguments have 'been overtaken by the fact that human rights have become hegemonic and therefore essentially global by fiat' (1997:568).

For academic or intellectual investigation into this fundamental international change, it is perhaps even more concerning that many commentators argue that critical discussion of the human rights framework itself is unproductive and dangerous. Louis Henkin asserts that seeking theoretical or philosophical justifications for human rights claims would be 'disruptive and unhelpful' (cited in Mutua, 1996:629). Mary Midgley acknowledges that for academics there may be uncertainties about the central justification for human rights, but warns that academics should not take an approach that is 'predeterminedly destructive'. Instead, they should be positive about the 'mysterious' power of the human rights concept which has emerged as a result of the 'immense enlargement of our moral scene' (1999:160–1).

As Richard Rorty has observed, 'human rights culture' is now 'a fact of the world' (1993:115–34). Indeed, former US secretary of state Madeleine Albright proclaimed that 'the concept of human rights reflects the very principle of civilization itself' (cited in Wagenseil, 1999:4). Human rights are seen in many respects to be beyond debate. As the UN General Assembly President noted, in December 1998:

> The quest for the basis of human rights to which philosophers, jurists and politicians devoted their interest and concern in the past has ... lost its significance. We can affirm today that human rights, beyond the theoretical concepts that justify the sacred and inviolable character of human rights, must be recognized and protected simply because this is what all humankind believes and desires, and because this has been the express will of the international community as reflected in the Universal Declaration. (UN, 1998)

From Kosovo to Kabul

The strength of the international consensus on human rights was highlighted by the Kosovo war and the international responses, both to Nato claims during the war and to the revelations after the war, which revealed a very different picture of the nature of the conflict. For many human rights advocates, the Kosovo war marked the beginning of the new age of human rights enforcement. Tony Blair expressed a much wider perception that this was a war fought not for self-interest but 'over the values of civilisation' (1999c). Similarly, the intervention in Afghanistan was presented as a war over civilised values on behalf of the 'world community'. Despite the fact that the Nato bombing campaign over Kosovo, conducted from high altitude, resulted in many targeting errors, the general opinion at the time was that the war was likely to be remembered 'not for its military and political misjudgements, but as the first war waged for ethical principles alone' (G. Robertson, 1999:387).

During the Kosovo conflict, the human rights consensus seemed particularly powerful to those who sought to question the policies forwarded by the advocates of rights intervention. Kirsten Sellars noted that questioning the altruistic motives behind the Kosovo bombing campaign was regarded as 'heresy': 'The consensus rules that anything done in the name of human rights is right, and any criticism is not just wrong but tantamount to supporting murder, torture and rape.' (1999:11) The use of available facts to challenge the case for war, found relatively little support or media space in this climate of consensus. This was true whether the issue at hand was the manipulation of the Rambouillet talks by US officials, to cut short peace negotiations by demanding Nato freedom of manoeuvre across the entire Federal Republic of Yugoslavia; or the fabricated stories during the bombing campaign of alleged evidence of planned genocide and fake German Defence Ministry documentation of 'Operation Horseshoe' (UKFAC, 2000c:par. 65; par. 93). For critical factual coverage of the conflict many people turned to non-Western media sources, where strongly researched articles were published in many countries, including Russia, China, India, Greece, Egypt and Israel (Hammond and Herman, 2000). It seemed that the facts on the ground mattered less to the Western advocates of intervention than the principle that a stand must be made on the side of the human rights cause.

This would appear to be confirmed in the responses of commentators to the revelations, in the years since the Kosovo war, that the claims of mass slaughter or genocide of Kosovo Albanians, which were the media focus during the bombing campaign, were an exaggeration. In August 2000, the ICTY put the preliminary body count of Serbs and ethnic Albanians that died in the civil conflict at between 2,000 and 3,000, raising doubts over the alleged 'proportionality' of the Nato military response of 12,000 high-altitude bombing raids, including the use of cluster bombs and depleted uranium munitions over heavily populated areas and destruction of much of the civilian economy of the region (UKFAC, 2000c). The leading British liberal broadsheet, the *Guardian*, editorialised in response that, yes, Nato may have 'lied' about its bombing campaign, and yes, massacre claims may have been 'exaggerated' and 'manipulated': 'Yet the sum of all these criticisms does not change the central issue. Was intervention needed?' (2000d) What the *Guardian* sought to defend was that 'the principle of intervention was right' rather than the practice of it or its outcome. It appears that once the discussion of international relations revolves around 'principles' rather than 'practices' the existing consensus on human rights activism can all too easily sidestep factual criticism.

This confidence in the justice of the cause of the Nato bombers, and of the principle they were seen to be acting on, reflected a profound transformation in the perception of international priorities. In fact, the most common criticisms of the Nato campaign, from human rights activists, were that it should have been launched earlier or that it should have been extended (against US opposition) to send troops in on the ground and to the Nato occupation of Serbia itself. Back in 1990, few people would have imagined that, within the decade, the international human rights community would be advocating the military occupation of independent countries on human rights grounds, the establishment of long-term protectorates, or the bombing of major European cities on a humanitarian basis. The clamour of support for military activism in the cause of human rights highlighted that Kosovo would, indeed, set a precedent for action on 'ethical principles' in the future. This precedent was to be trumped in spades in October 2001 when the world's biggest military power carpet bombed one of the poorest regimes on earth, with the open intention of removing its government. To the accompaniment of columnists and government advisers welcoming 'the new age of empire', George Bush's Republican administration declared that it would go further than Bill Clinton's Democratic administration in its pursuit of 'nation-building' in the cause of aiding the Afghan people (Cooper, 2001; Ferguson, 2001; *Washington Post*, 2001).

The Kosovo war was a catalyst in the shift away from the interstate framework of international relations, established at the end of the Second World War. It demonstrated the capacity of the human rights discourse to challenge and erode the Cold War framework of international law. The Nato attack clearly breached two central provisions of the UN Charter: Article 2(4) that 'all members shall refrain ... from the threat or use of force against the integrity or political independence of any state'; and Article 2(7) which prohibits intervention in matters essentially within the domestic jurisdiction of any state, subject to Security Council action under Chapter VII. The right of self-defence was not applicable as no Nato country was threatened by instability within Kosovo, and the Security Council did not invoke Chapter VII. The 78-day bombing campaign against Yugoslavia was an assertion by Nato countries of a right to intervene and to wage war without UN Security Council approval on the 'higher' grounds of human rights protection. The US-led intervention against Afghanistan demonstrated the shift towards a unilateral right of intervention with the outright rejection of the subjection of US force to any limitations from the UN Security Council (Sciolino and Myers, 2001; MacAskill, 2001a). The framework established in the Kosovo conflict was regularly used to legitimise the war against Afghanistan. Western government officials made comparisons with the justness of the cause of the military action in Kosovo, comparing the Taliban to Slobodan Milosevic and portraying the bombing campaign as part of a necessary strategy for bringing humanitarian assistance to the people of the decimated region (Straw, 2001b; Webster, 2001b).

In challenging the post-war framework of the UN Charter system, the Kosovo war and action against Afghanistan have underlined some of the differences between the developing human rights framework and previously accepted mechanisms of international and domestic regulation. Both military actions have raised the issue of the (re)definition of humanitarian action, with the conflation of military action and humanitarian aid (considered in Chapter 2). The support for the bombing campaigns across the political spectrum brings up questions about the reasons for the policy shift away from defending national interests towards an ethical foreign policy based on defending ideas and values (considered in Chapter 3). The lack of criticism of the wars from international relations academics, including many of those based at departments of 'Peace Studies', also raises questions about the transformation of international relations theory and the growing acceptance of a normative or moral basis for political policy-making (Chapter 4). Debate in the field of international law over the legality of the bombings and the increased calls for extended international tribunals presents questions about the changing nature of international justice and its relationship to international law (Chapter 5). Both conflicts have also sustained a debate on the right of military intervention and highlighted the growing acceptance of war as a 'lesser evil' to address 'human wrongs' (Chapter 6). Some of the broader theoretical concerns generated by the retreat from the principle of state sovereignty, as well as the increasing role in international policy-making of *ad hoc* 'coalitions of the willing' and the new consensus in favour of intervention to replace 'hostile' governments with international administrations are considered in Chapter 7.

FRAMEWORK

In this book I do not intend to present a history of the human rights movement, or of the development of international institutional powers. Neither do I wish to focus too much on a legal discussion about interpretations and developments in international human rights and humanitarian law. This work deals with the political basis for, and the political consequences of, ethical foreign policy and the developing human rights framework of regulation. It develops an analysis of why the ethical agenda of human rights has become widely accepted since 1990 and indicates areas in which there appear to be limitations or at least important questions over the implications of this shift in approach. The chapters that follow take a critical and questioning approach to both the aspirations and the ideas of human rights campaigners as well as to their positive claims regarding the international institutional changes outlined at the start of this chapter.

These criticisms are not based on more traditional critiques of human rights-based international policies. It is not the aim of this work to uncover the double standards involved in 'ethical foreign policy'. The economic and geo-strategic motivations, and limitations, behind decisions of whether, and how, to penalise selective human rights abuses have been discussed by many commentators who accept that ethical policy aims are inevitably blunted by *realpolitik* concerns of powerful nation-states (see, for example, Forsythe,

2000). Neither are the following chapters concerned with developing what could be categorised as an archetypal Left or 'anti-imperialist' critique of declarations of concern for human rights as a cynical cover for government intervention with the aim of economic exploitation of a particular region or as part of an inter-imperialist competition for power with other major states (for example, Chomsky, 1998; 1999).

This book attempts to develop a critique of human rights regulation that relies neither on the imputation of any 'hidden agenda' of Great Power motivations, nor on the bungled conduct or problematic outcome of particular 'humanitarian' interventions. A consideration of the broader political consequences of the theory and practice of the human rights discourse demonstrates the necessity for a more critical approach; one that can expose the elitist assumptions behind the human rights 'movement' and reassert the contemporary relevance of the universal values of political equality and democracy.

The first two chapters seek to establish the background to current debates on international policy-making. This chapter has outlined some of the claims of human rights advocates and has indicated the depth of the international consensus in the name of the human rights cause. Chapter 2 charts the development of the human rights discourse prior to 1990 and considers the shift in focus of the work of humanitarian NGOs and UN bodies through the extension and institutionalisation of long-term Western assistance in conflict resolution and development. It analyses the reworking of humanitarian ideas through the human rights discourse and emphasises how the shift from needs-based to rights-based aid provision has paved the way for today's conception of 'humanitarian militarism'.

The next two chapters attempt to establish an alternative framework for understanding the human rights discourse. Chapter 3 considers the shift in government and international institutional approaches towards ethical foreign policy, which prioritises human rights concerns. It examines why this shift occurred in the 1990s, and why the transformation of priorities has been so rapid. It also analyses whether governments have been pressurised to pursue these issues or whether ethical policy appeals directly to government interests. The chapter goes on to raise questions over the accountability of ethical policy-making. Chapter 4 considers the changing nature of international relations theory and the focus on normative analysis. This chapter looks at the differences in approach to rights and the human subject between the human rights discourse and classical liberal democratic theory, drawing out the consequences of these differences for new forms of international regulation supported by campaigning human rights advocates.

Chapters 5 and 6 analyse the impact of the human rights discourse at the international level, focusing on the challenge to the UN interstate framework and its priorities. Chapter 5 considers the development of international justice and the changing nature of international law. It establishes the historical context in which state sovereignty and the rights of sovereign equality were grounded and highlights the importance of the human rights critique of state sovereignty, considering the implications of this for weaker states. The human rights advocates' claims that the shifting international framework is an extension of international law are critically considered against concerns that the era of international law as the final arbiter of interstate relations may have passed. Chapter 6 extends the foregoing analysis to a consideration of the restrictions on the right of states to go to war. It looks at the arguments put against the UN framework of non-intervention and considers why world peace is no longer given such a high priority by human rights campaigners. The chapter also considers the potential for conflict between the goals of peace and of human rights promotion and the impact of UN peacekeeping reforms, which pursue the people-centred human rights approach.

The final two chapters turn to the wider political consequences of accepting the human rights framework. Chapter 7 considers the impact of the human rights critique of the political sphere, and the concept of political equality in particular, on relationships between major powers and non-Western states, at the level of interstate relations more generally and within the domestic political sphere in the West. Chapter 8 concludes the work, drawing out the political consequences of the human rights discourse from its initial starting assumptions about human potential and capacity for progress.

2   Human Rights-Based 'Humanitarianism'

There are those who say that we should halt the bombing to allow more food convoys in. I understand the concerns that lie behind these calls. But a pause in the bombing would only prolong the suffering of the Afghan people. The only things that can help the Afghan people are an end to the civil war, an end to this kind of regime and the start of reconstruction. – British Foreign Secretary, Jack Straw, 22 October 2001.

The human rights-based humanitarianism of the twenty-first century is very different in both content and form from the practice and principles of the nineteenth-century founders of the modern humanitarian movement. Until the 1980s the international promotion of human rights issues and the call for a more active humanitarian policy was a marginal cause of aid and campaigning NGOs such as Amnesty, Save the Children, Christian Aid and Oxfam (Armstrong, 1986). For the Left, the non-political stance of these groups, formally neutral in the struggle to liberate the developing world from Western imperialism, was condemned as predominantly conservative. For the Right, the neutral position of humanitarians was equally galling as NGO campaigns highlighted questions of Western economic domination and support for repressive regimes during the Cold War. Since the end of the Cold War, leading Western governments and political parties of both the Left and the Right have declared their support for human rights-led foreign policy activism and the profile and influence of campaigning humanitarian and human rights NGOs has been transformed.

The transformation of humanitarianism from the margins to the centre of the international policy agenda has been achieved through the reinterpretation of humanitarian policy and practice and its integration within the fast-growing agenda of human rights. The new international discourse of human rights activism no longer separates the spheres of strategic state and international aid from humanitarianism, but attempts to integrate the two under the rubric of 'ethical' or 'moral' foreign policy. As the humanitarian NGOs have been integrated into policy-making forums, the policy-makers have increasingly claimed to be guided by humanitarian principles. Today, there is a uniting of international institutions and NGOs in terms of both assumptions and staff. Commentators, like Alex de Waal, have noted the ease with which staff have crossed over between NGOs and international institutions and the 'marked convergence towards a common culture' (1997a:65).

The human rights NGOs, in conjunction with leading foreign policy strategists, have established a rights-based humanitarian consensus, the 'new humanitarianism', which has succeeded in redefining humanitarian policy. The universal principles, which defined the early humanitarian internationalists, are now widely criticised by their NGO successors as the language of universal humanitarianism has been reworked to pursue human rights ends. Today's humanitarians are concerned with long-term human rights outcomes rather than short-term humanitarian necessity. This transformation has led to the displacement of neutral humanitarian aid by more interventionist economic, political and military strategies of humanitarian assistance devoted to long-term strategic objectives. The 'new humanitarians' assert that their ambitious strategic ends inevitably clash with their earlier principles, which developed in an age when it was necessary to obtain consent from the states in which they operated and when the opportunities for more long-term involvement were limited (Duffield, 2001:31). Today, not only is this more interventionist approach seen as a legitimate response to the complex problems of aid provision, it is predominantly understood to be non-political and ethically guided.

This chapter is concerned with the process through which the core ethics of humanitarianism have been transformed, and an analysis of some of the consequences of this change. This chapter is not concerned with NGOs *per se*; it does not attempt to present a history of the rise of the humanitarian NGO movement, nor of the growing integration of non-governmental organisations into the policy-making and implementation of the major international institutions, such as the UN, OSCE and World Bank. The intended focus is the shift in the politics of humanitarian interventionism as advocated by non-governmental organisations during and after the Cold War. The following sections consider the non-political approach of traditional non-state humanitarian organisations and chart the development of more rights-based humanitarian NGOs, which have facilitated the mainstreaming of rights-interventionist policies. The chapter concludes by looking at how human rights-based humanitarian intervention has led to more coercive forms of 'humanitarian aid' and the growing acceptance of 'humanitarian militarism'.

HUMANITARIAN UNIVERSALISM

The traditional humanitarian values were seen as separate and distinct from the world of policy-making, peace and war. Beyond the conflicts of politics, humanitarian intervention sought to emphasise the universal nature of humanity, striving to reduce human suffering through famine relief, medical aid, the protection of prisoners of war, and so forth. These concerns, and the interventions motivated by them, were conceived as operating outside the sphere of politics. Humanitarian action strove to avoid interference with state-level geo-political competition as well as domestic political issues. Humanitarians were concerned neither with the rights or wrongs of national liberation, nor issues of economic redistribution, justice or democracy: this was the stuff of politics, not humanitarianism. Their sphere of involvement was focused on the protection of a basic level of human dignity in times of war or natural disaster.

The organisation that over the last century has most epitomised the values of humanitarian universalism has been the International Committee of the Red Cross (ICRC). The Red Cross movement was founded by Jean-Henri Dunant after witnessing the slaughter at Solferino in 1859 when the battle between France and Austria claimed 6,000 lives in one day with little concern for the sick and wounded. In 1864, sixteen governments met in Geneva, twelve of which signed the Geneva Convention, for wartime access to battle zones for neutral field hospitals, ambulances and medical staff. In 1901, Dunant won the first Nobel Peace Prize. By the First World War, the ICRC had become the largest humanitarian organisation in the world, responsible for monitoring the Geneva Convention, which codified the laws of war and the ground rules for the treatment of prisoners. The ICRC was not established as a pacifist or anti-war body, it made no claims to be able to solve humanity's problems, merely to reduce some of the suffering.

In 1965 the ICRC codified its work according to seven fundamental principles of humanitarian action: humanity, impartiality, neutrality, independence, voluntary service, unity and universality. Independence, voluntary service and unity relate to the inner integrity of the movement itself. Humanity, impartiality, neutrality and universality were held to be the underlying principles of any humanitarian intervention. The principle of humanity was based on the desire to assist the wounded and suffering without discrimination, recognising a common humanity and that 'our enemies are men'. The principle of impartiality was based on the desire to assist without discrimination except on the basis of needs, giving priority to the most urgent cases of distress. The principle of neutrality bound ICRC workers from taking sides in conflict or engaging in political or social controversies. The principle of universality claimed that the ICRC approach was the same the world over on the basis that the humanitarian values were shared universally. The principles of humanity, neutrality, impartiality and universality were predicated on separating the humanitarian from the political (Warner, 1999).

The avoidance of politics was essential to the definition of humanitarianism. Cornelio Sommaruga, as President of the ICRC, in his speech to the UN General Assembly in November 1992, made this clear: 'Humanitarian endeavour and political action must go their separate ways if the neutrality and impartiality of humanitarian work are not to be jeopardised.' (Cited in Warner, 1999) Jean Pictet, one of the ICRC's leading thinkers, warned that 'Red Cross institutions must beware of politics as they would of poison, for it threatens their very lives' (cited in Minear, 1999). As Michael Ignatieff notes, humanitarianism was at the core of the ICRC's non-political outlook: 'It made no distinction between good wars and bad, between just and unjust causes, or even between aggressors and innocents.' (1998:119)

Amnesty International, founded in 1961 with the aim of working for the release of 'prisoners of conscience', similarly pursued a universal campaign for the rights of political prisoners, regardless of whether they were persecuted by US- or Soviet-backed regimes. The politics of the prisoners were irrelevant, what mattered was that they were held captive for their religious, political or other consciously held beliefs or by reason of their ethnicity, gender or language. As well as working for the release of political prisoners, Amnesty also campaigned against capital punishment and the use of torture or inhuman punishment in all cases, not just for political prisoners. Amnesty was not concerned with the rights or wrongs of the politics or beliefs of the prisoners but with all prisoners receiving a minimum of universal standards of treatment.

The UN also established institutions solely for the purpose of humanitarian aid, such as the UN Relief and Rehabilitation Administration 1943–47, the UN International Children's Emergency Fund (UNICEF) in 1946 and the UN High Commissioner for Refugees (UNHCR) in 1950. The mandates of these institutions were explicitly humanitarian, not political. Private charity organisations were also involved in famine relief, many having been founded in response to the First and Second World Wars. Save the Children was established in the aftermath of the First World War. Oxfam was founded in 1942, initially as the Oxford Committee for Famine Relief, providing relief for the famine victims in German-occupied Greece where the Allied blockade had cut the country from its peacetime food supplies. This universal approach was a direct challenge to the British government policy of blockade, and the Oxford Committee was prevented from sending aid until 1943. These relief aid charities, like the ICRC, saw themselves as filling the gaps in humanitarian provision that temporarily, in the aftermath of war, could not be met through the political system. By the end of the 1940s the major relief charities established themselves in a more permanent role, addressing not only wartime distress but also international suffering in the developing world.

During the Cold War, the work of relief charities achieved a high profile precisely because of their universalist approach and political neutrality. They played an important role in providing aid where the international geo-political divide meant that leading Western states were not willing to assist those in need. The Biafra crisis in 1968 was one of the first examples of humanitarian aid NGOs mobilising in the face of British and international disapproval. In the 1970s, NGO relief intervention was repeated in Bangladesh, Ethiopia, the West African Sahel and Cambodia after the defeat of the Khmer Rouge government. In all these cases the NGOs campaigned against the lack of official institutional intervention. While the major powers pursued the *realpolitik* of the Cold War, humanitarian non-governmental organisations showed up the gaps in humanitarian provision. Cambodia was an example of this. With the refusal of Western powers to recognise the post-Khmer Rouge government and the absence of aid from international institutions, NGOs were able to play a dominant role. Their non-governmental nature meant that they could function despite political pressure. As Ben Whittaker notes, these cases demonstrated that Oxfam and other NGOs could 'operate where huge governments and international bodies were stymied as politically hamstrung' (1983:11).

This position gave humanitarian NGOs a radical edge, putting the interests of people above the strategic concerns of the East/West divide and providing aid against the wishes of Western governments. Agencies such as Oxfam, Impact, Concern and Save the Children became popularly identified with the cause of the developing world, providing these previously staid organisations with a new, more youthful and popular appeal. The high point of NGO humanitarianism came with the Live Aid campaign to raise funds for the Ethiopian famine of 1984–85. The aid agencies, in collaboration with Bob Geldof's Live Aid, were instrumental in defying the indifference of Western governments and launched a hugely popular relief campaign (Searls, 1995). Most importantly, relief aid was avowedly non-political, there were no strings attached. Relief NGOs did not seek to link aid to specific Western states or to dictate economic or social policy. Humanitarian relief was assumed to be given free of political conditions or association with foreign or defence policy, delivered purely on the basis of need. As Bruce Nicholls summarised: 'the two principles of nondiscrimination and political neutrality pervade both Geneva Law and the public face of modern humanitarianism. Without them, humanitarian practice would be indistinguishable from partisan political activity.' (1987:195)

For most of the Cold War period the division between state-led development aid, open to political considerations, and politically-neutral humanitarianism was clear and transparent. Particularly in the 1960s and 1970s, the problems of war and famine in the non-Western world were predominantly seen in the context of Western domination and Cold War clientelism. The existence of broad social and political movements based on solidarity with the developing world or critiques of Western market domination meant that the problems were seen in a broader international context. It was this wider focus on the relationships of power and dependency that meant that the potentially patronising aspects of charitable aid were contained and, at least publicly, there was little support for blaming or condemning recipients of aid or the non-Western governments facing a humanitarian crisis.

BEYOND HUMANITARIANISM

The key attribute that clearly demarcates today's rights-based humanitarianism from non-political humanitarian action is the end of the strict separation between strategic ends-based state assistance, which was often highly selective and conditional on certain economic and political policy choices, and needs-based NGO humanitarian activism, which was based on unconditional need. The conflation of these two approaches has become possible because, on one hand, the NGOs have either called for the politicisation of aid or been complicit in its politicisation, while, on the other hand, governments have sought to justify strategic policy-making through the ethical discourse of humanitarianism. The politicisation of aid reflects the more interventionist nature of external assistance to non-Western states, however the consensus of support for these more invasive approaches has enabled them to be presented increasingly within a traditional humanitarian context. The roots of today's human rights-based humanitarianism lie in the growing consensus of support for Western involvement in the internal affairs of the developing world since the 1970s.

There are two strands to the 'new humanitarian' interventionism that predate the post-Cold War consensus. Both these strands have sought to move beyond the traditional non-strategic humanitarian aims of saving human lives and reducing human suffering. The gradual build-up of pressure to aspire to achieve longer-term policy ends has reflected the changing perceptions of the NGO role in international situations and the increasing support for a more extensive rights-orientated involvement. The first strand, developed in response to conflict situations, was the extension of involvement from the provision of immediate assistance to victims of conflict to the greater commitment of solidarity and advocacy work for victims and concerns for the long-term protection of human rights for 'at risk' groups. The second strand, developed in response to problems of famine and drought, was the move of relief NGOs from emergency humanitarian aid to long-term development in the 1970s.

Until the early 1990s, the ICRC had a monopoly on the definition and elaboration of humanitarian principles (Leader, 1998:295). Since then there has been a proliferation of doctrinal changes, led by pressure from NGOs and institutional funders. For example, the 1993 Providence Principles, the 1993 Mohonk Criteria, and the 1994 Red Cross/NGO Code of Conduct. The pressure from the NGOs who argue for a more 'solidarity'-orientated intervention and those who are involved in development has been marked. Nicholas Leader, from the Overseas Development Institute, categorises these two challenges to the ICRC's principles as 'deepening' and 'broadening' the conception of humanitarianism. The NGOs who want a more committed 'solidarity' form of intervention in conflict situations have emphasised the need for protection or security as well as assistance. The developmental NGOs have argued that humanitarian intervention should also include longer-term assistance such as peacebuilding, capacity-building, empowerment and development as reflected, for example, in the Mohonk Criteria (WCC, 1993).

However, once the 'new humanitarian' NGOs focused on solidarity or long-term development it became necessary to make strategic choices regarding which aims to prioritise and which groups to work with. The desire to politicise involvement in aid provision without sacrificing their neutral and 'non-political' status led NGOs to seek to justify their strategic choices through the language of morals and ethics rather than politics. It was this conflict between evolving policy practice and the traditional humanitarian basis for involvement that laid the basis for the human rights discourse of today (see Table 1). The humanitarian NGOs were the first inter-national organisations who sought to use the terminology of human rights in an attempt to justify political policy choices in the language of ethics:

The ethical basis for making choices about solidarity and peace building is often a far more complex and political decision as it

Table 1: The operating principles of needs-based and rights-based humanitarianism

Operating Principles	Needs-based Humanitarianism	Rights-based Humanitarianism
Engagement with political authorities	Eschew political confrontation	Advocate controversial public policy
Neutrality	Avoid taking sides	Take the side of selected victims
Impartiality	Deliver aid using proportionality and non-discrimination	Skew the balance of resource allocation
Consent	Pursue as *sine qua non*	Override sovereignty as necessary

Source: Adapted from Thomas Weiss, 'Principles, Politics and Humanitarian Action', *Ethics and International Affairs* (1999), Vol. 13, p. 4.

implies decisions about rightness and just causes ... Although in some conflicts the 'just cause' is clear, in most this is not the case. If the principle of impartiality is rejected, who is to judge which is which? This is sometimes termed a shift from a needs-based to a rights-based humanitarianism. In many ways the deeper notion of humanitarianism that includes both protection and assistance is a rights-based humanitarianism. (Leader, 1998:298)

Deepening Humanitarianism

The birth of the modern human rights-based 'solidarity' movement has often been located in NGO responses to the Biafran famine in 1968 (Waal, 1997a; Weiss, 1999:3). The famine resulted from the independence war fought by Igbo secessionists of the state of Biafra in south-eastern Nigeria against the federal government. The secessionist struggle received no diplomatic support from the West, the Soviet bloc or other African states, which were concerned over the destabilising effects of questioning state borders. Within a few months the dominance of the government forces and the lack of outside aid had doomed the struggle to failure. As Alex de Waal notes, it was only by accident that Biafra became a *cause célèbre* for the human rights movement. The international attention stemmed from the famine becoming news through the publication of photographs of severely malnourished children. As Frederick Forsyth, at that time a journalist, recalled:

Quite suddenly, we'd touched a nerve. Nobody in this country at that time had ever seen children looking like that. The last time the Brits had seen anything like that must have been the Belsen pictures ... People who couldn't fathom the political complexities of the war could easily grasp the wrong in a picture of a child dying of starvation. (Cited in Waal, 1997a:74)

The media coverage of the first African famine to become headline news led to accusations that the British government's arms shipments to the Nigerian leadership and lack of support for the Biafrans was making it complicit in genocide by starvation. The lack of UN or outside government relief for the secessionists enabled the humanitarian aid effort to be monopolised, for the first time, by the NGOs. Biafra was the ICRC's first large-scale relief operation and Oxfam's second field operation. The first real test for non-governmental humanitarian organisations resulted in a split between the

Red Cross and major NGOs over the nature of humanitarian action. Oxfam broke its commitment not to act unilaterally and took an openly partisan approach claiming that 'the price of a united Nigeria is likely to be millions of lives' (cited in Waal, 1997a:75). Several international NGOs followed, arguing that breaking from the ICRC position of non-criticism was the only ethical way of assisting the population because if the Biafran people lost the struggle for secession they would face systematic massacre by federal forces.

The NGOs and the church-funded campaigns became the main propagandists and source of international support for the Biafran struggle. The Joint Church Airlift supplied aid and attempted to establish a Biafran air force, against Nigerian government opposition. This led to a federal ban on outside aid flights. The ICRC did not engage in any publicity and accepted the federal government's ban on aid flights. This position was condemned by the more interventionist and partisan aid NGOs. A leading critic was French doctor Bernard Kouchner, who declared that their silence over Biafra made its workers 'accomplices in the systematic massacre of a population' (cited in Waal, 1997a:76).

The Biafran war was not only notable for the creation of the new committed and increasingly invasive ethics of human rights intervention. It also set a much more worrying marker for the future of 'new humanitarian' rights-based interventionism. The war was already over when the famine became news, and the international interest was immediately used to rekindle the struggle. Speaking later, Paddy Davies of the Biafran Propaganda Secretariat explained:

> Biafra realised that this was an angle they could play on. It had tried the political emancipation of oppressed people, it had tried the religious angle ... but the pictures of starving children and women, dying children ... touched everybody, it cut across the range of people's beliefs. (Cited in Waal, 1997a:74)

For the Biafran government, the provision of aid was secondary to the propaganda and international standing gained from the aid agencies siding with the war aims of the secessionists. Internationalising the struggle put pressure on the Nigerian regime and enabled the Biafran leadership to prolong the war. The aid agencies took on trust the claims of the Biafran government, and its public relations firm Markpress, regarding genocide and 'thousands dying daily' and according to Oxfam's official history 'they fell for it, hook, line and sinker' (cited in Waal, 1997a:75). The secessionist line forwarded by Kouchner and other agencies, that the Biafran people would be faced with systematic massacre by federal troops if they lost the war, turned out to be unsubstantiated. In fact, de Waal notes that even as the international relief operation was being massively expanded there was already a large amount of evidence that there would be no genocide. In the large areas of Biafran territory taken over by the federal government there had been no government massacres (1997a:76–7).

In 1971 Bernard Kouchner established Médecins sans Frontières (MSF), which has since symbolised the 'new humanitarian' cause. There are two 'solidarity' principles, which were developed out of the Biafra experience and have since become central to the new rights-based humanitarianism. First, the 'freedom of criticism' or 'denunciation'. As James Orbinski stated, on accepting the 1999 Nobel Peace Prize on behalf of MSF:

> Silence has long been confused with neutrality, and has been presented as a necessary condition for humanitarian action. From its beginning, MSF was created in opposition to this assumption. We are not sure that words can always save lives, but we know that silence can certainly kill. Over our 28 years we have been – and are today – firmly and irrevocably committed to this ethic of refusal. (1999)

Second, the 'subsidiarity of sovereignty' or the 'right of intervention', the 'sans frontières' of the MSF movement. Many commentators have cited MSF founder and future UN governor of Kosovo, Bernard Kouchner, as the humanitarian official responsible for popularising the legal theory of French academic Mario Bettati, who developed the concept of the 'right of intervention' (Rieff, 1999a:184; Pugh, 1998:341).

Both these 'new humanitarian' principles challenge the ICRC work which depended on the consent of the parties in the area in which it worked. This more interventionist approach of 'solidarity' has received wide support, particularly since the end of the Cold War. As George Foulkes states: 'Humanitarianism ... demands that we stand firmly alongside those striving against oppression, and assist their struggle for dignity and basic human rights.' (Cited in Leader, 1998:297) However, the NGOs which choose to engage in advocacy and solidarity are of necessity eroding the principles of needs-based humanitarianism by subordinating needs to the strategic ends of human rights and the struggle against oppressive developing world governments (Pugh, 1998:340).

Broadening Humanitarianism

The 1970s and 1980s saw the direct government funding of NGOs like Oxfam, Christian Aid and the Catholic Fund for Overseas Development, the integration of international humanitarian NGOs in international institutions and their growth in numbers and influence. International NGOs were increasingly relied upon to administer government and institutional relief funds in disaster situations in the 1980s. By the mid-1980s 70 per cent of UK aid to Sudan and 50 per cent of British relief to Ethiopia was managed through NGOs (Searls, 1995). As they received wider recognition and took on greater responsibilities towards aiding the developing countries, they began to look at their own work in a more critical fashion. Many aid agencies became dissatisfied with the limited impact of relief aid on the plight of people in the developing world.

In order to address the problems of the developing world, the more radical NGOs turned to development, and argued for a long-term involvement in the South rather than short-term emergency aid. Most of the international agencies took up the Freedom from Hunger campaign maxim: 'Give a man a fish and you can feed him for a day. Teach him to fish and you feed him for life.' (Whittaker, 1983:21) By the end of the 1970s Oxfam was spending less than 10 per cent of its budget on emergency relief and over 50 per cent on development issues (Searls, 1995). However, by the late 1970s it was becoming increasingly clear that the state-led development strategies of the South were having little success. While a few commentators located the problems of development in the context of inequalities promoted by the world market system, most drew the lesson that developing world states could not be trusted to pursue development.

The humanitarian agencies campaigned against much of the international developmental aid for Southern states, arguing that in the Cold War context Western powers were more interested in shoring up corrupt elites than tackling poverty. While US diplomats focused on people suffering under communist regimes, humanitarian NGOs criticised United States development aid for authoritarian regimes in Africa and Latin America (Forsythe, 1989:27). State-led aid programmes were seen during the Cold War as tainted by superpower geo-politics, with no examples of purely humanitarian actions. As US President Nixon openly stated in 1968: 'the main purpose of American aid is not to help other nations but to help ourselves' (Whittaker, 1983:51). While the superpowers and state-staffed UN agencies may have shared the language of human rights and development aid with the NGO community, there was little in the way of shared assumptions over policy practice (Waal, 1997a:65).

In opposition to the development policies pursued by non-Western states, international NGOs focused on alternative grass-roots models of development. This approach is explained by David Korten, a former worker for the United States Agency for International Development:

> The widespread belief that development is primarily a task of government has legitimised authoritarianism and created major barriers to true development progress in the South and over the past four decades the people have been expected to put their faith and resources in the hands of government. In return governments have promised to bestow on the people the gift of development. This promise has proved a chimera born of a false assessment of the capacity of government and the nature of development itself. (1990:95)

As Southern states were crippled by the debt crisis and later by the World Bank Structural Adjustment Programmes, state provision of welfare collapsed in many societies. International relief NGOs, with Western government funding, attempted to fill in the gaps. As two Oxfam workers explained:

> Gallantly stepping into the breach come the NGOs very much in the neo-colonial role. Whole districts, or once functioning sections of government ministries, are handed over to foreigners to run especially in health or social services. This process is enhanced as Structural Adjustment Programmes bite even deeper ... 40 percent of Kenya's health requirements are now provided by NGOs ... The more the NGOs are prepared to move in the easier it is for government to reduce support. (R. Palmer and J. Rossiter, cited in Searls, 1995)

This people-centred approach to development, which often saw developing world governments as illegitimate representatives of particular elites, tied in with the structural adjustment conditions, justified by the IMF in terms of attempts to benefit exploited rural producers or the population as a whole against the state-centred concerns of ruling elites (Clapham, 1999:533). In fostering 'people-focused' approaches to development, concentrating on projects which attempted to help the poorest sections of society, the international NGOs developed the concepts of 'capacity-building', 'empowerment' and 'civil society' as they argued the need for a long-term involvement in society and a sphere of influence independent from the developing world state. As Edwards and Hulme note:

> NGOs and GROs [grass-roots organisations] have been awarded a key role in this process by donor agencies, and are seen as an integral component of a thriving civil society – an essential counterweight to state power, opening up channels of communication and participation, providing the training ground for activists, and promoting pluralism. (1994:4)

In the mid- and late 1980s, NGOs were encouraged to establish new indigenous NGOs in the South, which increasingly received direct funding. These Southern 'partners' allowed Western donors to create parallel structures of aid and relief distribution which further acted to undermine the already weak and under-resourced state structures (Burgerman, 1998:905). Nicholas Stockton makes the point that the central emphasis of the developmentalist, local 'capacity-building' approach of many NGOs was the assumption that the problems of conflict or of development could only be resolved by working outside the political institutions of the developing world state (1998:355). This search for 'civil society' solutions ignored the international context of conflict and economic restrictions and tended to lay the responsibility for policy failure on the non-Western state and its citizens (see also Middleton and O'Keefe, 1998; Duffield, 1996; 2001).

Nicholas Leader suggests that their involvement in long-term development work in the 1970s and 1980s shaped the approach of many NGOs to providing relief in conflict situations. A tendency developed for field staff to look for frameworks which would allow them to address the root causes of conflict, not just symptoms. He also suggests that, at a more cynical level, in the context of the withdrawal of donor funding, NGOs tried to strengthen their case for support by emphasising their capacity to meet a variety of strategic ends (1998:297). Today, many NGOs argue that they have a much broader social role to play: 'There is a need to re-focus policies so that they enhance the capacity of humanitarian agencies to prevent, mitigate and resolve the effects of violent conflict.' (Goodhand and Hulme, cited in Leader, 1998:297)

Joanne Macrae argues that 'humanitarianism strikes at the heart of the professional culture of developmentalists' (1998:312). The anti-state approach and focus on 'sustainable approaches' is hostile to short-term relief. Developmentalists argue that relief creates dependency and reduces the capacity of local communities, while long-term developmental support builds capacity. Macrae sees the 'neo-peaceniks', the conflict resolution and civil society-building NGOs as posing a similar critique of humanitarian aid as a barrier to 'capacity-building'. She makes the point that these critiques miss the point that humanitarian relief was never claimed to play a role in conflict resolution or sustainable development (1998:314). The engagement with 'political and social engineering' may aim to address the causes of suffering but this level of direct and long-term interference has little to do with the emergency relief of needs-based humanitarian aid (Pugh, 1998:340).

By the end of the 1990s, those activists who still argued for the prioritisation of emergency relief were forced on to the defensive by the domination of the developmental approach. As Max Boot argued in *Foreign Affairs*:

> Interventions such as these [Somalia and Haiti] that address symptoms (famine or repression, for example) instead of their causes (such as bad government) are doomed to disappoint. This is a lesson the Clinton administration learned belatedly in Kosovo and Bosnia, and perhaps even in Iraq. (2000a)

The Human Rights 'Victim'

The sphere of NGO goal-orientated rights-based humanitarianism set up crucial practical precursors for the more direct and invasive government-led human rights-based interventionism of the late 1990s. It also established an ideological framework for relationships between Western institutions and the developing world, which became crucial to the legitimisation of 'ethical' foreign policy. This framework enabled the Cold War system of international regulation to be reshaped on the basis of 'capacity-building' and rights protection. In this framework, non-Western governments tended to be seen as a potential threat to their states' economic and social development, incapable of rational policy development and prone to corruption and nepotism. The citizens of non-Western states were seen as easily manipulated by their corrupt and inefficient elites and ill-versed in the skills of political decision-making and economic exchange. Both the 'solidarity' NGOs, with a deeper commitment to international involvement in conflict resolution, and the 'developmental' NGOs tended to portray the non-Western subject as incapable of self-government and in need of long-term external assistance.

This approach led relief agency guides to take visitors to the worst places, stressing the dependence of the people on outside support and making exaggerated dire predictions of the future. Journalists and media editors knew in advance what a 'humanitarian story' looked like. The overall plot has been characterised by Benthall as a moral 'fairy story' (cited in Waal, 1997a:82–3). This 'fairy story' had three components, familiar because they are the essence of the human rights intervention 'stories' of the present. The first component was the hapless victim in distress. In the famine 'fairy story' this victim was always portrayed through film of the worst cases of child malnutrition in the worst feeding centres. In cases of civil conflict the victims were often war refugees who had been 'ethnically cleansed'. The second component was the villain, the non-Western government or state authority, which had caused famine and poverty through its corruption or wrong spending policies, or had consciously embarked on a policy of genocide or mass repression. The third component in the humanitarian 'fairy tale' was the saviour, the aid agency, the international institution or even the journalists covering the story. The saviour was an external agency whose interests were seen to be inseparable from those of the deserving victim.

The search for victims has dominated media coverage of humanitarian crises. The Kosovo crisis, for example, saw journalists 'impatient to find a "good" story – i.e. a mass atrocity' (Gillan, 2000). Many Western journalists were dispatched to Macedonia and Albania with the sole purpose of finding a rape victim. Benedicte Giaever of the OSCE was angered that 'almost every journalist who came to see her asked one thing: could she give them a rape victim to interview' (Gillan, 2000). This approach, which takes the humanitarian crisis out of a political context to tell a 'fairy tale' or moral story has been termed the 'journalism of attachment'. This style of journalism has been forcefully criticised:

Far from raising public understanding of the horrors of war, their reports mystify what conflicts are really about. By abstracting acts of violence from any wider conflict over political aims, they remove any possibility of people seeing what caused the war. The result of imposing a ready-made Good v Evil framework on every situation is that conflicts can only be understood as the conse-quence of man's atavistic, bestial urges. Instead of 'humanising' a war, this approach ultimately dehumanises all those involved. (Hume, 1997:15)

Alex de Waal terms the outlook of the international humanitarian agencies, and the media promotion of their cause, 'disaster tourism'; in humanitarian crises they selectively saw the worst and assumed the worst (1997a:82). The lack of knowledge of the severity of the famine, drought or civil conflict led to exaggerated predictions of the death toll, and, of course, the need for support for the agency's declared rights-based humanitarian aims. The predominant approach of humanitarian interventionists to the conflicts in former Yugoslavia and Rwanda demonstrates the dangers inherent in this perspective. The humanitarian NGOs have explained the civil conflicts as the products of local circumstances, from which it can only be concluded that the people of these regions are uncivilised, prone to violent and savage ethnic passions or at the very least easily manipulated by government propaganda because they lack inde-pendent critical faculties (see for example, Hartmann, 1999:54, and, for a critique, Collins, 1998).

The campaigning human rights-based NGOs did much to prob-lematise the non-Western state and legitimise Western activism through the creation of the incapable human rights victim. As Pierre Krähenbuhl notes:

The legitimacy of the humanitarian gesture is intimately connected with the ability to consider the 'other', the person in need, as a human being, something which the repeated use of the expression 'victim' tends to make more difficult. It strips of all human dignity the man, woman or child whom it is supposed to define. (2000)

While Cold War power-politics tarnished the idea of 'human-centred' state-led human rights activism, the campaigning and aid

NGOs revived the concept of 'ethical' Western involvement in humanitarian issues. As the late John Vincent noted:

> There is one sense, however, in which the arrival of the issue of human rights in international society may be regarded as wholly progressive. It is the sense in which the idea of human rights is borne by non-governmental organizations who act in defence of no sectional interest. (1986:264)

With the end of the Cold War the 'geo-political straitjacket' was removed and humanitarian agencies and human rights advocacy groups seized the opportunity to influence the international agenda (Waal, 1997a:133). The agencies that were able to do this most successfully were those that clearly pursued a rights-based 'new humanitarianism' and rejected the post-1945 humanitarian aid framework of ICRC neutrality and needs-based emergency relief. The NGOs made the running in the new order because they were less bound by either official mandates or Cold War orientations than international institutions. The lack of legal mandate and organisational flexibility has meant that it has been easy to adapt their perspective to be in tune with the times. The major exception to this shift has been the Red Cross, the only international relief organisation, apart from the UNHCR, tied to a mandate under international law (the Geneva Convention regulations).

This was a new sort of humanitarianism, which instead of operating separately from political mechanisms, saw itself as an alternative guide to policy-making. Far from being neutral in relation to the aspirations of both Soviet Communism and US-led market economics, both these perspectives were seen to be flawed because they put politics above people. The language of human rights was the perfect foil for advocating an NGO-led approach. Rejecting the political Cold War framework and the narrow strategic concerns of geo-political strategy, the immediate situation of the victims was held to be all that mattered. Michael Ignatieff quotes the disillusion of Don McCullin, a British war photographer:

> But what are my politics? I certainly take the side of the underprivileged. I could never say I was politically neutral. But whether I'm of the Right or the Left – I can't say … I feel, in my guts, at one with the victims. And I find there's integrity in that stance. (1998: 23)

Ignatieff astutely notes that this approach is a 'weary world away from the internationalism of the 1960s' when there was a political cause at stake and conflict and interventionism could be supported or opposed on the basis of Left and Right. Today, he states 'there are no good causes left – only victims of bad causes' (1998:23). Once every aspiration, whether it is for independence or for regional superiority, for equal rights or for separate development, is seen as a flawed and pointless exercise, the only sympathy is for victims: 'the twentieth-century inflection of moral universalism has taken the form of an anti-ideological and anti-political ethic of siding with the victim; the moral risk entailed by this ethic is misanthropy' (Ignatieff, 1998:25). This approach risks 'misanthropy' because the human rights activist sees little that is positive in the societies in which they work, only passive victims and evil or dangerous abusers.

On the basis of the incapacity of the human rights victim, the 'deepening' and 'broadening' of humanitarianism is often proclaimed to be a radical and progressive approach. Yet, in many cases, the transition from needs-based to rights-based humanitarianism is a striking example of this 'ethical misanthropy'. The extension of humanitarian action is driven by the liberal conviction that the non-Western state concerned lacks an adequate capacity for self-determination or self-government. From short-term emergency aid, the humanitarian impulse has been transformed into a framework of long-term involvement, assistance and capacity-building (Mackinlay and Kent, 1997; Hayes and Sands, 1997; Paris, 1997). This is reflected in the expanded UN agendas on peace and development which advocate long-term social engineering rather than traditional grants of aid or the placement of UN Blue Helmets to keep armies apart and monitor the peace (UN, 1992; 1994; 1995).

There are three related reasons for this transformation in the relationship of humanitarian assistance. First, the demise of social and political movements, which supported the cause of independence in the developing world and highlighted the inequalities of power inherent in the world market, has led to an increasingly localised focus on conflict and social problems, in isolation from the international political and economic context. Second, once the questions of humanitarian crisis were interpreted predominantly from a local as opposed to an international standpoint, the failure of Southern developmental strategies was seen as rooted in problems of the culture or mentality of non-Western political leaders and peoples. Third, this diminished view of the non-Western subject meant that humanitarian actors increasingly saw the involvement of themselves, and their Western government backers, as necessary for long-term political, economic and cultural change.

For some commentators the transition to rights-based humanitarianism is seen as an extension of the needs-based approach. This is clearly indicated in the terminology of 'deepening' and 'broadening' humanitarian action. The misanthropic danger in these developments is drawn out in the following section, which highlights the risk that, rather than supplementing traditional humanitarianism, rights-based intervention can lead to 'ethical' justifications for the denial of humanitarian aid. In place of unconditional emergency aid, accountable to non-Western governments, 'ethical misanthropy' leads to calls for the coercive external management of crisis situations by Western institutions.

FROM HUMANITARIAN NEEDS TO HUMAN RIGHTS

The 'deepening' and 'broadening' of humanitarianism brought into question the central principles informing the work of the ICRC. Nicholas Leader notes that with the principle of impartiality the ethical basis for humanitarian action was clear, that is, based on need and given in proportion to the need (1998:298). Once the range of humanitarian assistance was expanded the ethical basis of NGO intervention became human rights not human needs. The transformation of humanitarian work through the displacement of needs by rights has been crucial to the 'new humanitarian' discourse.

Neutrality

Human rights advocates, like Geoffrey Robertson, have led the calls for the reform of international humanitarian mechanisms, railing against the 'obsessive neutrality ingrained in UN personnel and procedures' (1999:xix). As Michael Ignatieff notes, 'the doctrine of neutrality has become steadily more controversial as the new politics of human rights has entered the field' (1998:119). He criticises the fact that the ICRC chooses still to 'go by the book' with its narrow adherence to the Geneva Convention, and sides with its critics in MSF who highlight the ICRC's conservative 'legalistic bias' and 'cautious, lawyerly neutrality' (1999a:203–4). In fact, the criticisms of the ICRC's stance have gone further as its position of neutrality led it to keep silent about knowledge of Nazi concentration camps during the Second World War (Moorehead, 1998). It has also been vociferously attacked for its stance of neutrality during the Bosnian war, and has been condemned for not sharing its knowledge of mistreatment of prisoners with The Hague and Arusha tribunals (G. Robertson, 1999:167). The modern human rights approach sees conflict in non-Western states not as a consequence of economic, political and social tensions, to be ameliorated by aid, but as a relationship of abuse. For every act of abuse, there are victims to be supported and abusers who must be punished: '[H]umanitarian intervention cannot be impartial between the Serb militiaman and the Muslim civilian, or the machete-wielding Hutu and the Tutsi victim. The ICRC's doctrine of discretion and silence ... has shaded into complicity with war crimes.' (Ignatieff, 1988:124)

As Jean Pictet noted: 'One cannot be at one and the same time the champion of justice and of charity. One must choose, and the ICRC has long since chosen to be a defender of charity.' (Cited in Minear, 1999) The prioritisation of neutral aid over political and social engineering has been condemned by the Red Cross's radical competitors. As merely a 'champion of charity', the ICRC is seen to be highly conservative and out of touch (Hutchinson, 1996). Ignatieff illustrates this problem very clearly in his observations of the ICRC's work in Afghanistan. Other relief agencies, including Oxfam, MSF, UNICEF and the UNHCR, ran programmes employing Afghan women and protested against Taliban decrees that suspended women from working. When they called on the Red Cross to join the appeal, it refused. For the Deputy-Head of the ICRC in Kabul, women's rights were not a humanitarian issue (1988:146). Women's rights were a political question, to be addressed by politicians not humanitarian agencies. In this sense, as Ignatieff recognises, the ICRC is a humanitarian organisation which remains politically neutral and makes no claims to human rights status.

The less interventionist perspective of the ICRC is easily criticised today as the modest morality of small deeds or the 'one more blanket' approach (Ignatieff, 1998:144). However, ICRC officers have defended the decision to remain neutral on the grounds that they would never have been allowed access to prisoners if camp authorities thought they would use this information in war crimes tribunals. The policy of neutrality meant that the Red Cross was able to help all those in need in conflict situations, not merely those held to be the most worthy. As a result of this approach, the ICRC was the only humanitarian organisation allowed to remain in Serb-held areas of Bosnia and Croatia during the 1995 Nato bombing which accompanied the Croat-Muslim offensive. This meant that it was able to assist Serb victims of the war when several hundred thousand refugees were forced to flee their homes in the largest single act of ethnic cleansing in the conflict, the Croatian clearance of the Krajina (Ignatieff, 1998:139).

The humanitarian ethic of neutrality was publicly undermined in the consensus of NGO support for Western military intervention in the wars of Yugoslavia's disintegration. Here it seemed clear that there was a moral scenario of good against evil, of strength against weakness, and that neutrality would mean being complicit in the defeat of good. As Ignatieff harangued the former UN Secretary-General Boutros Boutros-Ghali: 'Why insist on being neutral, in the face of a clear aggressor and a clear victim, when that neutrality daily undermines the United Nations' moral credit?' (1998:73) David Rieff similarly condemned the impartiality of those who wanted the intervention for peace as opposed to believing that the 'Bosnian government should be aided because it was in the right' (1999a:181).

Today, surveys of humanitarian relief organisations show that their officers agree with the shift away from political neutrality. As Hugo Slim has observed, after consulting all the UK's main agencies in the field, 'neutrality has almost become a dirty word' (cited in Fox, 1999). For many human rights activists neutrality has become 'a form of moral bankruptcy' (Weiss, 1999:8). Emma Bonino, European Commissioner for Humanitarian Affairs, noted in a September 1998 panel discussion that: 'I have my doubts ... that being neutral is still at all possible, or indeed ethically just.' In a forceful critique she questioned whether it was feasible that humanitarian agencies 'should be unable to distinguish right from wrong, the aggressor from the victim, the killers from the dead bodies? What absurd wisdom could call for this organised ethical confusion.' (Cited in Minear, 1999) As a 1999 Caritas Europa discussion paper states: 'Today neutrality is seen as undesirable. Either because it's considered amoral – remaining silent in the face of human rights abuses – or, simply because the central role of NGOs in highly political emergencies makes it impossible to achieve.' (Fox, 1999)

Alex de Waal, founder of Africa Rights, a staunch critic of partisan NGO intervention in the past, has vociferously attacked the 'elevation of the principle of neutrality' in Rwanda (1997a:192). Oxfam was among the first NGOs to use the term 'genocide' and campaigned publicly for greater international involvement, calling for UN intervention and a ceasefire. De Waal argues that peace was the wrong option: 'Waging war on the interim government was the only form of military intervention that would have contributed to stopping the genocide.' (1977a:194) He condemns the humanitarian NGOs for not taking sides with the Rwandan Patriotic Front:

> [T]he humanitarian proposals would not have halted the genocide and would almost certainly have contributed to further slaughter, the legitimation of the genocidal government, and impunity for genocidal criminals ... The demands of 'neutrality' overrode those of fighting against genocide. (1997a:195)

The 'new humanitarian' NGOs have a very different approach to the principle of neutrality and see their role as an engaged and radical one, aiming to fundamentally transform non-Western societies to tackle the underlying causes of violence. The 1990s codes for humanitarian conduct tend to avoid the commitments to strict neutrality of the ICRC. In the Providence Principles 'neutrality' is replaced by 'non-partisanship' while the Code of Conduct simply states that 'aid will not be used to further a particular political or religious standpoint' (Leader, 1998:299). While agencies like Oxfam, Save the Children and UNICEF have all adopted a 'new humanitarian' approach in recent years, the leading advocate of the new human rights-based humanitarianism is Médecins sans Frontières. Alain Destexhe, former MSF secretary-general, argues: 'Humanitarian action is noble when coupled with political action and justice. Without them, it is doomed to failure.' (Cited in Weiss, 1999:15) The award of the Nobel Peace Prize to MSF in 1999 was a highly significant statement in support of the transition to rights-based humanitarian aid. This was acknowledged by the agency's founder Bernard Kouchner: 'MSF's work was political from the start. I hope the prize marks the recognition of a type of humanitarian work which fights injustice and persecution, in contrast to traditional organisations.' (Cited in Fox, 1999)

Universalism

During the 1990s, humanitarian aid organisations have come under fire if they have followed a universalist approach of providing emergency aid solely on the basis of need rather than policy ends. It is now commonplace to read of humanitarian aid prolonging wars, feeding killers, legitimising corrupt regimes, creating war economies and perpetuating genocidal policies. Humanitarians have gone from being angels of mercy who can do no wrong to being seen as part of the problem. The British Secretary of State for International Development, Clare Short, has expressed concerns that aid agencies have prolonged the conflict in Sudan and has said she is 'haunted by the risk of relief maintaining conflict' (Fox, 1999). Similarly, the European Community's Humanitarian Office (ECHO) has decided to shift to a new human rights-based approach to humanitarian aid, as a result of sustained criticism: 'Business as usual for the Commission as humanitarian aid donor would mean courting the risk of growing criticism and isolation from the donor community, and a loss of credibility generally.' (Cited in Fox, 1999)

As the Caritas Europa discussion paper highlights: 'It is important to point out that a human rights-based humanitarianism will mean withholding aid in some cases.' (Fox, 1999) Michael Ignatieff argues that victims should no longer be seen as equal, whatever the justice of their cause, because the cause of ethnic cleansing and genocide means that some victims are more deserving than others (1998:124). This is confirmed in a 1999 ECHO discussion paper which clearly acknowledged that access to those in need would no longer be the overriding objective:

> From a rights perspective, access to victims of humanitarian aid is not an end in itself and will not, therefore, be pursued at any cost ... Access will be sought if it is the most effective way to contribute to the human rights situation. (Cited in Fox, 1999)

The new trend can best be seen in the controversy over the delivery of aid to the nearly 2 million Rwandan refugees in camps in Ngara, Goma and Bukava in Zaire. From the very beginning, agencies were condemned by human rights groups for saving the lives of 'genocidaires' who would survive to reorganise and re-invade Rwanda to 'finish off' the genocide (Waal, 1997a:195; Stockton, 1998:353). In an unprecedented move, humanitarian agencies, including MSF, withdrew humanitarian aid from these camps on the basis that there was a risk that relief would strengthen the armed forces and thus prolong the conflict. Leading figures from the international NGOs, like Africa Rights, even took issue with using the term 'refugee' to describe fleeing Rwandans. Alex de Waal argued that 'the moral complexities were hidden away and a simple charitable imperative (Give!) was presented to the media' (1997a:196). He condemned ethical justifications for aiding the refugees, citing the argument of Hugo Slim:

To have withheld humanitarian assistance in the hope that the regime might not be able to regroup and might not choose violence again would have meant working on the principle of 'doing evil that good may come' – a principle that has consistently been objected to in Christian moral theology and which would make an absurdity of the humanitarian mandate of relief agencies. (1997a:197)

For de Waal, however, preventable deaths among the refugees would have been preferable to providing support for forces responsible for genocide: 'the issues of genocide and justice slipped down Oxfam's agenda: an immediate humanitarian response for the "refugees" became its priority' (1997a:197). As James Orbinski stated on receiving the Nobel Peace Prize for MSF:

The moral intention of the humanitarian act must be confronted with its actual result. And it is here where any form of moral neutrality about what is good must be rejected. The result can be the use of the humanitarian in 1985 to support forced migration in Ethiopia, or the use in 1996 of the humanitarian to support a genocidal regime in the refugee camps of Goma. Abstention is sometimes necessary so that the humanitarian is not used against a population in crisis. (1999)

This perspective is often termed the 'do no harm' approach in which not providing aid to those in need is ethically defensible through the human rights discourse (Macrae, 1998:312). Short-term assistance is criticised for the potential long-term harm, either in fuelling conflict or legitimising and strengthening political factions (Leader, 1998:304–5). The result of this approach was the deaths of up to 200,000 people in Zaire, fleeing troops clearly intent on revenge for the genocide of 1994 (Stockton, 1998:353). Oxfam's Acting Policy Director, Nick Bloomer, has attempted to challenge the 'trend to start blaming humanitarian assistance for the conflicts'. He has warned that: 'We've seen a concerted political attack on the fundamental humanitarian principles and assistance for perpetuating wars.' (1999:20) By no means all refugees were guilty of genocide. As Nicholas Stockton notes, some 750,000 forcibly repatriated or 'lost in Zaire' were children under five, over 1.5 million were under 16 years of age (1998:354). He concludes that: 'The application of "do no harm" is tantamount to playing God – a deadly, perhaps totalitarian business to indulge in without the benefit of 20:20 future vision.' (1998:356)

This perspective of subjecting humanitarian aid to human rights conditions has, since the Rwandan crisis, become the official UK government position. Tess Kingham MP, a member of the International Development Committee, argues:

> Surely taking a view of the wider good – for the long term interests of people – to actually achieve real stability and development, that it may be better to withdraw aid now – to ensure that in the long term, it is in the best interests of the people. (Cited in Fox, 1999)

As noted above, Clare Short openly castigated British aid agencies for raising money for humanitarian relief during the 1998 famine in Sudan, arguing that what was really needed was a political solution and an end to the war. Similarly, in the case of Sierra Leone, the UK government called on humanitarian agencies to suspend relief because it would legitimise the military coup and postpone the return of democracy. Today, instead of feeding famine victims, aid may well be cut back (McSmith and Burke, 2000; *Observer*, 2000). This was highlighted when the UN World Food Programme suspended its shipments to Afghanistan immediately after the attack on the World Trade Center, despite the growing humanitarian crisis, because of fears that food would fall into the hands of the Taliban (McCarthy, 2001a; N. Cohen, 2001). Clare Short accused international aid agencies of being 'emotional' in their call for a halt to the Afghan bombing to allow aid through, arguing that the problem was that 'they are partly in need because they've got such a lousy government' (McCarthy, 2001b).

The restrictions on humanitarian aid and universal charity mean that those dependent on aid have even less opportunity for autonomy than previously. In Bosnia, human rights NGOs like the International Crisis Group have lobbied strongly for economic aid to be conditional on the implementation of the Dayton Accords and have argued that aid conditionality is the main source of leverage for the international community (Pugh, 1998:343; Chandler, 2000a). In Serbia, prior to the removal of the Milosevic government, European Union humanitarian aid programmes operated on the highly selective basis of providing fuel and provisions to opposition-run municipalities while applying strict sanctions to the rest of the country. This was challenged by the UN Office for the Co-ordination of Humanitarian Affairs in Belgrade and the International Federation of the Red Cross, which argued that aid should be given on the basis of need and irrespective of political party affiliation (Rozen, 2000a; 2000b). In Afghanistan, food aid, which was denied in the run-up to military intervention, accompanied the bombing campaign and was designed to weaken the Taliban government as part of the Pentagon 'hearts and minds' offensive to demonstrate international support for opposition forces (MacAskill *et al.*, 2001). The politicisation of humanitarian aid has led to even greater leverage over non-Western societies as NGOs and international institutions increasingly assume the right to make judgements about what is right and just, about whose capacities are built and which local groups are favoured. Where humanitarian aid started out as an expression of empathy with common humanity it has been transformed through the discourse of 'human rights and human wrongs' into a lever for strategic aims drawn up and acted upon by external agencies.

Attaching conditions to humanitarian relief on the basis of human rights objectives has brought into question the universal right of every man, woman and child to relief at times of disaster, which is enshrined in international law. The 'new humanitarian' approach of blaming the 'undeserving victims' has led to support for sanctions and the refusal of aid. This approach is advocated by the human rights campaigner Geoffrey Robertson, who argued that sanctions on post-war Serbia were justified because 'most of Serbia's eight million citizens were guilty of indifference towards atrocities in Kosovo' (2000:417).

Oxfam's Nick Stockton has spoken out passionately against the new vogue for 'deserving and undeserving victims' and has highlighted the dangers of human rights-orientated humanitarianism which abandons the universal right to relief:

> The concept of the undeserving victim is therefore morally and ethically untenable, and practically counter-productive. It represents an outright rejection of the principles of humanity, impartiality and universalism, fundamental tenets of human rights and humanitarian principles ... Withholding humanitarian assistance on the grounds that those in need *may* be criminals ... is the arbitrary application of punishment before trial and it constitutes cruel, inhumane and degrading treatment on a massive scale. Such treatment is arguably a crime against humanity. (1998:354–5)

Humanitarian Militarism

Once humanitarian intervention is conflated with rights-based strategic ends, defined by external agencies, the political ends are redefined as ethical and used to justify the denial of humanitarian principles. Almost overnight the universal humanist core of humanitarian action was undermined and humanitarianism became an ambiguous concept capable of justifying any form of external intervention. Today, leading commentators suggest that 'there is no general definition of humanitarianism' or ask 'What on earth does the word "humanitarian" mean?' (Ramsbotham and Woodhouse, 1996:9) As Peter Fuchs, the Director-General of the ICRC, has stated: 'the respective roles of politicians, generals and humanitarian actors are not clear anymore' (1999).

The traditional image of humanitarian assistance, of sending food parcels and blankets or granting asylum to refugees, is seen as a problem precisely because it is humanitarian; because it does not concern itself with a human rights solution beyond meeting immediate need. Gil Loescher, for example, condemns the UNHCR precisely for its narrow humanitarianism:

> A major obstacle to taking a more active role in refugee protection in countries of origin derives from the international refugee regime itself. The UNHCR was designed to appear to be non-political and strictly humanitarian ... UNHCR, as it is presently structured, is not mandated to intervene politically against governments or opposition groups. (1999:241)

The UNHCR, along with other humanitarian agencies, is being pressurised into redefining its role in crisis situations. Reflecting the 'new humanitarian' consensus, the UNHCR is downplaying its humanitarian role of aiding refugees, and taking on a new, more invasive role as a human rights actor assuming the right to address the root causes of refugee problems by directly influencing policy-making in non-Western states (Forsythe, 2000:74).

In fact, the strongest critique of needs-based humanitarian action is from the human rights movement itself, which argues that responding to crises by sending humanitarian relief is merely an excuse to avoid 'more vigorous responses' (Weiss, 2000:14). Humanitarian relief is increasingly seen as giving Western governments the appearance of 'doing something' in the face of a tragedy while providing an alibi to avoid making a riskier political or military commitment that could address the 'roots of a crisis' (for example, Roberts, 1999). Under the cry that humanitarianism should not be used as a substitute for political or military action, they are in fact arguing for a new rights-based 'military humanitarianism' (Stockton, 1998:356). As journalist David Rieff notes: 'humanitarian relief organizations ... have become some of the most fervent interventionists' (1999a:184).

The rights-based critique of humanitarianism provided the military in Western states with the opportunity to portray their actions as increasingly ethical in the 1990s. Ironically, this occurred at the same time as armed interventions moved away from the UN Blue Helmet approach that overlapped with the humanitarian principles of neutrality, impartiality and consent (Pugh, 1998:348; UN, 2000c). As Michael Pugh observes, 'military humanism' is no longer an oxymoron because military action has increasingly been justified through defending human rights goals (1998:342). From the perspective of the military establishment, this new role is important and the cultures of the military and the human rights activist are increasingly being brought together through the idea of helping the 'victim', as can be seen from recruitment advertising in Britain and the United States. The humanitarian motives for military action have been so heavily stressed that some critics have warned that the British Army is in danger of being flaunted as 'the military wing of Oxfam' (Norton-Taylor, 2000a).

This convergence between 'ethical foreign policy', carried out through military action, and humanitarian assistance was only made possible through the concept of human rights-based humanitarian intervention. Several commentators argue that the division between humanitarianism and militarism was decisively eroded in 1991 with Security Council Resolution 688 concerning humanitarian provision in Iraq at the end of the January–February 1991 war (Ramsbotham and Woodhouse, 1996:13). Under the banner of 'humanitarianism', the supporters of UN Resolution 688 linked human rights with international peace and security, arguing that failure to protect the Kurds would threaten the security and sovereignty of other countries (Mills, 1997:286). Once the protection of human rights was linked to international security the UN Charter framework of non-intervention in internal affairs was implicitly undermined. Matters of domestic jurisdiction could now be re-framed through the human rights discourse as 'just cause' for military action (Black, 1999b).

The military intervention in Somalia in 1992 and the dispatch of UN and Nato forces to Bosnia were also justified in the UN Security Council as a response to a 'threat to the peace' (Roberts, 1993:440). During the 1990s, the connection between rights-based humanitarianism and military intervention was cemented through the UN Security Council's broad definition of international peace to include concerns which would have been earlier classed as internal questions (Forsythe, 2000:57–62). Despite this manoeuvre, the Security Council did not recognise a formal right of military intervention purely on human rights grounds. The Nato assault on Kosovo was the first internationally sanctioned military action in the name of human rights and internal questions of governance, rather than international security.

The blurring of the distinction between military action and humanitarian intervention, through the human rights discourse, has seen the questioning of every traditional humanitarian principle (MacMillan, 2000; Thomas, 2000). The UNHCR has blurred the distinction between being a warring party or an impartial humanitarian actor by suggesting that because the Nato mandate is one of peace enforcement it is maintaining the principles of neutrality and impartiality. NGO analyst Ed van Mierop, however, notes that Nato dictated the terms of co-operation with the UNHCR and that the NGO community as a whole has accepted Nato co-operation (2000). As over Kosovo, the international military intervention against Afghanistan involved close co-ordination between aid-providing international NGOs, government agencies and the US-led military forces (MacAskill *et al.*, 2001). In fact, the Afghanistan intervention for the first time made militarism and humanitarianism part of the same strategic project, George Bush declaring that: 'As we strike military targets, we will also drop food, medicine and supplies to the starving and suffering men and women and children of Afghanistan'. (Wren and Steinberg, 2001) This twining of humanitarianism and militarism was also designed to generate domestic support for the military action with government-supported aid appeals timed to coincide with the start of the bombing campaign (Lawrence and Wells, 2001). As Robert Hayden observes, the concept of humanitarianism has been transformed: 'instead of protesting the application of state violence on non-violent dissidents, activists are demanding the application of massive violence on states deemed to be inferior'. He terms this development 'humanrights-ism' to demonstrate the repudiation of traditional humanitarian principles

(2000). Thomas Weiss also argues that the human rights community has redefined humanitarianism as its opposite: 'These actions are, by definition, coercive and partial. They are political and humanitarian; they certainly are not neutral, impartial, or consensual.' (1999:21)

The definition of humanitarianism has been transformed. Humanitarian intervention no longer seeks to save lives in the short term but to pursue a long-term 'greater good'. The full impact of the logic of human rights-based humanitarianism could be seen in the coverage of the bombing of Afghanistan in British liberal broadsheets like the *Guardian* and *Observer*. An *Observer* leader column, for example, argued that even if the bombing campaign led to an additional 100,000 children dying through starvation it would still be 'humanitarian' militarism because the Afghan people would be better off in the long term:

> UNICEF reported last week that 100,000 more children will die during this winter ... if bombing of the country continues ... One hundred thousand more deaths if bombing goes on. A greater good squandered if it ceases ... The only truly humanitarian outcome for Afghanistan's starving now requires the downfall of the Taliban government. (*Observer*, 2001).

If, in the cause of the 'greater good', the wilful deaths of 100,000 children can be described as 'humanitarian', there is clearly little left of the legacy of the early humanitarian campaigners.

CONCLUSION

From being based on the universal nature of humanity, which inevitably caused conflict with the Western agenda of the Cold War, today's 'new humanitarians' have challenged every principle that demarcated the traditional framework of humanitarian action. No longer do they advocate principled neutrality, nor defend the most basic level of humanitarian relief as a universal right if this threatens to undermine broader strategic human rights-based aims. Through the human rights discourse, humanitarian action has become transformed from relying on empathy with suffering victims, in support of emergency aid, to mobilising misanthropy to legitimise the politics of international condemnation, sanctions and bombings.

Today, a Western government playing to the rhetoric of 'ethical foreign policy' will find that it is more likely to receive the support of the NGO community for applying sanctions to human rights abusers than for granting development or emergency aid to regimes which may be criticised for one human rights infringement or another. It is a sad irony that the more the humanitarian movement jettisons its traditional principles and takes on a committed and invasive 'ethical' human rights agenda, the more support it receives from Western governments and leading international institutions eager to present themselves as guided by the spirit of humanitarianism.

Nato has now taken on a wide range of 'humanitarian' tasks from bombing to refugee support and the post-conflict reconstruction of roads, schools and hospitals. It seems that, having stepped into the limelight, the humanitarian NGOs may be squeezed out by the 'armed aid workers' and come to rue the end of needs-based humanitarianism. As de Waal notes, the interventionist discourse led by the 'new humanitarian' NGOs has 'legitimated the extension of a particular form of political action to areas formerly out of bounds': 'The results were dramatically successful: an enlarged humanitarian arsenal, and the assertion of new legal and ethical principles that justified unprecedented actions by international institutions.' (1997a:157–8)

The 'new humanitarian' NGOs may have helped to popularise the interventionist discourse around human rights, but they lacked the capacity to act on this without the support of leading governments in America and Europe. Chapter 3 considers why these governments, and the international institutions they operated through, were keen to take up the challenges of ethical human rights-centred foreign policy.

3   The Attraction of Ethical Foreign Policy

> As a Permanent Member of the UN Security Council and as a country both willing and able to play a leading role internationally we have a responsibility to act as a force for good in the world.
> – *UK Government Strategic Defence Review*, published 8 July 1998, Cm 3999, paragraph 21.

The declarations of ethical foreign policy emanating from the governments of leading world powers are often taken at face value as 'simply the right thing to do' (Blair, 1999a). Many human rights advocates believe that they have achieved a level of influence on Western governments, which are beginning to realise the need to prioritise human rights, even if they lack the commitment to pursue these aims consistently. This chapter questions some of the assumptions about the shift towards prioritising human rights issues in foreign affairs and looks at why ethical foreign policy has become increasingly central to government policy-making in the leading Western states.

The following section considers several explanations forwarded to explain the shift from pursing narrow national interests in foreign policy to focusing on human rights questions in areas where Western states have little economic or geo-strategic interest. It suggests that while international changes have provided the opportunity to present foreign policy in ethical terms, the main dynamic behind ethical foreign policy lies in the domestic sphere and the search for new forms of political legitimacy. Subsequent sections develop this analysis, considering the low costs involved in ethical foreign policy and the selective nature of its application, further suggesting that the lack of clear policy aims in human rights promotion reflects a desire to use foreign policy for domestic purposes rather than any concern with human rights issues *per se*.

WHY NOW?

Three reasons are usually considered in explanations of the change in importance of ethical foreign policy in the 1990s. The first is that the shift to implementing human rights protection is part of the gradual evolution of human rights concerns since 1945. The second is that the world is more dangerous with the end of the bipolar world of the Cold War, the nation-state is becoming increasingly fragile and there is greater need for international human rights protection with 'failed states', 'complex emergencies' and civil conflict. The third suggestion is that, with the growth of the communications revolution, we have become much more aware of abuses that are happening around the world and the 'CNN effect' is forcing governments to act to assuage the concerns of voters and civil society organisations.

Gradual Progress?

Advocates of the new human rights regimes have a marked tendency to rewrite history to present the internationalisation of human rights concerns as a process that has been central to international relations since the Second World War. Post-1945 history is often read backwards teleologically as a continuous movement towards the present, starting with the UN General Assembly's acceptance of the Universal Declaration on Human Rights and the Genocide Convention in 1948, moving through the completion of the two UN covenants in 1966, the Covenant on Economic, Social and Cultural Rights, and the Covenant on Civil and Political Rights, to the international tribunals of the 1990s. Geoffrey Robertson refers to the 'evolutionary process for international human rights law' after 1945 (1999:xiv). Often this 'evolution' is described as a number of stages. Thomas Buergenthal analyses three: the normative foundation of human rights in the UN Charter and the international covenants of 1966; followed by the stage of institution-building with the establishment of the UN Human Rights Committee and the Committee on the Elimination of Racial Discrimination in the 1970s; and the third stage, that of implementation in the post-Cold War era with the 1993 UN Vienna Declaration on Human Rights, which stated that the 'promotion and protection of all human rights is a legitimate concern of the international community' (1997).

Officials from the US State Department often offer an alternative approach which regards the current focus on human rights as an eternal part of US policy-making. This teleology starts from the Declaration of Independence, and is traced through the Bill of Rights and the Civil Rights Movement to the present day. This perspective makes some official contributions to academic and legal journals read like the anaemic tourist guide patter for the Philadelphia Liberty Bell:

> [M]uch of American history is the story of our own struggle to acknowledge and embrace the universality of human rights. The integration of human rights into American foreign policy is therefore a natural reflection of our interests and values ... Our dedication to universal values is a vital source of America's authority and credibility. We cannot lead and we cannot be a world leader without it. (Wagenseil, 1997:4)

These ideas of gradual progress towards institutionalising an international human rights agenda mask the transformation of the situation in the 1990s. The three, or occasionally four, stage analyses blur the qualitative transformation between the normative and institutional stages, where there was no attempt to raise human rights above the rights of state sovereignty, and the post-Cold War era. In the UN Charter of 1945, Article 2(7) established that states, rather than abstract human rights, would be the legal subjects of the international post-war system. The UN Charter provisions on human rights did not establish any obligation to guarantee human rights nor define what was meant by 'human rights and fundamental freedoms' (Buergenthal, 1997:707). The Universal Declaration of Human Rights of 1948 was a non-binding UN General Assembly resolution which promoted human rights in abstract terms and was not intended to be read as a statement of law or legal obligation (G. Robertson, 1999:30, 75; Mills, 1997:276; Corell, 1997:519). The Declaration was a moral one only, with no intended enforcement mechanisms and certainly nothing mandating member states to intervene in another state's affairs to stop human rights abuses (Ignatieff, 1999b). The 1966 Covenant on Economic, Social and Cultural Rights had no adjudicatory body, although the Covenant on Civil and Political Rights, with more support from Western states, actually did incorporate such a body, the UN Human Rights Committee (G. Robertson, 1999:146). Yet even this mechanism cannot be said to have prioritised human rights over state sovereignty. It involved the voluntary co-operation of states in the submission of government reports, which were followed up by 'suggestions' or 'general recommendations', with no institutional sanction to ensure adequate supervision or observance of the agreements. It was only in 1992 that the Human Rights Committee took the major step of even commenting directly on reports submitted by different states (Boerefijn, 1995).

The current attention paid to the Genocide Convention, adopted by the UN in 1948, is another misleading example of reading the history of human rights mechanisms backwards. The US senate did not ratify the Convention until 1988, 40 years later. While the Genocide Convention was a 'dead letter' during the Cold War, only five years after ratification the United States was at the forefront of forcing the UN Security Council to establish the International Criminal Tribunal for the former Yugoslavia. During the intervening 40 years many other international conflicts had taken place in which many more people had died and which could have been alleged to constitute genocide, yet there was little motivation to act on the part of the US or the international community (Korey, 1999:155).

Prior to the 1990s, it was only states with few political, strategic or economic interests abroad, such as Canada, the Netherlands and Scandinavian states, that claimed to base foreign policy on human rights, free from military and geo-political priorities (T. King, 1999:315). In the United States, President Carter's human rights policy, despite its change in emphasis, was limited to a few select countries, with little change in the relationship between human rights and foreign assistance under subsequent administrations, which prioritised economic relations and geo-political concerns. In Japan, Official Development Assistance switched to a human rights focus after a cabinet decision in 1991. The British government took longer to shift away from its Cold War approach; it was only in 1997 that a government White Paper required foreign aid programmes to build on human rights as a core policy aim (Montgomery, 1999:87).

While it can be argued that current human rights policies are a development from past proposals, it would be misleading to see this development as an inevitable or predetermined one. The new policies and institutional developments do not simply express ways of implementing or applying pre-existing ideas, but reflect a fundamentally different conception of the relative importance of human rights questions. The two other approaches considered below both argue that there has been a fundamental reappraisal of human rights, and locate this shift in qualitative changes in international society. The first argument suggests that the world has become more dangerous in the absence of the Cold War, with new types of disputes within nation-states, and the second, that the public in the

Western world has become more aware of human rights abuses, creating more pressure on governments to respond to crises.

A More Dangerous World?

The post-Cold War non-Western world is often presented as a depressing and chaotic distopic vision: 'The reality of our era ... is that torture is rampant, murdering civilians commonplace, and driving the survivors from their homes often the main goal of a particular military offensive.' (Gutman and Rieff, 1999:10) The UN Commission on Global Governance argues that: 'A disturbing feature of the contemporary world is the spread of a culture of violence ... Violence is sometimes perceived as an end in itself ... The world over, people are caught in vicious circles of disrespect for the life and integrity of others.' (CGG, 1995:16–17)

Violence is often the central focus of human rights reports and symbolic of what many commentators see as a broader cultural and civilisational failure in many non-Western regions. Daniel Thurer notes, regarding Africa, the 'brutality and intensity of the violence used' with 'the whole society – adults, young people and children alike – falling into the grip of a collective insanity following the breakdown of state institutions' (1999). It would be easy to assume that there were more war crimes and crimes against humanity than in the past, and that civilisation is breaking down in many parts of the world. Martin Shaw suggests that 'genocide has come to dominate the war strategies of many local states and state-like movements. From Bosnia to Rwanda, genocide has been a large part of the practice of war.' (2000)

The mainstream commentators assert that the nation-state is disappearing under the pressure of globalisation, that there are more human rights tragedies, more conflicts or more civil strife. The banner headline over the publication of the *Observer's* 'Human Rights Index 1999': 'Terrible climax to the century of horror', sums up most human rights advocates' views of the present. The Human Rights Index, launched in 1998, is held to demonstrate 'a worsening state of affairs ... [with] genocidal attacks on civilian populations in Kosovo and East Timor' (Beaumont, 1999). Bernard Kouchner argues: 'In a world aflame after the Cold War, we need to establish a forward-looking right of the world community to actively intervene in the affairs of sovereign nations to prevent an explosion of human rights violations.' (1999)

The statistics definitely make for grim reading. However, it is not often mentioned that the annual casualty figures from conflict are lower today than the global average for the entire period of the Cold War (Norton-Taylor and Bowcott, 1999). As Ken Booth notes, 'the world has not seen a sharp increase in armed conflict since the end of the Cold War' (1995:117). John Bolton, former US assistant secretary of state for international organisations, argues that the perception that barbarism is on the increase is largely down to the international human rights movement which has struggled to place conflicts at the centre of attention (1999). Of the 35 wars taking place in the mid-1990s only eight broke out in or after 1989, the other 27 began during the Cold War and were exacerbated by it. Although there are some brutal conflicts today none are as large as the wars in Korea, Vietnam or the Middle East during the Cold War and none have the consequences of 'superpower' nuclear conflict. As the UK Select Committee on Defence (UKSCD) noted in 1998: '[T]he United Kingdom does not face any credible threats to its own territorial integrity for the foreseeable future ... this country is probably physically safer now than at any other time in its recent history.' (UKSCD, 1998:par. 86) Not only is the world a much safer place than during the Cold War but many 'intractable' conflicts, such as those in Israel, South Africa and Northern Ireland, may be on the way to resolution (Booth, 1995:117).

Greater Sensitivity?

The predominant explanation for the policy shift in the 1990s is the success of normative values, with the development of a more human rights-aware population putting pressure on enlightened Western governments to act. There are two interrelated explanations for this shift in awareness: the growth of campaigning NGOs and the communications revolution, which has brought conflict into our living rooms through CNN and other 24-hour news channels. Geoffrey Robertson argues that the work of NGOs and the greater exposure of world events through CNN is rekindling the 'potent mix of anger and compassion' behind the establishment of the Universal Declaration 'and now produces a democratic demand not merely for something to be done, but for the laws and courts and prosecutors to do it' (1999:373). The combination of these two factors would indicate that the shift towards ethical foreign policy based on human rights is the product of popular demand. It is suggested that the human rights movement has millions of members throughout the world, including 12 million who signed a petition pledging support for the Universal Declaration in its fiftieth anniversary year. This 'indignant pity of the civilized world', transmitted to different democratic governments has allegedly impelled the international and UN response (G. Robertson, 1999:373).

While correctly understanding the qualitative nature of the shift towards ethical foreign policy, this argument is not easily substantiated. It is difficult to establish the nature of the relationship between government policy and the focus of NGO campaigning and international news coverage; it may well be that this relationship is a correlative rather than causative one. Both elements will be considered in turn.

First, the growth of NGO campaigns and civil society movements. Many human rights activists claim the credit for the transformation of international priorities, arguing that NGOs have been able to pressurise governments, which would otherwise be reluctant to act in the cause of human rights. In much of the academic literature on the question, there is some uncertainty over measuring the influence that NGO lobbyists have, relative to other factors that bear on government policy measures. One thing that is clear is that NGOs can only have an indirect influence. Ultimately, it is still states which approve international treaties, establish the monitoring mechanisms, decide the foreign assistance budgets, and decide troop commitments and priorities. While human rights NGOs can play an important role as conduits of Western funding in non-Western societies, they have few resources with which to influence their own governments. As David Forsythe notes, with neither a membership capable of influencing elections, nor the financial capacity to make donations or influence election campaigns, human rights NGOs lack the powers of traditional interest groups in the domestic political sphere (2000:169).

The growth of non-governmental organisations in the 1990s has been much remarked upon, but few commentators have pointed out that the influence of NGOs in international relations has changed cyclically, rather than undergoing a gradual increase. Steve Charnovitz's detailed study points out that emerging NGO 'international civil society' is not an entirely new phenomenon (1997). Non-governmental organisations tend to play a greater role during periods of transition in international institutions, the high points of international NGO influence being the 1850–1914 period, the 1920s and again in the last two decades. A central factor in this cycle has been the needs of governments and the creation and realignment of international institutions. The experimental development of new institutions and themes in the international order has involved the integration of NGOs, particularly in the policy areas which were not considered important during the Cold War, such as the environment, development, human rights and minorities (Charnovitz, 1997:269).

As Alvin Toffler noted in the 1970s: 'the careful, deliberate strengthening of the NGO sector and the integration of UN activities with the activities of the NGOs would go a long way towards replacing the present bureaucracy with a flexible, effective adhocracy' (cited in Charnovitz, 1997:285). Whereas politicians are formally bound by the legal and political constraints of international institutional frameworks, NGOs can be promoted as sounding boards for new ideas and organisational mechanisms (Bond, 2000:53). Paul Reinsch explains:

> States naturally move with caution ... and it is only when a need has become imperative and when means and methods have been worked out and shown to be safe and practical, that public authorities feel justified in entering into international administrative arrangements. (Cited in Charnovitz, 1997:269)

These studies suggest that it is governments and international institutions, experimenting with new forms of international regulation, that are controlling the agenda of NGOs, rather than the other way around.

Second, there is the role of the media, the expansion of forms of communications, e-mail and new technologies, which means that what happens on the other side of the world becomes headline news (P.M. Taylor, 1997). This is exemplified in the claims that there is a qualitatively greater 'CNN awareness' of human rights abuses around the world which has led to a public demand for human rights activism. As with NGO lobbying, the impact of new 'globalised' media and communications on government policy is difficult to assess fully. Nevertheless, opinion studies have shown that the idea that there is public pressure for human rights interventions has been exaggerated. For example, in the mid-1990s, polls showed that only a minority of the United States public backed human rights promotion as an important foreign policy goal, well behind stopping the flow of illegal drugs, protecting the jobs of US workers and preventing the spread of nuclear weapons (Forsythe, 2000:143). This finding is supported by the fact that President Clinton had to explain where Kosovo was on the map, before attempting to promote military action in 1999, because there was so little public interest in the issue. The 'CNN factor' should not be overrated. CNN coverage did not lead to US intervention in Rwanda or Zaire in the 1990s, and the extensive coverage of the Kosovo crisis created no public demand in the United States for ground forces to be sent in. In many respects, polls demonstrate that the Western public tend to share a more traditional view of foreign policy priorities, based on national interests, rather than the liberal 'crusading' perspective of their government leaders (Schwarz, 2000).

Alternatives?

The explanation for the rise of ethical foreign policy lies in transformations of both international and domestic political frameworks with the end of the Cold War. The transformation of the international sphere provides the possibility for declarations of support for universal ethics, but this chapter will suggest that a major impetus towards ethical policy-making also derives from changes in domestic politics. This is important to highlight as analysts of the new ethical world order rarely consider the domestic political advantages governments can gain through their promotion of ethical foreign policies.

Attempts to use universal ethics to justify the projection of national power abroad are hardly novel, and can be seen in the nineteenth-century expansion of British control over international waters to counter slavery or the US declaration of war on Spain in 1898 because of its oppressive rule over Panama and Cuba (G. Robertson, 1999:13). The point that is central to the current transformation in the language of international regulation is that the legitimacy of universal claims depends on the extent to which these are challenged by opposing social forces. After the Second World War, international institutions, established under US leadership, attempted to positively justify their regulatory power in the language of universal rights and freedoms encapsulated in the United States' claim to be the 'defender of the free world'. Some people may argue that little has changed, except that the Western states have now claimed for themselves the mantle of the 'global community' or 'international society' with the demise of the Soviet bloc.

However, the disappearance of the Soviet bloc from the equation has been of greater importance than merely facilitating the name change from 'the West' to 'international community' or 'global civil society'. The promotion of the authority of Western powers through the use of universal values such as democracy and human rights was, in the Cold War period, always open to challenge and often discredited in practice, for example, in the popular opposition to the Vietnam War or to the West's sponsorship of unpopular surrogate states such as Israel or South Africa. The existence of a superpower alternative to the West meant that instruments of international domination over other parts of the world were often exposed as oppressive, despite the attachment of the UN to formal equality in the international sphere. Since 1989, however, the Western powers have faced little challenge to their capacity to (re)define and promote universal values (Chandler, 1997).

What has changed with the end of the Cold War is the capacity of Western powers to politically legitimise greater intervention abroad. This capacity is rarely understood by international commentators who assume it to be a constant, and therefore understand the shift towards 'ethical' policy as a product of the decline of military competition with the Soviet bloc. For example, Mitchell Meyers notes:

> With the strategic and political restraints of the Cold War, no longer a near total albatross, a new paradigm of foreign policy is foreseeable. For instance, the United States can now intervene in more places where it perceives there has been an implied waiver of sovereignty [through human rights abuse], without fearing retaliation from a non-existent Communist bloc. (1997:904)

The Soviet Union did not just represent a military challenge to Western intervention in the developing world. The Soviet bloc and non-aligned states formally supported the anticolonial struggle and encouraged the possibility of independent economic and political development. The international framework of the Cold War, therefore, also reflected a political barrier to Western interventionism. The decline of support for the aspirations reflected in these international challenges to Western domination has enabled Western powers to morally and politically legitimise more direct interventions, rather than resorting to covert actions and the manipulation of dependent client regimes. This capacity to reorganise international relations on the terms of the leading

Western states was powerfully demonstrated in the 'remarkable new alliances' with states in the Middle East and Asia, cemented by US and British diplomatic activity preceding US-led military action against Afghanistan (Murphy and Wastell, 2001).

The possibility of using the international sphere to promote ethical universals does not fully explain why this path has been loudly proclaimed by the major industrialised powers. To explain the reasons for the shift in foreign policy perspectives, and increasingly militarised forms of international relations, it is also necessary to consider the problems of the domestic sphere.

One aspect that defines governments across the major industrialised states is a preference for an ethical re-framing of policy initiatives. With the end of the ideological framework of the Cold War it has become increasingly difficult to justify and legitimise policies on the basis of the traditional identities of capital and labour. This is reflected in the shift by governments in the US, Britain and Germany towards attempting to occupy the centre ground and redefine their aims in the language of the 'Third Way'. There is a rejection of political programmes based on traditional constituencies of the Left and the Right, in an attempt to find policies which appeal directly to individuals no longer engaged with or involved in the political process. Attempts to cohere the middle ground and connect governments with a citizenship alienated from traditional party politics have led to a focus on ethics and morality.

Ethical policy is a powerful mechanism for cohering a set of clear values and broad policy aims for Western governments when domestic policy-making has no ready-made constituency and easily leads to party divisions and public discrediting. In these days of increasing cynicism and doubt over government and politics at a domestic level, human rights promotion seems to be the one idea with the power to hold society together and point a way beyond the relativism and pessimism of our times. As Francesca Klug notes: 'the post-Cold War search for new ideals and common bonds in an era of failed ideologies appears to have contributed to a growing appreciation of human rights as a set of values' (2000b:147).

The attention to ethical foreign policy has been an important resource of authority and credibility for Western political leaders. The ability to project or symbolise unifying 'values' has become a core leadership attribute. George W. Bush's shaky start to the US presidency was transformed by his speech to Congress in the wake of the World Trade Center and Pentagon attacks, in which he staked out his claim to represent and protect America's ethical values against the terrorist 'heirs of all the murderous ideologies of the twentieth century' (Bush, 2001a). Tony Blair, similarly, was at his most presidential in the wake of the attacks, arguing that values were what distinguished the two sides of the coming conflict: 'We are democratic. They are not. We have respect for human life. They do not. We hold essentially liberal values. They do not.' (2001a) Peter Hain, Minister of State at the UK Foreign Office, also focused on the 'values that the terrorists attacked' in his call for political unity around 'tough action' (2001). It is for these reasons that high-profile intervention over Kosovo was considered very positively in the Blair government's leaked memos in the summer of 2000 (Wintour, 2000). Peregrine Worsthorne, a former editor of *The Times*, has argued that ethical foreign policy has become of central importance to the government's legitimacy at home: 'Like it or not, therefore, we realpolitikers must realise that a nation state which fails to try to do its humanitarian duty is likely to lose its *raison d'être*.' (1999) As former US vice-president Al Gore has stated, the focus on human rights means 'the United States of America stands for something in this world' (cited in Wagenseil, 1999:4). This sense of mission and policy coherence through ethical foreign policy was clearly articulated by Bush and Blair in the wake of the Pentagon and World Trade Center attacks. President Bush stating in his 20 September speech that 'in our grief and our anger we have found our mission and our moment' in the call to defend freedom (Bush, 2001a). Some commentators have interpreted the focus of both Bush and Blair on finding a sense of mission in foreign policy as an expression of the Western leaders' religious convictions and 'faith-based' approach, although these convictions appear to be much less evident in the domestic sphere (Sullivan, 2001).

The Labour government's Strategic Defence Review makes clear that the resources being put into foreign policy initiatives bear little relationship to any strategic threat faced by the UK. Since the Cold War, 'the UK can be more discriminating about those risks it chooses to address and the reasons for which it may address them':

> We could of course, as a country, choose to take a narrow view of our role and responsibilities which did not require a significant military capability ... This is indeed a real choice, but not one the Government could recommend to Britain. (Cited in UKSCD, 1998:par. 87)

This flexibility, in terms of freedom from Cold War restraints, allows foreign policy to be driven more directly by domestic needs than before. The British government felt that 'Kosovo matters to Britain' although 'it is clear that there is no direct and immediate threat to Britain's own national security from the situation in Kosovo' (UKSCD, 1998:par. 95). Kosovo 'mattered' not because of the importance of the situation on the ground in Kosovo, nor because of the depth of public support for Kosovo Albanians, who received little sympathy once they tried to take refuge in Britain as asylum seekers. As Mick Hume noted in *The Times*: 'The war against the Serbs is primarily about giving Mr Blair's Government an aura of moral authority and a sense of mission. It is about projecting a self-image of the ethical new Britain bestriding the world.' (1999)

The human rights discourse also provides a framework for the strident moral mission of the 'war against terrorism' declared by Washington and London after the September 2001 destruction of the World Trade Center. Leading Western states could claim the right to project their power abroad on the basis that they were acting for universal interests rather than their own. In George Bush's words: 'This is the world's fight. This is civilization's fight. This is the fight of all who believe in progress and pluralism, tolerance and freedom.' (2001a) Tony Blair assumed the mantle of 'the moral power of a world acting as a community' to argue that this moral mission would 'reorder the world around us' (2001b).

The search for ethical or moral approaches to the centre ground has inexorably led to a domestic shift in priorities making international policy-making increasingly high-profile. This is because it is easier to promote universal values and ethics in foreign policy than in domestic policy. There are three big advantages: first, the object of criticism is a foreign government; second, the British, or US, government is not so accountable for matching rhetoric to international actions; and third, credit can be claimed for any positive outcome of international policy, while any negative outcome can be blamed on the government which was the object of criticism. This chapter suggests that the lack of connection between rhetorical demands and accountability for policy-making or policy outcomes has made ethical foreign policy-making a strong card for Western governments, which need to consolidate their authority at home. The human rights approach enables Western governments to attempt to address domestic malaise through the sphere of foreign policy, focusing on international issues to resolve awkward questions of elite mission and political coherence.

FOREIGN POLICY OF CRITICISM

The focus of ethical coherence through foreign policy has been shaped through the human rights discourse. Makau wa Mutua draws out the distinction that has developed in the NGO field between civil rights and human rights campaigners (1996:609). Western human rights groups have focused on the abusive practices of what they see as repressive 'backward' foreign countries and cultures, while the agenda of civil liberty groups has concentrated on domestic issues. In popular culture the assumption was that human rights problems did not apply to 'people like us' but to societies which are 'different' (Kennedy, 2000:xiii; Klug, 2000b:5). This division was reflected in Cold War academia where civil rights were taught under domestic politics courses and human rights were studied under foreign or international courses.

Non-governmental organisation human rights work tends to focus on the cataloguing of abuses committed by foreign governments, as Henry Steiner notes:

> Given the ideological commitments of these NGOs, their investigative work naturally concentrates on matters such as governmental abuses of rights to personal security, discrimination, and basic political rights. By habit or established practice, NGO's reports stress the nature and number of violations, rather than explore the socio-economic and other factors that underlie them. (Cited in Mutua, 1996:622)

Virtually all reports by NGOs are catalogues of cruelties and abuses by governments, and their central campaigning method has been to publish reports that generate press coverage and place international attention on stigmatised governments (Burgerman, 1998:910; Posner, 1997:628). The NGOs campaigning against non-Western governments see their work as non-political, they just describe abuses and ask the international community to act. In this way, they present human rights as independent of the social, economic or political situation. Many NGOs are concerned that explaining why abuses occur may justify them or give credence to the claims of repressive regimes. If mitigating factors were to be brought into the account this would undermine the mission of seeking immediate compliance with human rights standards. Pressure is brought about by utilising key events or symbols such as a highly publicised massacre, like Srebrenica, or a 'poster child' to simplify complex issues for mass audiences (Burgerman, 1998:910).

This association of ethical human rights policies with the denunciation of the crimes or abuses of governments has led to a particularly one-sided perspective focusing on condemnation and punishment. It is assumed that the more 'ethical' the government or NGO group is the more forceful will be their calls for sanctions or other forms of punishment. In this respect the human rights campaigners distinguish themselves from the international agencies involved in democracy promotion and democratisation, which tend to see a long process of constructive assistance for reforms as necessary (see Chandler, 2000a:7–17). There is little evidence that condemnation and coercion is a more effective policy option than co-operation. Jeffrey Garten in *Foreign Policy* asks if human rights activists would deny that US trade links and commercial investment in states like China, India, Indonesia and Brazil have contributed to improved economic opportunities, communication freedoms and better education, health and working conditions (1996). He makes a strong case that 'the criteria for promoting human rights ought to be not what salves our consciences, but rather what works' (1996). However, the pragmatic 'what works' approach seems to be noticeable by its absence in the human rights NGOs' concern to denounce foreign governments and promote ethical coercion. As considered in Chapter 2, most high-profile human rights actions have involved selective condemnations, sanctions and military intervention; the policies of economic integration and aid have, in fact, suffered and are often seen as inimical to human rights promotion.

Unfortunately, the NGO approach of seeking 'worst cases' to highlight their work, through mounting a populist campaign of condemnation, has been willingly followed by Western governments. For example, in his ethical mission statement of July 1997, the British Foreign Secretary identified key aspects of ethical foreign policy. These measures all prioritised coercion over co-operation. They included support for measures to condemn regimes which 'grossly violate' human rights standards and 'repeatedly fail to respond' to demands to improve the situation; giving full support to sanctions applied by the international community to force human rights violators to improve their records; the support of multilateral conferences which criticised abuses of human rights; and support for the International Criminal Court and the provision of more resources for the international tribunals at The Hague and Arusha (UKFAC, 1998; Cook, 1997).

The association of ethical foreign policy with international condemnation and coercion was cohered during the Kosovo conflict. For Tony Blair this was a 'moral crusade' fought for moral values (1999b; 1999d). The ethical nature of the Kosovo war was also emphasised by Vaclav Havel, speaking in April 1999:

> But there is one thing no reasonable person can deny: this is probably the first war that has not been waged in the name of 'national interests', but rather in the name of principles and values. If one can say of any war that it is ethical, or that it is being waged for ethical reasons, then it is true of this war. Kosovo has no oil fields to be coveted; no member nation in the alliance has any territorial demands on Kosovo; Milosevic does not threaten the territorial integrity of any member of the alliance. And yet the alliance is at war. It is fighting out of a concern for the fate of others. It is fighting because no decent person can stand by and watch the systematic, state-directed murder of other people. It cannot tolerate such a thing. It cannot fail to provide assistance if it is within its power to do so. (Cited in Falk, 1999a:848)

The US-led assault on Afghanistan of October 2001 followed the same ethical logic. Again, it was a responsibility that 'no decent person' could fail to support. Unlike wars of the past, this was not about the narrow pursuit of national interests but about demonstrating responsible global citizenship and, above all, helping to protect the people of Afghanistan themselves. The Secretary of Defense, Donald Rumsfeld, suggested that 'to say these attacks are in any way against Afghanistan or the Afghan people, is flat wrong', while George Bush explained: 'This is our way of saying that ... we are friends of the Afghan people.' (King and Jaffe, 2001; Rumsfeld, 2001) The Western bombers could argue that they were the 'friends' of the Afghan people and could morally justify their interverntion through the condemnation of the human rights record of the Taliban government, Tony Blair arguing:

> Look for a moment at the Taliban regime. It is undemocratic. That goes without saying. There is no sport allowed, or television or photography. No art or culture is permitted ... Women are treated

in a way almost too revolting to be credible. First driven out of university; girls not allowed to go to school; no legal rights; unable to go out of doors without a man. Those that disobey are stoned. (2001b)

The politics of condemnation takes for granted that the problems of weak and fragile states (like Afghanistan) are internal matters of poor governance or questions of the mindset of ruling elites. This approach ignores the interntional context, for example, the impact of sanctions and international isolation. It also pays scant attention to the domestic social and political context, never asking how women can have equal rights, or high art and culture can flourish, in a society ravaged by war and intervention and now largely based on feudal backwardness and a subsistence economy. The foreign policy of criticism exploits the human rights framework to portray the carpet bombing of Afghanistan as part of the solution to the problems of international isolation and economic and social disintegration.

RHETORIC WITHOUT RESPONSIBILITY

The secret of the success of the human rights movement lies less in its roots in the radical humanitarianism of NGOs during the Cold War period than in the capacity of the discourse to provide legitimacy without accountability. The granting of rights which cannot be exercised by their subjects (considered further in Chapter 4) has allowed Western political elites to recast themselves and regulatory institutions at home and abroad through the creation of a new political subject which stands outside the political sphere, the human rights victim. The creation and prioritisation of these new 'ethical' rights and pseudo-political subjects has enabled the governments of Western states to supplement their problematic political mandates with a new ethical legitimacy.

There are two key aspects to the attempts to provide a non-political legitimisation of political power. Both involve the redefinition of the rights of citizens and the duties of governments. First, the universalising of the political subject: the governments of the West now proclaim they have a duty to others as much as to their citizens, downgrading the importance of legitimacy through the traditional political subject, the electorate. Second, the duty of the government to others is one that does not involve the right of accountability. As considered below, the decisions on what ethical policy actions to take reside with the government or are taken in co-operation with other Western states. Ethical foreign policy is one area in which the government can operate outside the traditional sphere of policy-making.

Accountable to Whom?

The concept of human rights intervention in the cause of protecting or promoting the rights of the vulnerable has a powerful but problematic appeal. As Nigel Dower notes, ethical foreign policy is a radical change in how political policy has been traditionally justified (1997:107). Ethical policy departs from the traditional lines of accountability in a modern democracy where the government was seen to have a duty to reflect the desires and priorities of its citizens in its policy-making. Ethical foreign policy is defined by an opposite set of justifications. It is based on the moral recognition that a government's duty is no longer to the electorate: '[O]nce we recognise that our duty extends towards those unknown, i.e. that we have a duty of more extended caring, then the unknown can be anywhere and anyone, irrespective of place, race, creed, sex or whatever.' (Dower, 1997:103)

Internationalising responsibility for human rights means that we are all responsible but at the same time no one is accountable. Human rights are the duty of everyone. Mary Robinson, UN Commissioner for Human Rights, argues that 'all of us are called upon to play a part in championing and defending human rights ... Individuals have a duty to put pressure on governments ... and to try to ensure the media spotlight is not turned off ... We are all answerable.' (1999) Kofi Annan, UN Secretary-General, makes the same point:

> When we recall tragic events such as those of Bosnia or Rwanda and ask, 'Why did no one intervene?' the question should not be addressed only to the United Nations, or even to its member states ... Each of us as an individual has to take his or her share of responsibility. No one can claim ignorance of what happened. All of us should recall how we responded, and ask: 'What did I do? Could I have done more? Did I let my prejudice, my indifference, or my fear overwhelm my reasoning? Above all, how would I react next time?' (Cited in Whitney, 1999)

As Alex de Waal notes: 'The "responsibility" of the UN agencies, NGOs and foreign governments is a vague and easily evaded moral responsibility – nothing more than an aspiration – rather than a practical obligation for which the "responsible" institution can be called to account.' (1997a:70)

Victim's Rights?

While ethical foreign policy is seen as not directly accountable to the electorate, it is often argued that there is a higher universal moral accountability in supporting the rights of victims. As Mary Robinson puts it: 'Everything begins and ends with a determination to secure a life of dignity – a truly human quality of life – for all the people in whose names we act.' (1997:25) However, the problem with universal moral accountability is that it can never be a replacement for political accountability. In fact, the claims for universal moral accountability undermine the notion of democratic accountability itself.

First, on the most abstract level, there cannot be universal victims' rights. The concept of victims' rights undermines universality by creating a special interest. In fact, the development of modern law depends on the removal of any particular or special rights of the victim. For example, victims of crime have no special rights as the criminal law is defended and applied in the interests of society, not as an individual act of revenge or retribution. The victims of crimes or abuses would, in a domestic context, be the last people to make a final judgement on action to be taken, or to establish a just solution. Victims of crimes would in many cases advocate the most barbaric punishments and be the least likely to support the rights of the accused. Similarly, 'victims' who may be inconvenienced or lose out through social changes brought about by economic development or environmental projects would have strong negative views which, while understandable, could not be the basis on which society should decide whether those developments should go ahead. It is clear that if the international community actually were to base policy on the claims or rights of victims it would be in an impossible position, supporting a highly coercive policy on behalf of an unrepresentative minority perspective. On this most simplistic level, it is clear that the universal ethic of action in the cause of victims' rights cannot sustain the ethical weight being attached to it by its advocates.

Second, human rights intervention to support victims' rights or needs tends to empower the forces that are acting on their behalf rather than the victims themselves. As Hannah Arendt noted, this relationship of external assistance for victims is the opposite of a right: it is a charitable act; there is no law or right that could force intervention of this sort (1979:296). As with all cases of claims not based on rights: 'Privileges in some cases, injustices in most, blessings and doom are meted out to them according to accident and without any relation whatsoever to what they do, did, or may do.' (1979:296)

Tony Blair's party conference speech following the World Trade Center and Pentagon attacks demonstrated the ease with which the human rights framework could legitimate an otherwise questionable claim to act on the behalf of others. Blair declared that he was not just concerned with British interests but that: 'The starving, the wretched, the dispossessed, the ignorant, those living in want and squalor from the deserts of northern Africa to the slums of Gaza, to the mountains of Afghanistan: they too are our cause.' (2001b) The British Prime Minister later stated that his government was committed to working with the people of Afghanistan 'to ensure a better, more peaceful future' (Perkins, 2001). Today, the governments of the United States and Britain declare they have a duty to protect the rights of the Afghan people. Tomorrow, they may claim the duty to protect the human rights of someone else. The problem is that there is no mechanism to make the actions of the world's most powerful states accountable to the citizens of the states they choose to intervene in. The claim to act on behalf of other people can create a dangerous blank cheque to justify the actions of Western governments. For example, Tony Blair could claim that the carpet bombing of Afghanistan was an action undertaken on behalf of Afghan citizens: 'This is not a conventional conflict. It is not a battle for territory per se or for the subjugation of Afghanistan. It is a battle to allow the Afghans themselves to retake control of their country.' (2001c) Of course, the Afghan people were to be given no choice over whether they were to be 'liberated' by US Air Force B52s or not.

International intervention in the Balkans also demonstrated that this process reinforces the inequalities of power between the international actors and the purported victims themselves. It was the intervening powers which defined the victim and prescribed the rights which they were choosing to uphold. The use of human rights to directly undermine democratic rights in this region was evident in discussions on the selective use of humanitarian aid in Serbia in 1999 and 2000. The European Union proposed to provide only certain types of humanitarian aid to Serbian municipalities run by opposition parties (see Chapter 2). The first selective aid programme was 'Energy for Democracy', where humanitarian shipments of heating fuel were directed to cities such as Nis, Kraljevo and Kragujevac. This was followed by similar aid programmes such as 'Schools for Democracy', 'Roads for Democracy' and 'Milk for Democracy' (ESEM, 2000; Rozen, 2000a). This selective approach of aiding some 'victims' while the rest of Serbia suffered international sanctions did little to empower the 'victims' but rather attempted to manipulate them to support a political project favoured by Western governments.

Perhaps the clearest example of the manipulation of victims' rights in the region was in response to the Kosovo crisis. The Nato powers established the need for intervention and a prolonged bombing campaign on the basis of protecting the human rights of the ethnic-Albanian community, alleged to be the victims of genocidal policies by the Serbs. During the bombing campaign the US Defense Secretary, William Cohen, claimed that 100,000 ethnic-Albanian men 'may have been murdered'; David Scheffer, the US envoy for war crimes, put the figure as high as 225,000 (Steele, 2000b). The lowest Nato government estimate of the number of ethnic-Albanians massacred by Serb forces, by Geoff Hoon at the British Home Office, was 'at least 10,000' (Steele, 2000a; 2000b). These figures were in marked contrast to the ICTY's preliminary conclusions, in August 2000, that the final total death toll of the civil conflict would be between 2,000 and 3,000.

The victim status of the ethnic-Albanians that allowed them to gain the support of Nato states was not enough to allow them a say in the post-war government of the province. Once the Serb state had been forced to relinquish sovereign powers over the territory, Nato was concerned that the victims would 'fill the vacuum' with their own institutions (Zizek, 2000:59). After waging war for ethnic-Albanian rights to autonomy and self-government, Nato and UN officials felt that the ethnic-Albanians could not be trusted to rule in their own name, let alone take over the administration of schools, hospitals and the media (Chandler, 2000b). An extensive bombing campaign that was waged for the rights of Balkan victims, as the most public example of ethical human rights-led foreign policy, resulted in little gain for the people of the region. Michael Mandelbaum makes the point in *Foreign Affairs* that 'Western leaders declared that they were fighting for the sake of the people of the

Balkans, who nevertheless emerged from the war considerably worse off than they had been before.' (Cited in Littman, 1999:ii–iii)

Once ethical policy is presented as action in the cause of others, any policy failure can only have limited political repercussions. This was demonstrated time and again over Balkan policy. Even the worst results of international meddling in the region were interpreted not as evidence of US and Nato policy failure but rather, in the words of President Clinton, as 'we gave them a chance to make their peace and they blew it' (Rose, 1998:65). One month, if developments in the region looked positive, it would be 'a test case' of the United States' ability to promote human rights; the next month, if things were going less well, the Balkans would become 'an intractable "problem from hell" that no one can be expected to solve' (Woodward, 1995:307). Any complaints over policy outcomes were met with the moral exculpation that 'we' tried and 'they' failed to make the most of it (Ignatieff, 1998:99). It seems that the process of buck-passing over Balkan policy will be repeated in relation to Afghanistan. The United States and Britain appear keen to make the UN responsible for delivering on their promises that they will help rebuild Afghanistan after the war. The United Nations is unwilling to be set up for a fall and has little desire to take responsibility for addressing the consequences of the ill-thought-out US intervention in the region. The UN administrators will no doubt blame the economic, social and political problems of any future regime squarely on the Afghan people and their representatives (MacAskill, 2001b; Judah, 2001).

POLICY SUCCESS GUARANTEED

Failure is Not Possible

When dealing with pariah states, the starting assumption that genocide is inevitable, or that a 'culture of violence' is to blame for the crisis, means that policy failure on the part of human rights interventionists is easy to ride out. Whatever happens in the targeted states, under international sanctions or military action, it can be alleged to be better than non-intervention. As both Tony Blair and the *Guardian* argued in response to the Nato slaughter of ethnic-Albanian refugees: 'Milosevic is determined to wipe a people from the face of this country. Nato is determined to stop him' (*Guardian*, 1999). Short of killing every ethnic-Albanian in Kosovo, Nato's haphazard bombing campaign was guaranteed to be a success.

The House of Commons Foreign Affairs Committee (UKFAC), although dismissing the idea that there was a Serb policy of genocide in Kosovo, still concluded that:

> The issue in Kosovo was ... whether in the absence of Nato intervention, the Serb campaign would have continued over many years, eventually resulting in more deaths and instability in the region than if Nato had not intervened. We believe that it would. (UKFAC, 2000c:par. 123)

The belief that it would have been even worse without international action provides a hypothetical *post facto* excuse that is difficult to disprove. Of course, in the realms of hypothetical possibility there are few limits to the academic imagination. John Gray, professor of European thought at the London School of Economics, asserts that:

> The result of Nato doing nothing would have been a newly divided Europe, with much of the Balkans consigned forever to an outer darkness in which human rights count for nothing ... If it had not intervened, Europe's Orthodox and Muslim regions would have ended up beyond the pale of civilised life, prey to ruthless tyranny and subject to gross abuses of human rights. (2000)

As the *Guardian* editorialised after more facts emerged into the public realm in relation to the Kosovo crisis: 'Excessive optimism about the success of the bombing was matched by excessive pessimism about the horror of Kosovo.' (2000d) The discourse of human rights establishes a framework of Western intervention which inevitably encourages a positive view of intervention in the face of exaggerated fears of non-intervention.

A similar misplaced optimism about precision bombing and the effectiveness of large-scale military action accompanied the military assault on Afghanistan following attacks in the United States. The direct cruise missile hit on Afghanistan's main mine clearing agency in a village two miles from Kabul, which killed four UN civilians, was an early indication which highlighted the gap between the public relations media exercise launched by Western governments and the reality on the ground (Jenkins, 2001; Harding, 2001). After another couple of weeks which saw the 'collateral' deaths of many more Afghan civilians as 'stray' missiles hit hospitals, mosques, civilian convoys, anti-Taliban villages as well as pro-Taliban villages, civilian economic installations and Red Cross supply stores, all without any clear military gains, Western governments still emphasised that stopping the bombing would be even worse. Clare Short raised the 'nightmare scenario' of the Taliban taking over Pakistan's nuclear capability, while Tony Blair went a step further to warn that Osama bin Laden's terrorist network could have already acquired nuclear materials and pose a nuclear threat to the world (McCarthy, 2001b; Webster, 2001a). Media commentators produced a long list of 'terrifying' scenarios that could take place if the bombing of Afghanistan were to stop prematurely. These ranged from economic concerns of losing control of Saudi oil-reserves to Polly Toynbee's conviction that, if left in power, the Taliban would 'slaughter their own people in numbers greater than the likely casualties of this war' (Ferguson, 2001; Toynbee, 2001). There was, therefore, little questioning when Tony Blair claimed that military action was justified, regardless of whether it succeeded or failed: 'Whatever the dangers of the action we take, the dangers of inaction are far, far greater' (2001b).

The methods used in international interventions and the final outcome are no longer relevant once an ethical human rights framework is established. Joy Gordon draws on comparisons with the Nuremberg and Tokyo trials after the Second World War, which asserted an essential distinction between 'evil human beings and righteous ones' (1998:783). In denouncing the moral crimes of the states which lost in the war, the acts of Western powers were seen as excusable:

> What Nuremberg tells us is that, measured against the moral and political imperative of denouncing atrocities, all competing moral or legal imperatives are completely without weight ... What is important to note is how this project of denunciation trumped all other moral issues and did so absolutely – not only the judicial illegitimacy of the tribunals themselves, but also the Allied war crimes, the use of Atomic weapons and the callousness and anti-Semitism of the many countries which denied refuge to Jews fleeing the Holocaust... We inherit from Nuremberg the idea that when there are atrocities to denounce, we need not look at the acts of the denouncers themselves. (1998:786)

Gordon continues, to note that: 'We inherit from Nuremberg the notion that moral denunciation of human rights violations does not have rules or limits, or ambivalence or ambiguity' (1998:787). The

Kosovo case was by no means exceptional in this regard. Because the human rights discourse establishes such a moralised view of 'ethical' interventions, it is difficult for critical views to gain a hearing. Today's human rights advocates tend to portray every 'ethical' inter-vention against selected pariah states as on a par with the Allied war effort against Nazi Germany, the template for a moralised view of conflict. This ethical connection is mythologised through the human rights teleology that connects 'ethical foreign policy' to the Genocide Convention of 1948 and the 1949 Geneva Conventions, which 'were intended to establish a firebreak between civilization and barbarism' (Gutman and Rieff, 1999:8).

Acting is What Counts

When coercive action is taken over alleged human rights concerns, these actions then become tests of resolve to strictly apply an 'ethical' approach, and the reputation of states and international institutions is held to be on the line. When human rights issues become the subject of a state's ethical foreign policy and become internationalised, they automatically gain significance. As the British House of Commons Select Committee on Defence noted: 'The sources of instability that affect our fundamental interests, therefore are often driven more by how we, our allies and partners choose to react to particular crises, rather than the crises themselves.' (UKSCD, 1998:par. 103) Kosovo, which initially was of little vital interest to Britain, became so once it was a focus for ethical policy-making. As the Select Committee noted, 'the very act of introducing British forces into a situation transforms any crisis from the UK's perspec-tive into something more fundamental, because, if nothing else, the safety and reputation of the UK's Armed Forces are then at stake' (UKSCD, 1998:par. 104). After intervention has been undertaken: '[I]t is not only the security of Europe, in its widest sense that is at risk ... So too is the credibility of Nato in its newly developing role, and so too is the effectiveness of the United Nations.' (UKSCD, 1998:par. 95) The same 'logic' was followed in the Afghanistan war, where aid agency and UN calls for a halt to the bombing to allow aid through were seen to send 'a terrible message' to terrorists about a lack of Western resolve (Wintour, 2001b). A rational call for a pause in the bombing was broadly held to mean challenging the credibil-ity of the intervention itself.

In this situation, international policy-making becomes quickly divorced from the immediate concerns of people in the targeted state and is seen to be a matter of broader principle. Further, it becomes increasingly symbolic, based more on the concern with 'image management' than the long-term consequences. Because there is little national interest at stake, governments are chiefly looking to capture positive headlines and increase their credibility at home. James Woolsey, former director of the CIA, has argued that recent US administrations have had 'a propensity sometimes to reason backwards from public relations to policy, to the facts one was looking at' (Harnden, 2001). This makes policy vulnerable to shifts and turns as it is dictated more by domestic concerns than events on the ground. This is why international action, based on short-term considerations, often appears half-hearted or ill thought out. Rather than resolving a crisis, intervention driven by domestic or institutional concerns is as likely to provoke or to extenuate one. It is this tendency that inevitably meant that US-led military intervention in Afghanistan created a humanitarian crisis, rather than resolving one (Steele and Lawrence, 2001), repeating the same destabilising process that led to international policy over Kosovo transforming 'a relatively small scale conflict into a regional humanitarian crisis' (Michael Barutciski cited in Pugh, 2000:232).

Human rights interventions, in these circumstances, are much less rational, even in their military dimension, than traditional state *realpolitik*. The entirely irrational course of the Kosovo war, in *realpolitik* terms, from diplomacy at Rambouillet, to military strategy, to economic devastation of the region, provides support for the view that being seen to act mattered more than the action itself. This point was reinforced to me during the Kosovo crisis when a lead writer for the *Observer* contacted me at the start of the bombing campaign. The paper had been urging the government to commit to military force but, now that it had, was concerned about the consequences. Because of previous support for a tough moral stance the editors believed that, despite their doubts, the paper had to give full support to the campaign as the only way forward (see *Observer*, 1999a). Just as Nato's credibility was allegedly on the line so was the *Observer*'s, and that of every other media journalist and human rights advocate who had called for intervention. Once the issues became ones of moral principle it was much more difficult to step back and advocate an objective policy approach.

As soon as the human rights framework is established, there is an inevitable assumption that external intervention is the only moral solution. The problem with this framework is that intervening powers rarely consider the long-term consequences. As Madeleine Bunting writes in the *Guardian*, there is a 'Disneyfication of reality' as Western leaders play the 'fantasy game' Nation Builder, deluding themselves in the 'belief that attacking a poor, desperate, brutalised country will, in the long run, be good for it' (2001). The irrational policy-making which marked the Kosovo intervention was repeated in Afghanistan. Once again, the offer of negotiations was roundly rejected and the military intervention lacked any consistent aims with apparently little thought given to military or political strategy or the disastrous humanitarian consequences for the people of the region (Burke, 2001). Eminent military historian Professor Sir Michael Howard was one of many commentators who could not understand the rationale behind US and British military actions, arguing that the bombing of Afghanistan was like 'trying to eradicate cancer cells with a blow torch' (Branigan, 2001b).

Because the ethical agenda of human rights intervention is drawn up by international institutions, under pressure from governments wishing to be seen to be 'doing something', policies in areas of activism often bear little relationship to needs. One clear example of this was the dropping of aid and food supplies by the US military at the start of the military campaign against Afghanistan. The food supplies, parachuted down in canary-yellow food packets labelled 'This is a food gift from the people of the United States of America', which included tomato ketchup, peanut butter and strawberry jam, were widely condemned by aid agencies as being totally inappropriate for people suffering from malnutrition (Fletcher, 2001; AFP, 2001). Thomas Gonnet, head of Afghan operations for French aid agency Action Against Hunger, described the food drop as 'an act of marketing, aimed more at public opinion than saving lives' (AFP, 2001; see also Monbiot, 2001a). Even the military strategy was shaped as much by the domestic concern with image management as tactical needs on the ground. One example of this was the actions of the US Navy F18 fighters, in the first few weeks of the campaign, which made purely symbolic attacks on the Taliban front lines, at the same place every day, playing to the large media corps based in the Northern Alliance territory (Meek, 2001). This attention to media image could also be seen in the staged blanket coverage of the first US special forces raid against abandoned Taliban installations, selected in order to make a good impression on the viewing audience back home (Hume, 2001). There has been a lot of media commentary on the 'propaganda war' and attempts by the UK and

US governments to control media exposure (Wells, 2001; Watt and Denny, 2001; *Times*, 2001). However, less attention has been given to the broader policy consequences of economic, political and military intervention strategies which are led by PR concerns rather than needs on the ground. One area where some disquiet has been raised over false priorities is that of post-war international involvement. In many cases, there has been harsh criticism that the allocation of human rights spending seems to be unrelated to the requirements of those on the ground (Jenkins, 1999b). This is demonstrated by the skewering of international assistance to states which are the focus of media attention. The first year of the United Nations mission in Kosovo cost an estimated $456 million, yet little of this went to meet humanitarian needs. As Iain Guest noted, 'the massive concentration of international aid in such a tiny country has had a devastating impact' (2000). The takeover of Kosovo by aid agencies and UN administrative officials has resulted in the collapse of ethnic-Albanian social organisations and actually undermined 'capacity-building'. Recovery has been set back by inflation caused by high-spending international officials pushing house prices beyond reach, while the distortion of salaries means that professionals like teachers or doctors can earn ten times more as drivers and interpreters. Huge sums, like a $10 million grant made available for the Kosovo Women's Initiative, have led to people establishing NGOs just to obtain donor money as social and economic life is reshaped around the funding requirements of external institutions.

As Thomas Carothers observes, it seems that 'the case for foreign assistance generally, may at times depend less on the specific impact of the assistance on others than on what the assistance says and means about ourselves' (1996:132). Michael Ignatieff draws out the dangers of this self-serving approach:

> [W]hen policy was driven by moral motives, it was often driven by narcissism. We intervened not only to save others, but to save ourselves, or rather an image of ourselves as defenders of universal decencies. We wanted to show that the West 'meant' something. (1998:95)

With regard to the Balkans, a few critics did attempt to argue for a rational foreign policy concerned with results more than declarations. John Casey wrote: 'It is reckless of the Government to pretend that the Nato bombings can be justified irrespective of any policy for the settlement of the Balkans.' (1999) Simon Jenkins argued that the Labour government was 'merely playing with imperialism' and at best 'half-hearted' (2000). As Susan Woodward told the UK House of Commons Foreign Affairs Committee: 'there was not a clear political goal', in fact the policy goal 'was so weak that it changed over the period of time that we were bombing. We kept changing goals and you can follow the rhetoric of leaders to see that.' (UKFAC, 2000c:par. 74) The Committee concluded that 'it seems reasonable to assume that Nato was not clear about its objectives' (UKFAC, 2000c:par. 76). A similar lack of clarity about possible war aims in the attack on Afghanistan following the destruction of the World Trade Center led to nearly a month of uncertainty as the US and British governments delayed any action, choosing to focus on high-profile 'consensus-building' with other world leaders (Borger *et al.*, 2001). When the military assault started on 7 October the fact that bin Laden could not be located meant the claimed objective changed to destabilising the Taliban regime (Watson and Whitworth, 2001). After nearly a month of bombing without any evidence of bin Laden's whereabouts or any military advances against Taliban-held towns, Western leaders sought to shift the focus, Admiral Sir Michael Boyce, Chief of the UK Defence Staff, stating that the war could last three or four years because 'we're fighting a concept, not a state ... The al-Qaida organisation is not tangible' (Evans, 2001).

However, critics who advise caution and the need to consider the consequences of ethical coercion are often seen as opponents of the human rights cause. In relation to Kosovo, Jonathan Freedland, among others, argued that, by not intervening, Western governments would be 'bystanders to evil' (1999). The emphasis was on the nobleness of the cause rather than the policy results. As Susan Sontag stated: 'There is a radical evil in the world, which is why there are just wars. And this is a just war. Even if it has been consistently bungled ... Stop the genocide. Return the refugees. Worthy goals.' (1999) Under these circumstances, action is what counts. The morality is in taking action rather than the final outcome or consistency. Peregrine Worsthorne wrote:

> [I]t is not at all surprising that Messrs Clinton and Blair are getting more credit from public opinion than from the experts for how they are handling the Kosovo crisis. For a morally driven foreign policy ... has to be judged by different criteria to a traditional foreign policy – which is what the experts understand – based on considerations of national security. While practical results are

central in any realistic assessments of the latter, noble intentions are central to any realistic assessment of the former. Ideally, of course, the noble *intentions* should produce noble results, but if that – for reasons beyond our control – proves impossible, then it is at least something to be proud of to have had the noble intentions. (1999)

He argued that the national interest had been redefined by the international humanitarians to include the 'nation's interest in being able to go to bed at night with a clear conscience'; in which case, a bungled international intervention was preferable to none: 'Better in the national interest, therefore, to try to help, and fail, than not to try at all.' (1999) Ken Booth, in his criticism of 'philosophical sceptics' who emphasise the dangers of international meddling without any clear aims, clearly favoured 'confused' policies of intervention over caution:

Meanwhile, flesh is being fed or famished, and people are being tortured or killed … Unless academics are merely to spread confusion, or snipe from the windows of ivory towers, we must engage with the real. This means having 'the courage of our confusions' and thinking and acting without certainty. (1995:113)

THE LIMITS OF ETHICAL FOREIGN POLICY

At the level of public declaration, human rights, or rather the promise to ethically refuse to trade or aid regimes which fall below certain human rights standards, has taken centre place in the foreign policy agendas. This can be seen from the new agendas of every international institution, from the UN to the World Bank, every regional association of states, from the European Union to the Organisation of African Unity, and every Western government. However, the policy impact of these universal commitments to act against human rights abusers has been a highly uneven one.

The aspirations of the human rights commentators, for the punishment or isolation of human rights abusing states, could never be consistently put into practice without bringing international relations to a standstill. The isolation of selected peripheral states is a possibility but anything further would bring international chaos. As David Rieff argues, universal action against human rights abuses would be a recipe for 'war without end' (cited in Longworth, 1999). With scores of states practising torture it is unlikely that there could be concerted agreement on sanctions and international punishments. And even if there was, it would seem problematic to assume that bringing the leaders of all these states to the International Criminal Court or imposing blanket economic sanctions would be organisationally possible, let alone that it would bring any benefits to their benighted people (Holbrook, 2000). The United States is widely held to abuse a variety of human rights, for example, by practising the death penalty, but international sanctions would seem an unlikely way to change public or government opinion on the issue. Similarly, the European Union's sanctions and political ostracism of Austria after the success of Jörg Haider's Freedom Party in the October 1999 elections, did little to change the public support for his views and was highly impractical for the collective mechanisms of the EU. The Austrian example shows clearly that there is a difference between making a high-minded declaration in support of human rights and actually acting on it. In September 2000 the EU quietly decided to drop the sanctions without conditions.

The problems of universally applying the coercive policies of the human rights discourse are particularly revealed in the selective discussion about war crimes. Truth commissions are considered fine for countries like South Africa, El Salvador, Guatemala or Chile, where there is an international consensus on the need for stability and no desire to upset delicate local political arrangements (Bosco, 2000; Wright, 2000). On the other hand, in international pariah states, like Yugoslavia, the moral absolute of human rights comes into play despite the recognised fact that criminal trials can prolong or rekindle animosity and prevent peace and reconciliation (Astier, 2000; Crossette, 2000). Even when 'principled' human rights policies are enacted against pariah states, *realpolitik* and the need for stability often intrude. This was demonstrated in October 2000 when the UN Secretary-General's special envoy to Yugoslavia, Jiri Dienstbier, publicly suggested that, for the sake of stability, Milosevic should be offered immunity from the UN's criminal tribunal if he stepped down from power. He argued that: 'The real question is if we are more interested in Milosevic ... or the future of 10m Serbs and probably the Balkans.' (Cited in MacAskill and Traynor, 2000; Boot, 2000b). Similar concerns arose in disagreements between the EU and the United States over whether aid for the Kostunica regime should be dependent on handing Milosevic over to The Hague (Carroll *et al.*, 2000).

The untenable nature of the coercive demands on ethical foreign policy means that there is inevitably a stark contradiction between the universal moral and ethical claims made for government policy and the more pragmatic policy outcomes. In the select cases where strong economic, diplomatic or military action is taken, usually against economically marginal states where few strategic interests are at stake, it is easy to make the media headlines and claim the moral high ground. When there is no action taken because of the expense involved, the lack of international or regional agreement on policy, or geo-strategic or economic interests, then pragmatism is defensively justified as 'the conscious policy of Critical Engagement – the pursuit of political dialogue wherever it can produce benefits' (UKFAC, 2000b:par. 13).

Government policy-makers often argue that there can be no straightforward accountability for 'ethical' policy-making because there is no set of guidelines which can be applied automatically regardless of context (UKFAC, 2000b:par. 13; 1998:par. 94). Government officers suggest that human rights policies should be implemented internationally on a case-by-case basis because for some states, sanctions or military intervention may be the best policy, while for others, quiet diplomacy may produce the best results (Scheffer, 1999; see also Forsythe, 2000:228–9). Naturally, many commentators are sceptical of these arguments that justify the case-by-case basis of government policy-making, allegedly on the grounds of pragmatism, in the cause of human rights promotion. There are two critiques of this ethical selectivity, both of which do little to point out the irrational nature of aspirations to international 'ethical' coercion.

The main critique of double standards is from the supporters of ethical foreign policy themselves. These critics argue that double standards are not inherent in the irrational demands of the coercive human rights discourse, but are, in fact, a product of the 'narrow' interest of governments in maintaining international trade and stability. They argue that it is these 'narrow' interests that restrict ethical policy-making. This is demonstrated by observing that there has been little real change in commitment to coercive policies during the 1990s. For example, the European Union had applied limited economic sanctions for human rights abuses twice before 1990, against the Soviet Union over martial law in Poland in 1981 and against South Africa over the 1985 state of emergency. Despite the 1986 Declaration on Human Rights and increased rhetorical centrality of human rights to European Union affairs, little changed in the 1990s. As one study concludes:

> Although human rights are supposed to lie at the heart of the CFSP [Common Foreign and Security Policy], in practice the [European] Union's response to grave violations of human rights in Rwanda, Zaire, Nigeria, Burma and East Timor has been minimal and ineffectual. The Union's human rights diplomacy has in general remained limited to issuing condemnatory declarations. (T. King, 1999:335–6)

The reasons for the reluctance to act against human rights abuses were those of strategic and economic interest. As David Forsythe notes, there is an 'enormous gap between the liberal legal framework on human rights that most states have formally endorsed, and the realist principles that they often follow in their foreign policies' (2000:139). These included: concerns over instability in states with close relations to particular European powers; economic concerns that European banks and companies would be affected by actions against Nigeria or China; and fears that economic relations with states from the Association of South East Asian Nations would be affected by action against Burma or Indonesia (T. King, 1999). As Labour MP Diane Abbott noted, the British government had a 'temptation to be strong [on human rights] in weak countries and weak in strong countries' (BBC, 1998; see also UKFAC, 1998:par. 98).

In the United States, the Clinton administration's human rights declarations were also highly selectively applied. Aryeh Neier, former executive director of Human Rights Watch, charged that the administration willingly denounced human rights violations in 'pariah states or the governments of countries that are not considered politically or economically important' but refused to condemn repressive governments deemed to be economically or strategically important for the United States (cited in Apodaca and Stohl, 1999:194; see also Neier, 1996). The evidence shows that the United States has been happy to take a lead in denouncing human rights abuses which occur in states such as Cuba, Iran, Iraq, Libya, North Korea, Serbia, Sudan and Syria, but unwilling to condemn similar, or worse, abuses in geo-politically or economically significant states such as Egypt, Israel, Mexico, Saudi Arabia, Turkey, Brazil, Indonesia, Russia, India or China (Neier, 1996). As David Rieff notes, the US administration has 'voraciously embraced' the new agenda of human rights on the rhetorical level, but has simultaneously insisted this agenda is entirely consistent with the traditional global interests of US hegemony (1999b).

Despite the rhetoric of the universality of human rights, the reality is that the impact of action on human rights is a highly selective one. As the British House of Commons Foreign Affairs Committee notes:

> There are relatively few regimes which so 'grotesquely violate human rights and repeatedly fail to respond to demands for an improvement in standards' that they occasion concerted action on the part of the international community in the form of condemnation or the imposition of political or economic sanctions. Regimes such as Myanmar and the Federal Republic of Yugoslavia are guilty of flagrant and repeated breaches of human rights standards, and properly stand condemned. However, there are other regimes which arguably have comparable human rights records and yet, for reasons which may be strategic or commercial, do not attract the opprobrium or condemnation of the international community to such a degree, if at all. (UKFAC, 1998:par. 92)

From the perspective of the human rights advocates, the aspiration of universal condemnation is a courageous one, which should come before *realpolitik*. There is a clear recognition that ethical policy-making is in direct opposition to traditional economic and political concerns. However, these critics seem to have no sense of the value of *realpolitik* for the international order or of the problems that would be caused by actually ignoring the dictates of economic, political or military stability. In the past, this attempt to ignore the realities of the world order would have seemed mad or at least utopian, yet today these ethical crusaders have the capacity to put governments on the defensive.

The alternative critique of the double standards of ethical foreign policy is that offered by the Left. For many Left critics of ethical condemnations, ethical foreign policy is not in opposition to *realpolitik* but a way of acting on it. They agree with the human rights advocates that the reluctance to impose coercive policies on many states is due to real interests of economic and political stability. However, they imagine that where states are scapegoated as human rights pariahs this is because they are either resisting the world market, or have economic resources that have to be directly exploited or are in geo-strategic positions that Western powers seek to have direct control over. Instead of revealing the counter-productive and irrational impact of human rights coercion, the Left often rationalise these policies as if they were long-term strategies consciously followed and meticulously planned (see, for example, Chossudovsky, 1997; Clark *et al.*, 1998; Monbiot, 2001b).

The freedom to declare ethical policy, without universal rules to govern any actions taken, gives Western governments a very flexible remit: a freedom to choose which cases to turn into examples and which to ignore. This does not mean that governments are pursing an entirely 'realist' agenda of power politics. In fact, the motivations for high-profile human rights intervention are often revealed to be very different from the traditional motivations of imperialist power, which concerned economic and strategic interests. Nevertheless, as Simon Jenkins notes, 'ethical' policy-making does revolve around 'enlightened self-interest'; a self-interest in proclaiming adherence to the moral high ground, displayed in occasional demonstrations of tough policy (UKFAC, 1998:par. 84). As David Rieff astutely argues, the attraction of ethical foreign policy does not lie with policy outcomes either in terms of human rights promotion or some other more conspiratorial agenda:

> The fact that it is so easy for us to poke holes in the doctrine should give us pause, not lead us to pat ourselves on the back. It should, at the very least, make us wonder where humanitarian intervention fits in and why it has become (along with human rights) a central rhetorical plank of so-called Third Way politics in the West ... [H]umanitarian intervention is important because it is central to the post-Cold War West's moral conception of itself ... And in this context what is important about humanitarian intervention is an idea, rather than a practice ... [T]hose who oppose the doctrine should not console themselves with the thought that by refuting its practical applications they have accomplished much of anything. (2000a)

CONCLUSION

It is only post-1989 that the agenda of human rights intervention-ism has become both possible and necessary with the end of superpower rivalry and the old international political framework. During the 1990s, the ethical human rights agenda has become an

important mechanism for cohering Western governments and international institutions, bereft of any clear political agenda of their
own. This drive to resolve questions of legitimacy and coherence
through ethical policy, has led national governments and international bodies to institutionalise the once marginal concerns of
human rights advocacy groups and international lawyers.

The lack of accountability involved in *ad hoc* denunciations of
human rights abuses and the ease with which this leads to selective
actions against targeted states, has been facilitated by the human
rights discourse considered in Chapter 2. Pushing the idea of the
victim to the fore and presenting a much diminished view of the
capacity of societies to rule themselves, the rights-based NGOs
presented a coherent picture of the degraded non-Western subject and
thereby legitimised a new sphere of 'ethical' or non-political policy-
making (Johnstone, 1998). By blurring the boundaries of domestic
and foreign policy they have facilitated the creation of a new sphere
of activism for institutions and governments seeking to demonstrate
their importance and legitimacy in the post-Cold War world.

The ethical foreign policy of criticism is an 'aspiration' or 'principle',
which stands on the moral high ground. However, the ethics of
coercive universalism have resulted in an increasingly divided world
in which a few select states are held up for condemnation,
punishment and external intervention. Even in the select cases, where
coercive action is taken in the cause of human rights, it seems that the
motivation for these actions has less to do with the development of
human rights in these countries than the symbolisation of what
Western states and institutions stand for. The sanctions and denunciations are more for the purposes of domestic and international
credibility than intended to improve the situation for the worst-off
citizens in the targeted states. The reality of selective scapegoating and
irrational policy-making is obscured by the human rights discourse,
enabling the human rights roadshow to move on from Somalia to
Bosnia to Kosovo to East Timor to Sierra Leone to Afghanistan with
'demands for action' and little accounting of the outcome of intervention (Chomsky 1999; Maren, 1997; Chandler, 2000b).

4 The Limits of Human Rights Theory

> In sum, the argument for a universalist approach to human rights rests on the universality of human wrongs; the latter are universal social facts that derive from our animal nature and social character to date. – Ken Booth, in Tim Dunne and Nicholas Wheeler (eds) *Human Rights in Global Politics* (1999), p. 64.

There is a strong consensus today among international relations commentators that supports the concept of universal human rights as a guide to ethical international policy-making. This is a relatively recent development. For the first 20 years after the Second World War one of the major journals on international relations, *Foreign Affairs*, did not carry one article on human rights (Korey, 1999:151). Until the 1980s, the majority of academic commentators and policy-makers were not convinced that human rights concerns or ethical considerations were an appropriate subject for study when assessing a state's foreign policy (Shestack, 1997:565; Donnelly, 1999:5; Dower, 1997:86; T. King, 1999:314). Only during the 1990s did the ethical and moral dimension of international policy-making become treated as a legitimate factor, which could and, in fact, should influence and shape national and international policy-making.

Since the end of the Cold War, there has been a dramatic shift in the emphasis of analysis in the international relations field, away from the realist study of power relations and towards a focus on normative human rights theory. This focus has been welcomed for bringing morality into the analysis of international relations (F. Robinson, 1998:58; Müllerson, 1997:180). Its advocates argue that in an increasingly globalised world, we need universal standards that are based on the idea that we are human beings first and citizens second. Instead of rights being granted by an accident of birth, depending on which state we live in, human rights should transcend and subordinate national governments.

This chapter seeks to examine some of the claims forwarded in normative international relations theory, which is centrally concerned with developing a universal human rights agenda. Normative theory can be broadly defined as covering 'all political theorising of a prescriptive or recommendatory kind: that is to say, all theory-making concerned with what ought to be' (Stoker, 1996:1). The consensus on the need for the development of normative theory has developed in response to the 'realism' or *realpolitik* of the Cold War era, in which the focus was on power politics and there was little room for moral precepts in the understanding of the world (Forsythe, 2000:3; Donnelly, 2000:161–92). Philip Allott, for example, argues that traditional international relations theory is based on Machiavellism, 'the overriding of general moral duty by *raison d'état*', a paradoxical 'morality of immorality' (1999:34). For Allott, this privileging of the political sphere over the ethical meant that international relations theory became innately conservative and uncritical:

> Machiavellism was ... a calculated negation of a long tradition which conceived of values that transcend the power of even the holders of the highest forms of social power. Those ideas – especially ideas of justice and natural law, but also all those philosophies which speak of 'the good' or 'the good life' – were transcendental and aspirational and critical in character; that is to say they were conceived of as an *ideal* which could not be overridden or even abridged by the merely *actual*, and in relation to which the actual should be oriented and would be judged. The ideal makes possible a morality of society. (1999:35)

In contrast to realist approaches to politics and international relations that have been accused of justifying the status quo, normative theory sets out a radical agenda of criticism. Normative theory can have a radical appearance because it starts from the identification of certain moral precepts, the values which should be upheld by institutions or actors, and then submits institutions to critique in so far as they fail to match the normative ideas. Ken Booth asserts that the narrow focus on the political sphere of state interests and interstate rivalry in international relations theory has been a barrier, rather than a solution, to the problems of the international arena: 'What is needed must have *moral* at its centre because the fundamental questions of how we might and can live together concern values, not instrumental rationality.' (1995:110) He argues:

To my mind the twenty-first will be the century of ethics, and global ethics at that. What I would like to see is a shift in the focus of the study of international relations from accumulating knowledge about 'relations between states' (what might be called the 'dismal science' of Cold War international relations) to thinking about ethics on a global scale. (1995:109–10)

Andrew Linklater similarly argues that international relations theory needs to develop a 'bolder moral standpoint' (cited in Wheeler, 1996:128). The moral standpoint chosen by the majority of normative theorists is that of human rights and human wrongs:

How can we envisage greater attentiveness to claims advanced to mitigate or eliminate human wrongs? ... One response is by way of reorienting inquiry into the character of world politics, injecting moral purpose at the centre of our evaluative procedures; international relations is a social construction, and its normative emptiness is not a necessity. (Falk, 1999b:191)

David Beetham breaks down the complex activity of normative theory into a number of distinct elements (1996:28). These elements will form the structure of this chapter, drawing out the strengths and weaknesses of the theoretical attempts to place human rights at the centre of a critique of international society. First, the analytical or conceptual component will be addressed, the meaning of universal human rights and the criteria for being able to tell whether or not these have been achieved in practice. Second, the justificatory component will be considered, looking at why human rights should form the basis of an understanding of the international sphere. Third, the critical aspect, considering the nature of the normative critique of the existing international order, together with the practical aspect, the new institutional arrangements which are proposed and the guarantees, if any, that they will be more effective. And finally, the question of agency, the social or political groups which are envisaged as acting as the bearers of these normative ideas.

WHAT ARE UNIVERSAL HUMAN RIGHTS?

It is generally accepted that the modern human rights movement was born during the Second World War. American writers usually focus on President Franklin D. Roosevelt's famous 'Four Freedoms' speech of 1941, while British commentators often cite H. G. Wells'

1940 publication *On the Rights of Man* (Buergenthal, 1997:706; G. Robertson, 1999:20–3; Forsythe, 2000:35). Human rights ideas were important in cohering the Allied war effort, symbolising the values that the Allied powers stood for in the struggle against Germany and Japan. These early declarations of support for 'essential liberties and freedoms' maintained their cohering importance at the end of the war as the cornerstones of a new global order. This normative framework was intentionally abstract, as the new international order shaped by the leading world powers was still fractured by a division into sovereign states. All the leading powers were keen to defend the freedoms of national sovereignty for themselves as well as to construct an international framework based on the nation-state (Lewis, 1998:89). This framework will be considered further in Chapter 5.

As upheld in the UN Universal Declaration of Human Rights, agreed by the General Assembly in December 1948, these rights could be claimed or aspired to with either market or state-regulated economies and abstracted from the political questions of what societies' priorities should be. This substantial ground of agreement, on 30 human rights, could be achieved as the UN did not claim to be describing rights that were universally recognised in every state, nor did it attempt to enact these rights within universal law. Human rights were held to exist, not as legal rights but as universal moral rights (Nickel, 1987:4; G. Robertson, 1999:30). As Louis Henkin stressed:

> When international law speaks of 'human rights,' it does not refer to, establish, or recognize them as international legal rights in the international legal system. By establishing interstate rights and duties in regard to 'human rights,' international law indicates its adherence to the morality and moral values that underlie them and strengthens the consensus in regard to that morality. (1981:269)

One reason why there was little concern with developing normative theory to legitimise a conception of universal human rights, as distinct from civil and political rights, was the highly selective nature of US policy-making on the issue (Müllerson, 1997:104). The human rights agenda was an openly political one, rather than guided by ethics or morals, inconsistently deployed for strategic and political ends. The focus was on Cold War opponents, such as the Soviet

Union and the states within its sphere of influence in Africa and Latin America, rather than those states within the US sphere of influence, such as Egypt, Israel, Turkey, Saudi Arabia and Kuwait. A second, and more important, reason for theoretical neglect was that the Western conception of human rights concerns, as largely synonymous with liberal democracy and the free market, meant that there was little demand for any separate theoretical defence for human rights as distinct from territorially-bound political and civil rights.

During the Cold War, the United States government and the human rights organisations that it funded consistently downplayed the economic and social aspirations of the Universal Declaration. In the West, human rights became synonymous with the campaigns for political freedoms in the Soviet bloc. The Helsinki Charter of 1975, which established the OSCE, gave prominence to human rights issues as a way of pressurising the Soviet bloc, but these were defined from an entirely Western perspective (Heraclides, 1993:5; Szafarz, 1992:17). The seventh of ten guiding principles was 'respect for human rights and fundamental freedoms, including the freedom of thought, conscience, religion or belief' (OSCE, 1995:3). The concerns expressed prior to the end of the Cold War were focused on political and civil freedoms, such as freedom of movement and information and the right to leave and return to one's country (Brett, 1993:143).

Prior to the 1990s, the leading Western states prioritised rights in the political sphere, civil and democratic rights, on the basis that these rights were of a qualitatively different standing to economic and social claims. The reluctance of major Western powers to go beyond abstract moral commitments to economic and social rights led to the establishment of two separate UN committees in the 1950s. These produced two separate international covenants in 1966, one on civil and political rights, and the other dealing with economic, social and cultural rights. The opposition of leading Western states to rights in the economic and social sphere was demonstrated in 1986 when the UN General Assembly adopted the Declaration on the Right to Development and the United States, Britain, Germany and Japan either voted against or abstained (Mutua, 1996:606–7).

This approach was reflected in the human rights NGO community. As late as 1993, the Director of Human Rights Watch, Aryeh Neier, stated that: 'I regard economic equity and economic misery as matters of enormous significance. I just don't think that it's useful to define them in terms of rights.' (Cited in Mutua, 1996:618) Expanding the idea of rights beyond the civil and political realm was felt to be problematic, concerning questions of distributive justice and matters of policy rather than principles. Human rights advocates felt that their claims to objectivity and neutrality would be compromised if they directly entered the sphere of domestic policy priorities (Mutua, 1996:618). Human Rights Watch, for example, did not abandon its long-standing opposition to the advocacy of economic and social rights until September 1996 (Korey, 1999:172; Mutua, 1996:619).

The meaning of human rights was clear during the Cold War, when the concept was widely seen as a propagandistic representation of the central tenets of Western democratic systems. The 1990s approach moved away from this substantially, through a critique of the centrality of political rights, which had been prioritised during the Cold War years. Since the end of the Cold War, human rights proponents have attempted to revive the spirit of the UN Charter and assert the importance of normative claims for universal rights, which stand independently from specific political systems of government. The UN Secretary-General, Kofi Annan, writing in the *Harvard Human Rights Journal*, argues: 'Civil, economic, cultural, political, and social rights are essential for harmonious relations among individuals, groups, and nations and are universal, indivisible, interdependent and interrelated.' (1997a:1)

Today, human rights advocates uphold both political and social claims for human rights as equally important to the satisfaction of minimum conditions for human dignity. In a direct attack on the privileging of political rights, it is held that the freedom to vote is meaningless without food and shelter while the right to social and economic benefits is meaningless if there is no say in government (G. Robertson, 1999:145). Henry Shue, for example, asserts that once one basic human right has been accepted, that necessarily implies further rights to security, subsistence and liberty to ensure that it is effectively implemented (1980:5–87). Similarly, David Beetham suggests that while civil and political rights are central to democracy, their acceptance implies the need for economic and social rights, which are necessary for civil and political equality, and also cultural rights, which are necessary for equality of citizenship (1999:114). This shift in approach away from the centrality of the political sphere is highlighted in Britain by civil liberties organisations such as Liberty and JUSTICE reinventing themselves as human rights organisations (Klug, 2000b:6). In the international sphere this shift is demonstrated in the UN Committee on Economic, Social and Cultural Rights' submission to the 1993 Vienna World Conference on Human Rights, which asserted that: 'there is no basis whatsoever to assume that the realization of economic, social and cultural rights will *necessarily* result from the achievement of civil and political rights' (cited in Beetham, 1999:107; see also Hammarberg, 1998). In this respect all rights, whether politically derived or morally grounded, are self-standing and equally important because they all contribute to the satisfaction of basic human needs.

While the advocates of human rights today all agree that state-based political rights are not enough on their own, there is very little agreement on what the content of universal human rights should be. Jack Donnelly argues that there is 'nothing fixed or inevitable' about the list of rights (1999:20). This is reinforced by Will Kymlicka and other rights theorists who suggest that the basic right to well-being and quality of life cannot just be determined on the basis of universal external standards. For these commentators, it is also necessary for needs to be assessed 'from the point of view of the person living it' (Freeman, 1995:34). The content of human rights is then only limited by the degree of perceived human wrong, which it is necessary to abolish in order to guarantee human dignity to all. This depends on the level of economic, social and cultural change human rights advocates feel is essential to reach the goal of a society which meets human needs. David Beetham, for example, does not quite go so far as to argue for complete economic levelling but is nevertheless determined that human rights should go beyond guaranteed access to the necessities of life, such as means of subsistence, shelter, clean water, sanitation and basic health care, to include education and also the right to work (1999:97–8).

Once rights are extended to the provision of goods necessary to remove any barriers to human flourishing, whether defined subjectively or through a universal measure, it becomes very difficult to determine rights from aspirations or desires. Milan Kundera expresses this well in *Immortality*:

> [T]he more the fight for human rights gains in popularity, the more it loses any concrete content, becoming a kind of universal stance of everyone towards everything, a kind of energy that turns all human desires into rights. The world has become man's right and everything in it has become a right: the desire for love a right

to love, the desire for rest a right to rest ... the desire to publish a book the right to publish a book, the desire to shout in the street in the middle of the night the right to shout in the street. (1991:153)

Many human rights advocates accept that there is little possibility of intellectual agreement on what constitutes human rights. Nevertheless, they make a powerful case for the possibility of moral agreement on human wrongs. Mary Midgley feels that 'whatever doubts there may be about minor moral questions and whatever respect each culture may owe its neighbours, there are some things that should not be done to anybody anywhere' (1999:160). For Ken Booth, the meaning or content of universal human rights can only be drawn out by the focus on 'human wrongs':

What finally binds all this together and gives a firm anchorage for universal human rights is the universality of human wrongs. Human wrongs are everywhere; all societies find it easier to recognise and agree upon what constitute wrongs elsewhere than they do rights; wrongs are universal in a way rights are not; and a concentration on wrongs shifts subjectivity to the victims by emphasising a bottom-up conception of world politics. (1999:62–3)

It is through this emphasis on 'human wrongs' that the redefinition of rights away from the narrow focus on the political sphere acquires a radical edge. As will be considered in the following section, there neither is, nor can there be, a moral content to political, civil and democratic rights. There is no external end or goal beyond the process of self-government of politically equal citizens. Democratic rights or civil rights are only the legal codification, or expression, of a right of self-government. Therefore, the freedoms of the political and public sphere, the right to freely trade, vote, associate, speak, and so forth, are entirely negative or value-neutral ones, there is no positive content. These rights do not establish how people should use their freedoms. Even when these rights are defined through legal expression, for example as in the laws of censorship, they are still negative, delineating a (restricted) sphere of freedom for self-government.

For the advocates of human rights, the lack of content of state-based political rights is problematic, in that the sphere of freedom necessarily provides no guarantees of ends or outcomes (Klug, 2000b:99). For example, constitutional law does not specify the content of government decisions, only how they should be made. There is no guarantee that an elected government will not enact policies, which will make some people worse off or damage the environment. The egalitarian assumptions, upon which civil and democratic rights stand, concern means and not ends, processes not final policies.

The content of universal human rights is concerned with making up for the perceived deficiencies of narrowly political rights. There is a human rights consensus that traditional democratic rights to civil and political freedoms are no longer, or never have been, adequate to safeguard the public or individual 'good'. The essence of human rights is the ring-fencing or protection of certain 'rights' that are too important to be left without guarantee. For human rights advocates, the lack of content involved in political liberties means that they cannot ensure the same level of protection for the individual as universal human rights can. Rights are redefined to favour policy ends over the political decision-making process. Everyone has a right that his or her fundamental needs should be met: a right to human dignity and respect.

Today's human rights theorists are happy to make the most of the ambiguities inherent in the human rights concept. They distinguish the importance of universal human rights *vis-à-vis* democratic 'state-based' rights on the grounds that rights that transcend elected governments are necessary, as political rights are morally indifferent to needs. But they often seek to legitimise transcendental human rights claims on the basis of similarities with state-bound political and civic rights, seeking to establish that there is no clear theoretical divide between the 'richer content' of human rights and the narrow content of political rights. The distinction between the 'means' of democratic rights and the 'ends' of human rights is intentionally blurred or ignored in various approaches. This can be done through the simple assumption that all rights claims are good *per se* and, therefore, contribute to the good of society. In this approach, considered earlier, it is best 'to think of rights as rights' merging to build 'an integrated, composite whole' (Forsythe, 1989:41).

An alternative approach, which claims a little more theoretical subtlety, is the dismissal of any qualitative distinction between state-bound rights of political theory and transcendental rights of moral theory. Several human rights commentators challenge the idea of a qualitative distinction between 'positive' and 'negative' rights. They observe that civil and political rights, which demarcate a sphere of individual or collective autonomy for citizens, are seen to be 'negative' rights, while economic, social and cultural rights, which require the positive action or interference of the state or inter-national community, are seen as 'positive' rights. They then assert that to see this distinction as a fundamental one would be a 'serious confusion' and 'patently flawed' because both sets of rights are of equal standing (F. Robinson, 1998:64; Nickel, 1987:173–4; Beetham, 1999:125; T. Evans, 1997:125).

Human rights theorists challenge the idea of a qualitative dis-tinction through two separate theoretical approaches. One method is through conflating the legal expression of democratic and civil rights with the right itself. This enables them to assert that the exercise of civil and political rights requires positive action on behalf of the state to establish and enforce the legal code, thereby making all rights about the 'positive' assertion of regulatory control (Donnelly, 1998b:25; Forsythe, 1989:14; F. Robinson, 1998:64). The alternative approach is to separate the process of electing a government from the policies that it enacts. It can then be argued that, because states have the right to restrict liberty for social goals, political rights theory itself privileges policy ends, or 'positive' rights over democratic and civil rights (F. Robinson, 1998:64).

This conflation of rights of individual and collective autonomy, essential to democratic government, and rights as moral claims for positive state action, which are above the political sphere and not subject to democratic discussion, is central to the claims made for human rights theory in the 1990s. As John Gentry notes, the creation of new rights has led to a focus on the assurance of outcomes rather than processes (1999). The following section considers the justification for this radical critique of the centrality of political and democratic rights to policy-making.

JUSTIFICATIONS FOR TRANSCENDENTAL RIGHTS AND FOR POLITICAL RIGHTS

The lack of clarity over the content and meaning of universal human rights is further highlighted in attempts to substantiate or justify why human rights are a necessary addition to the territorially-bound conceptions of political and civil rights, the democratic rights, upheld, at least rhetorically, by the Western powers during the Cold War. As considered earlier, the advocates of human rights in most cases assume that there is no contradiction between the rejuvenated moral conception of universal human rights and the political conception of civic and democratic rights; that either they may be distinguishable but are closely related and mutually supportive or that the category of human rights subsumes and includes all other rights. In the few cases where commentators are aware of a contradictory relationship between the two sets of rights they assert that human rights have a stronger justification, are better than, or have priority over, narrowly political rights.

Initially, it would appear that there is little justification necessary to uphold the importance of universal human rights. Human rights are commonly understood, literally, as the rights we have because we are human and from this flows their universality. They must be equal rights because either one is a human being, and therefore entitled, or not. It also follows that human rights are inalienable, as one cannot stop being a human being, and they cannot be denied, or put aside.

This approach seems to be the one taken in the major international treaties and statements which are the founding documents for human rights campaigners. The Universal Declaration, the UN covenants and the Vienna Declaration only provide a 'thin' answer to the basic conceptual and theoretical justification for human rights (Donnelly, 1999:8). The source of internationally recognised human rights is identified as the inherent (moral) nature of the human being. Every person, simply as a human being, is entitled to human rights. The Universal Declaration, Article 1, states: 'All human beings are born free and equal in dignity and rights.' The Economic, Social and Cultural Covenant and the Civil and Political Covenant of the UN assert that 'these rights derive from the inherent dignity of the human person'. The Vienna Declaration, in similar wording, states that 'all human rights derive from the dignity and worth inherent in the human person'. The same terminology is used by the UN Secretary-General, Kofi Annan, who asserts that: 'they derive from the intrinsic value and dignity of each and every human being' (1997a:1). 'All human rights for all' was the motto of the Office of the High Commissioner for Human Rights for 1998, the fiftieth anniversary year of the Universal Declaration (Donnelly, 1999:10).

The need for some theoretical grounding or justification for transcendental human rights arises only when one seeks to go beyond the circular reasoning of having human rights because we are human. When the advocates of human rights seek to use the concept to question the international political order, they are confronted with the need to go beyond abstract justification for their demands. It is here that some problems become apparent. Although human rights are assumed, by definition, to be universal and indivisible there is little unanimity over their universal grounding. State-grounded political rights, as considered below, assume as their foundation an individual capable of self-government. The advocates of human rights start from the assumption that this is a false universal subject. There are a number of well established theoretical approaches that lend support to their critique of the political rights thesis. It is undoubtedly true that the equality of political and civil rights relies on the formal separation of the public and private spheres. The formal equality of the legal and political sphere necessarily abstracts from differences and inequality in the social and economic domain.

This separation forms the basis of the radical critique that the sphere of formal political rights excludes and marginalises many people that lack the capacities and resources necessary for self-government. Before a court of law or at the ballot box every citizen is treated as an equal, equally capable of taking responsibility for their actions and their political decision-making. Yet, this does not mean that the inequalities of the private setting will be progressively overcome. Inequalities in the social and economic arena are not necessarily resolved through political rights and many would argue that they are perpetuated through them. David Beetham, for example, suggests that the proper subjects of human rights, as distinct from civil and democratic rights, are those individuals who lack the capacities to act in a politically independent way. He argues that political and civil rights are 'of little value if individuals lack the personal capacities or resources to make use of the freedoms in question, and that legally established rights will be largely formalistic if the means necessary to exercise them are beyond people's reach' (1999:96). As Michael Ignatieff notes, we are increasingly made aware that it is the wretchedness of human beings that necessitates the universal protections of human rights:

> Nothing good has come of these experiments [in international intervention] except perhaps the consciousness that we are all Shakespeare's 'thing itself': unaccommodated man, the poor, bare forked animal. It is 'the thing itself' that has become the subject

– and the rationale – for the modern universal human rights culture. (1998:5)

Neil Stammers also observes that the idea of human rights is premised on the '*vulnerability* of individuals ... people require human rights to protect them from potential violations arising from the social contexts in which they find themselves' (1995:491). Ken Booth, who locates the subject of human rights in 'ethical communities' defined by exclusion from the political process, rather than political communities bound by the state, takes the same approach:

> Universal human rights are supposed to be invalid because there is no universal ethical community. But there is: the ethical community of oppressed women, the ethical community of under-classes; the ethical community of those suffering from racial prejudice; the ethical community of prisoners of conscience; the universal ethical community of the hungry ... and on and on. (1999:61)

This perspective is given greater weight by a feminist critique of the political rights tradition which sees the majority of the population, women as a whole, as marginalised and oppressed and, therefore, denied the formal capacities claimed by the democratic rights thesis. A slightly different approach is to assert that the problem lies not with a lack of recognition of the marginalised or oppressed groups within society but with the concept of the self-governing individual itself. James Nickel, for example, claims that even the individuals who are able to play a full role in policy-making lack the moral capacity for self-government. In this case, the need for human rights derives from the fact that 'unaided conscience will not generally provide fully adequate beliefs about how people ought to behave and how society ought to be organized' (1987:41).

The rejection of the concept of the self-governing political subject of necessity brings us back to the problem of grounding human rights on the basis of the innate characteristics of being a human being. This universal capacity has been theorised in a diverse variety of ways. For example, on 'an identification of the needs and capacities common to all humans, whatever the differences between them'; a universal 'capacity for moral understanding and progress'; the 'thin' conception of rationality proposed by John Rawls; or the speech and listening capacities identified by Jean-François Lyotard

(Beetham, 1999:93; Nickel, 1987:41; Mendus, 1995:14; Lyotard, 1993:138). For many of today's human rights advocates this essentially boils down to a capacity for moral reciprocity, 'feeling the pain' of others, or in the words of Michael Ignatieff: 'imagining the pain and degradation done to other human beings as if it were our own' (1999b). However, having rejected the universal grounding of political and democratic rights for exaggerating human capacities or for ignoring the social and economic inequalities in society, the 'common needs and capacities' are necessarily those at the lowest level of human society. This approach inevitably tends towards a reductive view of the human subject, where capacities are minimised and needs maximised (for example, Gerwith, 1981; Doyal and Gough, 1991).

Whichever approach is chosen, the human rights-bearing subject is qualitatively different from the subject of state-based political rights. The universal subject of human rights has much less capacity, for either self-government or self-determination, than the rational individual assumed by modern representative democracy. It is this perspective of the minimal subject, incapable of meaningful action in the political sphere, which leads to a pre-political justification for human rights (Zizek, 1999:171). All advocates of universal human rights necessarily have to posit a moral dimension to their claims for universal rights. As Nigel Dower notes: 'Since a human right is independent of actual conventions in society, the basis for its existence must be found elsewhere, and the natural place to find this is moral theory.' (1997:88) For example, Jack Donnelly asserts that human rights can 'be relatively easily derived from many moral theories'. He suggests that they could be derived from natural law or that teleological ends-based theories may be able to ground human rights in their tendency to further human good or flourishing (1999:12). Donnelly is not unusual in his reluctance to substantiate which moral grounds he is actually standing on. Attempts to ground abstract human rights in an overtly moral context reveal the problems of deriving a modern conception of right from the pre-political or anti-political sources of moral philosophy.

Modern conceptions of rights, the state-based civil and political rights, can only be justified on the basis of the political equality of rational self-governing individuals, and necessarily eschew any moral basis of external judgement. Moral philosophy sets itself as above or prior to political conceptions of equal rights between self-governing subjects. For this reason, it is not possible to argue cogently for political rights on a moral basis. Neither the categorical imperative of Kantian theory nor the ends-based teleology of Bentham's utilitarianism, for example, would justify universal human rights claims. For Kant, duty comes before human rights and for Bentham the good of society would come prior to human rights. Moral philosophy can logically derive duties but not rights, it can morally justify a universal duty to the common good but can justify neither universal human rights nor political and civil rights, which depend on the capacity for self-determination (Freeman, 1995:31). As Donnelly is forced to concede, the category of rights-based moral theories has 'historically been an empty one' (1999:12).

The concept of human rights appears to straddle the division between morality and politics in a way that prevents a consistent moral or political grounding to the subject of the rights concerned (Henkin, 1990:6). It has been widely noted that the lack of theoretical cogency has been no barrier to the revival of human rights theory, creating a gap between political theory and political practice (Mendus, 1995:10). As the vast majority of governments have accepted the concept of human rights, despite the lack of plausible fundamental principles, many influential commentators openly state that the question of theoretical consistency is of little importance (Bobbio, 1996:10; Rawls, 1993:68). This uncritical acceptance of human rights is highlighted by the public disavowal of theory in the resort by some theorists to the tautology of grounding human rights solely 'in the fact of their recognition' or by 'leaving open the question of justification' (Chesterman, 1998:117; Nickel, 1987:9; Waldron, 1987:163).

In fact, the conceptual ambiguity of human rights allows advocates of the concept to have the best of both worlds. The moral 'human' emphasis helps to abstract the concept from disputed political terrain, while the political 'rights' side of the concept helps to skate over the divisions within moral philosophy. The abstract subject of human rights appears to be the perfect moral/political category because the inherent ambiguity within it means that it can be taken up across the moral and political divisions of society. As Donnelly notes, the vague grounding of universal human rights helps overcome disputes over moral foundations and provides a common ground between different political perspectives (1999:13, see also Charvet, 1998; Klug, 1997).

However, there is a fundamental difference between deriving rights from the capacity of human subjects and deriving them from the incapacity of human subjects. The central component of all democratic systems of rights or legal systems, and their theoretical starting point, is the individual's capacity for self-government. The subject of the modern law is a person assumed to be a moral agent or self-willing actor. As a rights-bearing subject the person is not simply coerced into accepting the law by forces outside their influence. The law is seen to be freely accepted and to derive from their own will. The framework of regulation of the modern democratic system is historically and logically derived from the formal assumption of equal self-governing individuals, responsible and accountable for their actions and capable of rational decision-making. All modern doctrines of the enforcement of contract, the punishment of crime, the election of governments and the state system of international law rest on this core assumption (Heartfield, 1996). This can be usefully highlighted by a brief consideration of the different facets of a modern state's rights-framework or legal system.

Civil law is the clearest expression of the derivation of the law from the will of the self-governing subject. In enforcing the law of contract, civil law does not impose an alien or external goal onto individuals. In fact, the civil law only binds individuals to their word; this is an expression of the will of the legal subject as the contract is voluntarily made. There is no compulsion to higher policy goals or ends; the only object of the law is the contract between two equal contracting parties. Of course, it could be argued that it is unfair to hold a person to an earlier word against a later decision, however, that word was part of a social contract with another person who acted on the basis of it. The law is justified in holding an individual responsible and accountable for a promise freely given and the basis of another's actions. The implicit assumption is that we are not only all equally free to engage in contractual obligations but that we are all equally responsible for keeping our side of a contractual promise, that is, we are all equally moral and autonomous agents.

Criminal law also assumes the equality and free will of the legal subject. The accused is represented at the court in the same way as for breaches of civil law. The citizen has the right to defend his or her interests in court equal to any other citizen. The law is binding on the individual as if it were a contract, although there is no formal contract beyond the assumption of assent to membership of a law-bound community (mythologised in social contract theory). This is clearly only notional assent, but it is through this fiction of consent that the equal rights of defendants before the law are enshrined. The defendant is recognised as a moral agent, responsible for his own actions. Just as under the civil law, punishment is for a free act of will; there is no liability if the defendant acted without free will, for example, under duress or if suffering from mental impairment. Despite the lack of voluntary contract, the criminal law formally enforces the will of the offender, as a law-abiding citizen, against his or her actions. As a moral agent, the offender is responsible for his decision to break the law, just as if he had broken a civil contract. The possibility of punishment, as opposed to mere repression, derives from this recognition of the autonomy of the offender. The law is legitimate and not repressive because it is based on the assumption of a free autonomous and self-determined individual.

In constitutional law, the notional social contract is given content. As a people, the electorate is the subject from which the authority of the state is derived. There are many forms of deriving constitutional authority from the people, including, for example, constitutional monarchies, presidential systems, or consociational federal bodies, and within these a variety of forms of separation of powers between the executive, legislature and the judiciary. For all its limitations, the principle of popular sovereignty is a thoroughly radical conception of authority from the people. It argues that the state's authority derives exclusively from the people, without any external source of either power or legitimacy.

This idealised picture reveals the centrality, to all aspects of the modern framework of rights, of the rights-bearing individual with the capacity for self-government. The source of particular state-based rights is the autonomous legal subject, rather than abstract humanity. As the German MP Uwe-Jens Heuer and his colleague Gregor Schirmer point out:

> [T]he sphere of law ('Right') and human rights are (conceptually) separated from the state and from politics. But Right, and with it law, is a social product, the result of social struggles, and only comes to be when it is set out as law and sanctioned by the state ... But the separation of Right from the state and politics leads to its mystification. It now seems to come from the heavens above. (1998:8)

As Hannah Arendt noted, the 'inalienable rights' of abstract humanity would mean claimants falling back 'upon the minimum fact of human origin' (1979:300). She cogently argued that the concept of rights could not exist independently of political society. For Arendt:

> Equality, in contrast to all that is involved in mere existence, is not given us, but is the result of human organisation ... We are not born equal; we become equal as members of a group on the strength of our decision to guarantee ourselves mutually equal rights. (1979:301)

Even if the universal subject of human rights were clearly identifiable, it would be impossible to connect the abstract universal denominator of humanity with the concept of rights in any coherent way. Norman Lewis notes:

> Placing the concept 'human' in front of 'rights' may represent a quantum leap up. But this is only in the abstract. No matter how these rights are presented, what they have in common is the fact that they are not derived from legal subjects. (1998:85)

This central distinction in approach to the rights-subject explains why the two different rights approaches have an opposing conception of the importance of the political sphere and its institutions at the level of the state and international society. This difference is underlined in the following section, which considers the radical nature of the human rights critique of the political sphere and the problems this poses for any practical alternative.

THE POVERTY OF NORMATIVE PHILOSOPHY

As David Beetham notes, the essence of normative theory is the 'critical component' which asks two questions: 'How far are the criteria or principles entailed by the concept realised in a given situation or set of institutions? and How far does practice measure up to a justifiable normative standard or ideal?' (1996:28) The normative critique of international society, based on the challenge of human wrongs is a very powerful one. Nicholas Wheeler, for example, describes 'a world where, protected by the non-intervention principle, 123 states practice torture or ill-treatment of prisoners; where genocide occurs and goes unpunished; where 40,000 children die daily of preventable diseases; and where millions – especially women – live hopeless and wretched lives' (1996:131).

As long as there are victims of human wrongs then existing institutions and legal frameworks are open for criticism and seen as vulnerable to the call for change. The commitment of normative international relations theory to 'placing the victims of the society of states at the centre of theorizing' has produced a stark moral critique of international society, sometimes referred to as 'critical international society theory'. Wheeler argues: 'Critical international society theory places suffering humanity at the centre of its theoretical project exploring how the society of states might become more hospitable to the promotion of justice in world politics.' (1996:127) For Ken Booth, this approach is 'an ethics for the emancipation of victims across the world' (1995:116). This theory is not just thoroughly critical, it is also thoroughly radical, against the realist concern with power relations and states: 'especially important here is critical theory's project of placing the powerless and dispossessed at the heart of theory and emancipatory political practice' (Wheeler, 1996:128).

The moral critique of existing practices is always a radical one. But, as with any critique that starts from ethics rather than existing society, there is little need for serious consideration of the real and the profane:

> Westphalia, in its time, had represented a sort of anchorage, after the ravaging wars of religion. But the grammar of the system of state sovereignty and statism constructed from the seventeenth to the twentieth century led inexorably to the Holocaust and atomic warfare ... In the killing fields at the apogee of Westphalia – Dachau and Hiroshima – 'Hell was here'. (Booth, 1999:65)

According to this study, it is the striving for democracy and state sovereignty, allegedly the 'amoral' politics of 'realist' Machiavellism, which has led to the horrors of the twentieth century. If the political sphere is the cause of warfare and oppression, there is clearly little positive about politics or democratic government. The human rights critique is in many ways a stunningly confident attack on the political sphere under the cover of ethics and morality. Transcendental moral values are portrayed as the progressive solution to the problems of the narrow political sphere: 'This is the hope of progressively leaving behind the politics of the concentration camp – the ultimate sovereign space – for a cosmopolitan democracy aimed at reinventing the global human being – being human globally ... and badged with a common humanity.' (Booth, 1999:65–6)

This point is the exact opposite of that made by Hannah Arendt in her acclaimed study *The Origins of Totalitarianism*, originally published in 1951. She made the vital point that state rights were taken away from the Jews and other minorities prior to their internment, that in fact it was the loss of political and legal rights that were the crucial precondition for the horrors of the concentration camp (1979:296–7). She further demonstrated, that for those lucky enough to escape, the stateless refugees, 'the only practical substitute for a nonexistent homeland was an internment camp'; in reality the only guarantor of rights was the nation-state (1979:284). The truth of this was confirmed by my grandfather's experience on escaping Buchenwald concentration camp for British India, when he was interned in Ahmadnagar, one of the original concentration camps established by the British during the Boer War. Because human rights can only imply dependency on others, persecuted people, from the Jews in the 1940s to the Kosovo Albanians in the 1990s, claimed not human rights but political rights, illustrated in the demand for a state of Israel and for an independent Kosovo (1979:292–9).

Normative human rights theory, however, argues for a rejection of the existing framework of international society and the political sphere of the states which compose it. The theorists who are most critical of existing international society are those who are more concerned with blueprints for a future moral world order than an analysis of the problems of the existing one. This theory is powerful as a critique but the problems appear when the theory addresses alternatives, the institutional arrangements which can be derived from the starting moral precepts (Beetham, 1996:29). Human wrongs are the central empirical support for this critique, which condemns the fact that 'many states do not provide for the security of their citizens' (Wheeler, 1996:127). However, the description of 'wrongs' provides little explanatory depth and the link from being critical of human wrongs to a positive human rights framework is not straightforward, even in theory let alone practice. As Mary Midgley notes:

> To talk of rights is, by contrast, to talk directly about the people who need relief. It aims to lay a burden publicly on anyone who stands in the way of relieving them – a burden which cannot be dodged by passing the can. The quasi-legal language invokes the

broad impersonality of the law. It makes it much harder to say 'this is none of my business'. (1999:167)

The problem is that, having written-off states from acting in a morally responsible way, the moral agent, whose 'burden' or 'business' it is to enforce human rights, is difficult to locate. Where the political rights of the public sphere are non-specific as to ends or content, the human rights thesis is non-specific regarding the means of guaranteeing or implementing rights. For the founders of political and civil rights theory, rights could only be guaranteed by the subjects of the rights themselves (Rosenberg, 1999). If a right could not be protected, or exercised, by its bearers then it could no longer be a right, an expression of self-government. Democratic rights theorists developed this conception of the active and self-determining subject of rights in opposition to pre-modern hierarchical conceptions of rights as privileges bestowed on the deserving from above.

For the advocates of human rights, the legitimacy of the claim stands independently of, and sometimes in inverse relation to, the capacity of the subject. Because the human subject is defined as being without autonomy some external source has, of necessity, to be looked to. The theorists of human rights find it difficult to come up with a cogent answer as to the external source that can be trusted to implement and guarantee human rights. In reinterpreting rights as a moral category, as opposed to a legal or political one, a contradiction appears between the enforcement and guarantee of human rights and the formal legal and political framework. The ambitious nature of the concept of human rights, which establishes the content of those rights independently from the capacity of its subjects, means that this gap between claim and capacity lies at the heart of the question of implementation.

The lower the capacity of the human subject the greater the need for some form of external assistance or grant of resources or regulatory power, yet the incapacity of the subject makes this grant entirely arbitrary and by no means guaranteed. Fiona Robinson rightly argues that 'the right to food' or the 'right to housing' cannot guarantee anything more than an absence of discrimination, a formal freedom. To make these rights a duty of provision by the state or another actor, they require much more than a statement of right (1998:65). The 'right to food' or 'the right to housing' or 'right to development' are meaningless in terms of rights, as they are abstract claims which say very little about who or what must act to ensure they occur. As David Beetham notes, the International Covenant on Economic, Social and Cultural Rights 'can at most be a statement of aspirations or goals rather than properly of *rights*' (1999:116):

> They confuse the fundamental with the merely desirable or with that, which is specific to the advanced economies (holidays with pay, free higher education, and the continuous improvement of living conditions). Even those that are fundamental can not be defined in a justiciable form. At what level can the deprivation of nutrition, sanitation or healthcare be sufficient to trigger legal redress? (1999:116)

With little agreement on the substance of human rights, or the means of implementing them, it is easy to see why the claims made are often declared to be normative 'wish lists'. To achieve the good ends of human rights advocates, as Donnelly notes, is 'to reshape political and social relations so that this moral vision will be realised': 'Human rights thus are simultaneously a "utopian" vision and a set of institutions – equal and inalienable rights – for realizing at least an approximation of that vision.' (1999:16)

The lack of an autonomous human subject means that human rights advocates' aspirations for a better and more just society must necessarily focus on a beneficent agency, external to the political sphere, to achieve positive ends. There may be a duty to act to fulfil human rights needs but there is no politically accountable institution that can be relied upon. In order to help bridge this gap, between the ideal critique of the real and solutions which are necessarily part of the profane reality, human rights advocates tend to privilege the role of institutions which can stand above politics.

In the world of realist political and international relations theory, the focus is on existing institutional arrangements. This focus makes it difficult to accept the possibility of institutions that stand independent from social and political pressures. When addressing practical alternatives, the advocates of human rights are forced either to take existing political institutions, at state or interstate level, out of the political sphere or to posit some form of alternative institutional arrangement, which is independent of politics. For some theorists of human rights, the solution is to bring the state back into the analysis. But, of course, only if the political sphere is subordinated through the institution of forms of regulation independent of elected government. This can occur through political actors being bound by a bill of rights and, therefore, capable of acting morally, that is, independently from the economic pressure of the world of business and the political pressure of parliamentary competition.

The idea of the state acting morally to guarantee a set of moral ends seems to fly in the face of the democratic political conception of the state, based on the need to achieve consensus between competing interests within society. To justify the subordination of politics to moral ends, human rights theorists often stress the protective and morally progressive role of the state as the guarantor of democratic political rights as well as potential human rights. Donnelly, for example, as considered earlier, asserts that the 'negative' anti-state conception of political rights is misplaced as the state has to play a central role in the implementation of civil and political rights. Active institutional intervention is seen as necessary to implement legislation against discrimination, to ensure the procedural rights of individuals in the courts, and to create an environment conducive to the development of civil and political freedoms. Once democratic rights and civil liberties are seen to be dependent on the beneficent nature of state protection, as opposed to the reflection of the self-governing activity of the historical subject, it is then easy to assert an external mandate for the state, or other institutions, as the guarantor of human rights. The anti-political critique of the human rights theorists, shifts from condemning the 'concentration camp' of the politically-tied state to concluding that the morally-engaged state can be the guarantor of human rights. For some commentators, for example David Held (1995), Martin Shaw (1994), Bikhu Parekh (1993), Michael Walzer (1997) and Fred Halliday (1994), the leading Western states can act as the moral agents of humanity and have the duty to ensure the protection of human rights in those states that cannot be so easily trusted (see further Chapter 5).

Once the distinct guarantor of democratic rights, the active rights-bearing subject, is removed from the analysis, rights of self-government become indistinguishable from privileges granted by the tolerance and understanding of the powerful. As Neil Stammers notes, the imperative of action to defend human rights ironically entails a *realpolitik* which is highly state-centric and, in fact, not only reflects but also reinforces the highly uneven balance of existing power relations (1999:992). Under the logic of the human rights discourse, determined by the abstract and ahistorical view of

a degraded subject, even the 'negative' freedoms against state interference are seen as guaranteed by the state itself. Once this
tautological conception is accepted, rights to 'freedom' are indistinguishable from a licence for external regulation. If 'negative'
freedoms entail dependency on an external will, human rights,
regardless of their specific content, would necessarily entail far
greater external regulation as the breadth of their moral claims
makes their implementation a far more ambitious project. As A.
Belden Fields and Wold-Dieter Narr note:

> If people are not aware of the historical and contextual nature of
> human rights and are not aware that human rights become
> realized only by the struggles of real people experiencing real
> instances of domination, then human rights are all too easily used
> as symbolic legitimizers for instruments of that very domination.
> (Cited in Stammers, 1999:980)

Not all human rights theorists are willing to grant the state the
capacity for moral action. For more radical international relations
theorists the Western-led 'international community' is still too tied
to the political sphere and incapable of being led by the moral
human rights impulse:

> We could be much more confident about military interven-
> tion/peace enforcement by the 'international community' if this
> so-called international community were more than a term of
> propaganda used by the governments of the G7 states ... [F]or the
> most part the phrase 'international community' is a platitude,
> trotted out by the powerful when they want to legitimize a
> particular action ... The cosy phrase 'international community'
> often represents the diplomatic equivalent of honour among
> thieves. Look at some heads of government or heads of state. Can
> we hope that this 'community' of dignitaries and states will deliver
> the world from massive human wrongs? (Booth, 1995:121)

For the more radical human rights theorists, if even the leading
Western states cannot be trusted to act morally, then there is little
hope that international society as it is constituted can guarantee
human rights:

> If the morality of international society depends upon the assumption that all states are morally valuable places, the daily reality of human rights abuses suggests that international society is failing as a 'guardian angel' ... [T]he failure of the society of states to protect 'basic rights' fundamentally calls into question its moral legitimacy. (Wheeler, 1996:127)

For these radical theorists, the practical alternative to the 'real' remains in the sphere of the 'ideal'. They agree with their less radical colleagues that the international domain, or 'the global', is the key political space in which the solution to state-based politics can be found. Yet, instead of institutional perceptions of the 'global' grounded in Western political power, they counterpose the non-political institutions that are held to compose 'global' or 'transnational civil society' or help to constitute the network of inter-locking realms of 'cosmopolitan democracy'. The problem is that 'civil society' and 'cosmopolitan democracy' are not political insti-tutions, they are moral aspirations. As Mary Kaldor concedes, 'the concept of transnational civil society is less a descriptive or analytical term and more a political project' (1999a:195). The 'ideal' alterna-tive is to engage in struggle against 'the "realists" who still believe in the nation state as the centrepiece of international organisation and the main instrument for stability' (Kaldor, 1999a:209). Ken Booth can only describe the solution in similar terms as a struggle against the 'real': 'the enemy of cosmopolitanism is statism' (1995:120). For Booth: 'Cosmopolitan democracy, if operationalised, would be a stronger safeguard against totalitarianism ... than the ideals of Westphalia.' (1999:57) Yet, as the world is organised today, 'cosmo-politanism' is an ideal not an active agent.

Unable to get beyond 'wish lists' or the compromise of bringing the state back in through 'civil society' or 'cosmopolitan democracy' (considered further in Chapter 5) the practical solutions are where the normative agenda of universal human rights appear weakest. Many of the most ardent human rights advocates are quite willing to admit that their anti-political project is 'ridiculously utopian', but they would rather criticise with moral conviction than compromise their principles with an involvement in the profane world of politics (Kaldor, 1999a:212).

THE PROBLEM OF AGENCY

Underlining the consequences of the human rights discourse's dismissal of the active political subject is the question of agency:

'which social or political groups might plausibly act as bearers, prot-agonists or beneficiaries of the values in question?' (Beetham, 1996:29) At first appearances the human rights thesis seems to adhere to the view of the historical agency of collective humanity. For Ken Booth: 'The discourse of human rights is potentially crucial to human history because it is part of the language of the human species' self-creating emancipation from natural and societal threats.' (1999:31) A deeper consideration reveals that this is far from the case.

What was lost in the promulgation of human rights theory in the 1990s was the connection between rights and subjects who can exercise those rights, which was at the core of political accountabil-ity and democracy. Once the historical and logical link between rights and the subjects of these rights is broken, then democracy is a meaningless concept. The epistemological premise of democracy is that there are no final truths about what is good for society that can be established through the powers of revelation or special knowledge. As David Beetham argues: 'the only criterion for the public good is what the people freely organised, will choose, not what some expert or prophet decrees on the basis of superior knowledge' (1999:35). If we accept that people are the best judges of their own interests, then only self-determination can be the basis for collective self-government. Democracy, therefore, is only a means to an end, to the realisation of the public good because it allows people to define what that good is, as well as to control the process by which it is realised (Beetham, 1999:13).

Democracy does not guarantee that everyone will equally support, or equally gain from, the outcomes of collective decision-making. Democracy merely ensures that everyone has an equal say in that outcome. The predominance of some form of majority say in policy-making, through the electoral process, is a product of the underlying principle of equality, the basis of 'everyone counts for one and none for more than one'. If we are all equal, but have an infinite variety of different individual views of what the public good should be, and how it should be served, the only way to decide is by process of an equal say. The system of representative government attempts to ensure that the individual perspectives of the public good coalesce into a wider social perspective through a variety of processes by which a public will is manifested. There are a several stages in approximating this public will, which can vary with constitutional frameworks, but usually include political party competition at the polls and the debate and vote of elected members of the legislature, or parliament, on legislation.

Fiona Robinson's treatment of the problems of human rights gets to the heart of the issue, the difference between democratic rights without moral ends and human rights defined by moral ends. Robinson privileges ends over means in a direct way through the introduction of a distinction between 'the right' and 'the good'. She defines 'the good' as a substantive moral goal, or end in itself:

> '[T]he right' by contrast, is that which is decided simply by its instrumental significance for achieving that good. The right is a negative, procedural, rule-like notion; the 'good' by contrast, is that which gives the point of the rules which define the right. (1998:65)

If human rights, 'the goods', stand on their own as a moral end then there is little need for 'rights' in the decision-making process. Donnelly, similarly, recognises the implications of the human rights discourse for democracy. He argues that democracy is concerned with who ought to rule and human rights are concerned with what the rulers of the people do and how they rule. He asserts that in this sense human rights are 'profoundly anti-democratic', because their aim is to frustrate the will of the people when it diverges from human rights (1999:41). This separation of rights from their subjects leads to the redefinition of both rights and subjects through the human rights discourse. In fact, the logical conclusion of human rights policy would be the end of politics as a sphere for the resolution of social questions of the distribution of goods and policy-making. Even David Beetham, a leading proponent of the human rights thesis, balks at its consequences:

> While we may reasonably require of them [non-Western governments] to refrain from torturing their citizens, it is not obvious that we can equally require them to guarantee them all a livelihood, adequate accommodation and a healthy environment. Moreover, for them to do so, it is contended, would require a huge paternalistic and bureaucratic apparatus and a corresponding extension of compulsory taxation, both of which would interfere with another basic right, the right to freedom. (1999:116)

All human rights advocates share the view that social justice, the righting of 'human wrongs' should stand above the formal political equality of liberal democracy. The protection of women, national minorities, children, the environment, peace, multi-ethnic society and many other rights-causes are considered, by their advocates, to be too important to be left to the traditional instruments of domestic and international government. Whereas representative government works to realise the derivation of the state from the will of the people, human rights theorists seek to subordinate the will of the people to ethical or moral ends established by a less accountable elite. The traditional conservative critique of democracy was that of the 'despotism of the multitude', today's human rights advocates dress these nineteenth century arguments in the twenty-first century garb of normative rights theory.

Wheeler's critical international society theory places an important emphasis on public involvement in the 'ethical content and purpose of foreign policy' (1996:128). But not the public as constituted through the political process. In place of the democratic participatory society, assumed as the basis of the political conception of rights, the role of the individual is a much less empowered and passive one. In place of politics, we have the moral advocacy of a liberal elite. The voices of the human rights victims and politically excluded are not expressed through the ballot box but are the raw material for their self-appointed liberal advocates in the media, academia and the international NGOs.

The preference for elite activism over democratic involvement has been central to the anti-politics of the normative human rights revival. The elite assumptions behind this approach were expressed clearly in Michel Foucault's address at the launch of a human rights initiative to send naval vessels into the Gulf of Thailand on behalf of the Vietnamese boat people, at the Intercontinental Hotel, Geneva, in June 1981:

> We are here only as private individuals, who have no other claim to speak, and to speak together, than a certain shared difficulty in accepting what is happening ... Who, then, has commissioned us? No one. And that is precisely what establishes our right ... Amnesty International, Terre des Hommes, Médecins du Monde are initiatives which have created this right: that of private individuals actually to intervene in the order of international politics and strategies. The will of individuals has to inscribe itself in a

reality over which governments have wanted to reserve a monopoly for themselves – a monopoly which we uproot little by little every day. (Cited in Keenan, 1997:156–7)

It is no coincidence that Michel Foucault, one of the leading postmodern theorists, should pen what *Libération* later described as 'a new Declaration of the Rights of Man' (Keenan, 1997:158). This new 'right' for self-appointed and unaccountable liberal intellectuals to intervene in international affairs was premised on the postmodern dismissal of the collective political subject. These views were first developed by the French intellectual Left, as they dramatically shifted their perspective on the agency of social change, following their break with the French Communist Party after 1968. This ideological shift explains why the French liberal academics and NGO activists were at the forefront of the intellectual development of the human rights discourse in the 1970s and early 1980s (Mészáros, 1989:52–7).

For Booth, the problem with those who are critical of the moral advocacy of the liberal elite is that they are too concerned with the political framework of the state system to be sensitive enough to appreciate the emerging moral and ethical constituencies of the human rights discourse. These NGOs and liberal cosmopolitans are the basis of the 'new social movements' which the human rights advocates claim to represent:

> Universal human rights are solidly embedded in multiple networks of cross-cutting universal ethical communities. The fundamental weakness of the critics of universality is that they take too territorial a view of the idea of human community, human political solidarity and human social affinity. Their perspective is conservative, overdisciplined by constructed notions of states and cultures. (Booth, 1999:61)

'Global civil society' is to be the moral arbiter of policy, not the party competition and struggle for representation of the political sphere (Archibugi, 2000). Policy 'is best tested by listening to victims and trying not to offend global civil society, the nearest we have to a conscience of world society' (Booth, 1999:57). For Mary Kaldor, 'global civil society' can be located in 'the cosmopolitan young people to be found in almost every city from Sarajevo to New York' or the people active in NGOs, international organisations or the international media. The list goes on:

Or they may simply be cosmopolitan-minded; they may be people who join organisations like Greenpeace or Amnesty International, who join protests about the war in Bosnia and the construction of motorways, who offer voluntary contributions to cosmopolitan causes, who read international journals. Equally, if not more importantly, however, are those courageous territorially tied people who attempt at a local level to combat racism or other forms of exclusivism, who engage in various solidaristic activities, who try to sustain civic values in schools, hospitals and other local institutions. (1999a:209)

The human rights advocates, who listen to the voices of the oppressed and the cosmopolitan-minded, envisage themselves as the moral gatekeepers to policy-making discussion, under the guise of empowering the excluded. Mary Kaldor expresses this preference for liberal opinion to replace representative democracy in choosing who is entitled to have a say in policy discussion:

Civil society thus consists of groups, individuals and institutions which are independent of the state and state boundaries, but which are, at the same time, preoccupied with public affairs. They are, in effect, the guarantors of civil behaviour both by official institutions (states and international institutions) and in the world at large. Defined in this way, civil society does not encompass all groups or associations independent of the state. It does not include groups which advocate violence. It does not include self-organised groups and associations which campaign for exclusivist communitarian concepts. Nor does it include self-interested private associations. (1999a:210)

To be granted the right of inclusion into the policy debate, Kaldor insists people must pass the test of respect for 'global human rights culture'. Naturally, this test involves agreement with the all the ethical causes that Mary happens to espouse herself (1999a:210). This makes a mockery of the globally inclusive rhetoric of human rights theorists, like Ken Booth, who assert that 'a good place to start thinking about politics is to ask the victims'. The question of agency reveals the central flaw of the normative human rights theorists.

Their replacement of an historical social subject of rights with an abstract ethical subject inevitably leads to their own self-appointment as agents of change. Far from giving a voice to the excluded, the elite advocates are empowered on the basis of their vicarious association with moral causes.

CONCLUSION

Highlighting the centrality of the self-governing or autonomous human subject to the concept of rights sharply reveals the flaw of the burgeoning human rights discourse and the reason for its inability to establish a foundation for the substance and character of the new rights it proclaims. The redefinition of rights from neutral means to ethical and value-laden ends, or claims on an external authority, removes the universality and democratic content of rights. Neither the discussions over the substance or content of human rights, nor the means of implementing and guaranteeing them, are resolvable through democratically accountable mechanisms because these political questions of power and distribution are reposed as moral absolutes open to external or juridical interpretation through international institutions or domestic and international courts.

Once humans are universalised, not as competent and rational actors capable of determining their own view of the 'good' but, as helpless victims of governments and the forces of the world market or globalisation, then democratic freedoms and civil liberties appear meaningless. Under the guise of 'ethical' universalism the human subject is degraded to the lowest level, in need of paternalist guidance from the 'great and the good' who can establish a moral agenda of human rights to guide, educate and 'empower' the people. The assumptions and processes of representative democratic government are turned on their head.

For many advocates of human rights, the degraded view of the subject and the diminished view of the worth of democracy and state sovereignty are legitimate conclusions drawn from the problems of our modern globalised and dislocated era. It is for this reason that the following three chapters leave the realm of theoretical discussion to return to the empirical realm, to explore the consequences of this perspective for political relations between states and within the domestic political sphere.

5 International Law and the Challenge of Human Rights

> Whether Nato action was lawful is a very different question from whether Nato action was right ... We believe that, while legal questions in international relations are important, law cannot become a means by which universally acknowledged principles of human rights are undermined. – Proceedings of the UK House of Commons Foreign Affairs Committee, published 23 May 2000, paragraph 137.

Since the early 1990s, international relations have been transformed through the development of new norms and practices established with the intention of protecting human rights by extending the reach of 'international justice'. Justice and rights protection no longer stop at the borders of the nation-state. As the UN Secretary-General, Kofi Annan, has noted: '[W]e are living through a remarkable period in the advancement of international law. Great strides have been made in refining its writ, expanding its reach, and enforcing its mandate.' (1997b:363) The establishment of The Hague tribunals, dealing with crimes committed during the Bosnian war and the civil conflict in Rwanda, the House of Lords judgment against Pinochet, and the international indictment against a sitting head of state, Slobodan Milosevic, are all held up to indicate the trend towards 'international justice' and the prioritisation of human rights.

The extension of 'international justice' has reflected a widely welcomed decline in the legal weight attached to state sovereignty as a barrier to external judgement and intervention in a state's affairs. State sovereignty, the recognition of self-government and autonomy, is perceived to be increasingly dangerous or inadequate for many states and peoples. International intervention in Iraq, the decision to extend international regulation in Bosnia, and the establishment of protectorates in Kosovo and East Timor are seen to herald a new set of precedents that suggest a modified approach to state sovereignty. *De facto* rule over a territory is no longer held to legitimise the denial of justice or the abuse of human rights. An elected government should no longer have the final say on what constitutes justice and rights for its citizens.

For human rights advocates, this positive shift in international relations is best highlighted by the war over Kosovo in the spring of 1999. Under Nato leadership, major Western powers allegedly fought a war over the denial of justice and abuse of human rights of the ethnic-Albanians of Kosovo. As considered in Chapter 3, this war was not justified through a threat to international peace and security, nor in self-defence of a neighbouring state. It was widely greeted as the first war for human rights, a cause taking priority over the sovereign rights of the Federal Republic of Yugoslavia. It is little surprise that in the wake of this conflict commentators have declared that 'international justice' and human rights have trumped sovereignty (Longworth, 1999). This appeared to be dramatically confirmed in the international response to the Twin Towers attacks, when US and British officials openly claimed tht it would be legitimate for them to depose the Afghan government for harbouring suspected terrorists.

The Kosovo and Afghanistan conflicts are often held to have demonstrated some of the most positive characteristics of the new era of human rights protections, and more modestly defined sovereignty, but they also raise two questions that indicate potential problems with these new trends. First, while both conflicts may have demonstrated the triumph of 'international justice' over sovereignty they also raise the question of the relationship between 'international justice' and international law. The US-led military campaigns, without UN Security Council authorisation, were widely held to have breached formal international law (F.A. Boyle, 2001; Mandel, 2001; Holbrook, 2001; Henkin, 1999b; Wedgewood, 1999; Charney, 1999; Chinkin, 1999; Franck, 1999; Simma, 1999, Cassese, 1999; Littman, 1999, UKFAC, 2000c; O'Connell, 2000). The legal consequences of these breaches are not yet clear: some legal commentators argue that military intervention is warranted today, but only in exceptional situations; others argue that there are now a number of precedents for a more flexible interpretation of international law (G. Robertson, 2001a; Steele, 2001; Simma, 1999; Cassese, 1999; O'Connell, 2000; UKFAC, 2000c).

Second, the Kosovo and Afghanistan conflicts raise a question over the perceived end of sovereignty. With the sidelining of the UN, and dispute over its final authority regarding the use of force in international affairs, it may be that we are seeing a redistribution of sovereign power; or rather, the acceptance of sovereign inequality. The growing acceptance of a moral right of some states to unilaterally or collectively exercise military power to uphold 'international justice' and human rights indicates that sovereignty, or the exercise of state power, is being transformed. While, for some states, sovereignty is being limited, for others, it is increasingly free from traditional international constraints. This could be clearly seen in the Western response to the New York and Washington attacks in September 2001, where it was assumed that the US and Britain had the right to remove the Taliban from power in Afghanistan; Tony Blair promising the following month to 'sort out the blight' of the African continent (2001b). These declarations of less restricted sovereign power were flagged-up in the earlier discussion over British military engagement in Sierra Leone in May 2000. The *Guardian*, for example, saw that 'the intervention is the duty owed by a wealthy and powerful nation to, in this case, one of the world's poorest countries ... Britain is right simply to do what it can, where it can, when it can, within the limits of its power and self-responsibility.' (2000a) *The Economist*, similarly, argued that Sierra Leone demonstrated the 'hopelessness' of the African continent and that the Western forces had the moral right to fight and stay on 'to win the peace', as in the Balkans (2000a).

This chapter attempts to address these two questions, and suggests that the terminology used to describe the current shifts in international relations is necessarily opaque. Most commentators talk about 'international justice' rather than international law and the end of state sovereignty rather than the end of sovereign equality. This language downplays the fundamental connection between international law and sovereign equality, and the consequences of the human rights discourse for international relations. The rest of this chapter seeks to draw out the fundamental distinction between the new underpinnings of human rights-based 'international justice' and the traditional basis of international law, highlighting the centrality of the conception of sovereign equality to this distinction.

INTERNATIONAL LAW AND SOVEREIGN EQUALITY

Many studies of the post-Cold War international order trace the weakening of state sovereignty from the classic Westphalian model, of the seventeenth century, through the establishment of the UN, to the current trend towards a global regime of 'international justice', rights-regulation and cosmopolitan democracy. Advocates of human rights-based justice often see the concept of sovereign equality as an integral part of the long-standing doctrine of state sovereignty (Held, 1995:78; Weiss, 2000:13). In fact, the doctrine of sovereign equality is of much more recent provenance.

The classic state system is said to have emerged with the treaties of the Peace of Westphalia, in 1648, at the end of the Thirty Years War. In these treaties the secular claims of German princelings were recognised above the religious claims of the Papacy. There was no secular right of external power above the sovereign (Philpott, 1999:579–82). This formal recognition of the principle of territorial sovereignty became the basis of an interstate system of international relations. Although there was the beginning of an interstate system, there was no international law in the modern sense as the rights of sovereignty were restricted to the European powers. While interstate relations were regulated between mutually recognised sovereign states in the West, there was no explicit framework of international society, which formally limited the exercise of state sovereignty. The regulation of interstate relations could not go beyond voluntary agreements between a select group of sovereign states (Allott, 1999:42). These treaty agreements were based upon interests of preserving state power through strategic alliances and the limited geo-political stability of a balance of power.

The age of the classic 'anarchical' state system, with no limits to the sovereignty of the major powers, was also the era of colonialism (Bull, 1995). The states included in this interstate system were those that could exercise power in the international arena through ruling over their territory and defending it from the claims of other sovereign states. It was, therefore, also quite logical and consistent to see that in those areas outside Europe, which could not demonstrate 'empirical statehood', sovereignty could not apply (Jackson, 1999:441–4). Under this system the right of intervention in the affairs of other states was granted to states which were capable of acting on, and enforcing, this right: the Great Powers. As Christopher Clapham notes:

> Westphalian sovereignty provided the formula under which territories which did not 'count' as states according to the criteria adopted by the European state system could be freely appropriated – subject only to their capacity to conquer the incumbent power holders – by those which did count. (1999:522)

The major Western powers directly regulated their territorial acquisitions in Africa and India. Elsewhere, for example, in China, Japan and the Ottoman Empire, they refused to recognise or be bound by domestic legislation under the principle of extraterritoriality (Donnelly, 1998a:4). 'Might became right' under the Westphalian system as force was the final guarantor of claims to sovereignty (Held, 1995:78–9).

The Westphalian model of state sovereignty had its critics throughout the modern era, particularly as the leading non-Western states modernised and grew in importance. The fear of Western decline and the need to stabilise growing international society led to new experiments in international relations. The first Hague Conference, in 1899, saw the attendance of China, Japan, the Ottoman Empire, Persia and Siam. Japan's defeat of Russia in 1905 was a powerful shock to European imperial confidence, because this confidence was closely bound up with a notion of racial superiority (Furedi, 1998:29–30). The second Hague Conference, in 1907, was the first international gathering of modern states at which non-Europeans outnumbered the Europeans. The descent of European powers into the barbarism of the First World War did much to undermine the idea of Great Power international security. The fear of imperial decline and the expectation of resistance from the colonies led Western policy-makers to speed the process of transformation away from 'might is right' towards international law in an attempt to contain the threat of war between the Great Powers as well as anticipated anticolonial revolt.

The First World War settlement began the process of developing a legal concept of sovereignty as opposed to the Westphalian concept of sovereignty based on power. At the 1919 Paris Peace Conference, US President Woodrow Wilson affirmed the principle of national self-determination for the newly created states of Central Europe. The attempt to legalise or formalise international relations was a direct consequence of the collapse of the Russian and Austro-Hungarian Empires during the war and the Bolshevik revolution of 1917. The Soviet leader Lenin's declaration of the right of nations to self-determination and the Soviet Union's propaganda linkage of war with the imperialist outlook of the Great Powers put the Western policy-makers on the defensive. Instead of the discredited system of international power politics, post-First World War international relations became legitimised on the basis of formal equality between states (Pupavac, 2000a). International regulation sought legitimacy in natural rights principles of rights-bearing individuals coming together through a social contract, expressed in 'a self-policing system of collective security' (Levin, 1968:4; Mayall, 1990:44).

The case for empire had become problematic and the principle of equality was gaining ground both at home and in the colonies. The expansion of the concept of territorial sovereignty beyond the principle of 'might is right' was a highly controversial one within policy-making circles. Robert Lansing, US Secretary of State, recalled his doubts in his diary:

> The more I think about the President's declaration as to the right of 'self-determination', the more convinced I am of the danger of putting such ideas into the minds of certain races. It is bound to be the basis of impossible demands on the Peace Conference and create trouble in many lands.
> What effect will it have on the Irish, the Indians, the Egyptians, and the nationalists among the Boers? Will it not breed discontent, disorder and rebellion? Will not the Mohammedans of Syria and Palestine and possibly Morocco and Tripoli rely on it? (1921:87)

This 'danger' was a central concern of the inter-war settlement. The League of Nations initiated the process of formally restricting the sovereignty of the Great Powers. For example, colonial powers were no longer entitled to act as they liked but were mandated to advance the interests of their subject peoples. The mandate system, which implied that colonial rule could only be temporary, was the first open admission that empire was no longer a legitimate political form (Furedi, 1994:6). However, the concept of sovereign equality was still a heavily restricted one, and the West rejected Japan's attempt to include a clause on racial equality in the League of Nations' Charter. The major European imperial powers were not in a position to consistently uphold the rights of sovereign equality. This inability was expressed by Harold Nicholson, one of the members of the British delegation to the Paris Conference:

> The most ardent British advocate of the principle of self-determination found himself, sooner or later, in a false position. However fervid might be our indignation regarding Italian claims to Dalmatia and the Dodecanese it could be cooled by a reference, not to Cyprus only, but to Ireland, Egypt and India. (Cited in Cobban, 1969:61)

The development of a universal legal conception of sovereign equality had to await a further European conflagration.

After the Second World War, the United States' dominance of the world economy enabled the construction of a new system of international regulation. As Justin Rosenberg notes, the US planners realised that 'the British Empire ... will never reappear and that the United States may have to take its place' but, that in the face of growing nationalism and the discrediting of empire, new institutions of management of international relations would be necessary to 'avoid conventional forms of imperialism' (1994:37). Central to this new mechanism of international regulation was the conception of sovereign equality.

The discrediting of international regulation based on power and colonial domination led, through the two World Wars, to one based on sovereign equality. The Nazi experience and the rise of non-European powers had undermined the elitist ideologies of race and empire and led to the defensive acceptance of a law-bound international system. As Norman Lewis notes:

> The impact of the war and the sense of a loss of legitimacy ended what had, until then, been the inter-war consensus upon the non-applicability of the right to self-determination to colonial peoples ... However, this consensus could no longer be sustained in the face of the new legal order, the ideological conflicts of the Cold War and the rise of nationalism within the colonial world. (1997:11)

The political pressure on the leading world powers meant that the 1945 settlement, preserved in the principles of the UN Charter, was a decisive moment in the transformation of the Westphalian system. The sovereignty of the Great Powers was restricted, while the right of sovereignty was granted to new states which would have failed the Westphalian test of 'empirical statehood', and hence have been dismissed as 'quasi-states' (Jackson, 1990). The UN Charter system, the first attempt to construct a law-bound international society of states, recognised all nation-states as equal. Article 1(2) calls for 'respect for the principle of equal rights and self-determination of peoples'; Article 2(1) emphasises 'the principle of sovereign equality' of member states; and Article 55 stresses 'respect for the principle of equal rights and self-determination of peoples' (cited in Ramsbotham and Woodhouse, 1996:38). The UN system did not realise full sovereign equality in its own internal workings. The five permanent members of the powerful Security Council, the United States, Britain, France, Russia and China, were obliged to reach a consensus on policy, thereby giving the major powers the right of veto. Nevertheless, sovereign equality was formally recognised through equal representation in the General Assembly and through the principle of non-interventionism.

Sovereign states were clearly unequal in terms of power, wealth and resources. However, despite these limitations, the universal recognition of sovereign equality was a thoroughly radical conception of the authority of the non-Western state. Its authority was derived exclusively from its people and, as a consequence of this, the international order became one in which non-Western states had the same legitimacy as the more developed Western states, despite the inequality of economic and military power. This equality was confirmed on many occasions in UN resolutions, notably the Declaration on the Inadmissability of Intervention in the Domestic Affairs of States and Protection of their Independence and Sovereignty of 21 December 1965 (Resolution 2131 (XX)) and the Declaration on Principles of International Law Concerning Friendly Relations and Co-operation among States in Accordance with the Charter of the United Nations of 24 October 1970 (Resolution 2625 (XXV)). The latter declaration making it clear that: 'All States enjoy sovereign equality. They have equal rights and duties and are equal members of the international community, notwithstanding differences of an economic, social, political or other nature.' (Cited in Mills, 1997:269) The official commentary to the document stated:

> No State or group of States has the right to intervene, directly or indirectly, for any reason whatever, in the internal or external affairs of any other State. Consequently, armed intervention and all other forms of interference or attempted threats against the personality of the State or against its political, economic and cultural elements, are in violation of international law. (Cited in Littman, 1999:33)

'INTERNATIONAL JUSTICE' OR INTERNATIONAL LAW?

Today, the advocates of 'international justice' are heralding the emergence of a new human rights-based order of international relations. They assert that the post-1945 UN framework of interstate relations, 'international society', is being eclipsed by the new ethical demands of the human rights discourse. Few would disagree with Camilleri and Falk's position that 'there is a pressing need to rethink the concept and practice of sovereignty' (1992). Andrea Bianchi argues that the values and principles governing international law are under challenge:

> The two opposite poles of the spectrum are evident. On the one hand, there stands the principle of sovereignty with its many corollaries ... on the other, the notion that fundamental human rights should be respected. While the first principle is the most obvious expression and ultimate guarantee of a horizontally-organized community of equal and independent states, the second view represents the emergence of values and interests ... which deeply [cut] across traditional precepts of state sovereignty and non-interference in the internal affairs of other states. (1999:260)

Martin Shaw puts the question in stark terms:

> The crucial issue, then, is to face up to the necessity which enforcing these principles would impose to breach systematically the principles of sovereignty and non-intervention ... The global society perspective, therefore, has an ideological significance which is ultimately opposed to that of international society. (1994:134–5)

The core concept behind international law, sovereign equality, is seen as a legal fiction for abusers of power to hide behind. Human rights theorists argue that 'sovereignty is not a fact but a theory' which is wrongly seen as a 'foundational truth' (Allott, 1990:302; Camilleri and Falk, 1992:39). For the advocates of 'international justice', international law is just an 'anachronism' or historical hangover:

> It still talks, illogically, of violation of 'state rights', when it is *human* rights that are being violated. Some of its classic doctrines – sovereign and diplomatic immunity, non-intervention in internal affairs, non-compulsory submission to the ICJ [International Court of Justice], equality of voting in the General Assembly – continue to damage the human rights cause. (G. Robertson, 1999:83)

Leading human rights advocates see sovereign equality as the central barrier to peace and justice, asserting that this provides a 'cloak of impunity' (Urquhart, 2000). Andrew Linklater states that 'to respect sovereignty is to be complicitous in human rights violations' (2000). Geoffrey Robertson's highly regarded human rights history, *Crimes Against Humanity: The Struggle For Global Justice* (1999), sees 'the movement for global justice' as a 'struggle against sovereignty' (1999:xviii). Robertson sharply puts the case for abolition of the UN's position of sovereign equality:

> The reality is that states are not equal. There can be no 'dignity' or 'respect' when statehood is an attribute of the governments which presently rule Iraq and Cuba and Libya and North Korea and Somalia and Serbia and the Sudan. (1999:372)

Ken Booth asserts that Westphalian sovereignty is 'a tyrant's charter' (1995:116). Max Boot argues in *Foreign Affairs*:

> [M]ost of the world's nations do not have Westphalian legitimacy in the first place. They are highly artificial entities, most created by Western officials in the twentieth century ... There is no compelling reason, other than an unthinking respect for the status quo, that the West should feel bound to the boundaries it created in the past. There is even less reason why the West should recognise the right of those who seize power within those borders to do whatever they want. (2000a)

Few critics actually wish to abolish the legal form of sovereignty *per se*, many realise the importance of sovereignty for legitimisation of the domestic and international system. The attack on sovereignty is usually reserved for states that are judged to lack Western democratic credentials. In fact, several human rights analysts astutely suggest that human rights norms legitimise and bolster powerful Western states while delegitimising non-Western ones (Barkin, 1998; Forsythe 1989:6). It is the legal conception of sovereign equality that is being undermined not sovereignty itself (Glennon, 1999). This is confirmed through a consideration of the impact of international regulation on human rights.

In international practice, the effect of human rights regulations on state sovereignty is a highly uneven one, even at the purely formal level. For example, the 1977 Geneva Convention protocols, which authorise the Red Cross to provide assistance in wars of national liberation and in internal campaigns of disobedience, have not been ratified by the US or Britain on the grounds that the ICRC's presence would legitimise the insurgents at the expense of the sovereign state (Ignatieff, 1998:128). Similarly, the OSCE regulations for the protection of minority rights have concentrated on Central and Eastern European affairs because of a concern to protect the right of sovereignty in Western states (Forsythe, 2000:126; Chandler, 1999). The United States has not recognised many central human rights conventions, for example, it has never ratified the UN Covenant on Economic, Social and Cultural Rights or signed up to the UN Convention on the Rights of the Child. It has also opposed the establishment of the International Criminal Court (Forsythe, 2000:145).

Of course, at the level of social, political and economic influence this inequality is more pronounced. The less economically or geo-politically important states are most at risk of intrusion from the new human rights bodies and institutions. There is a consensus that there should be much greater flexibility in practice, to 'allow for degrees of sovereignty' so that states can be treated as '*more* or *less* sovereign' (see discussion in Mills, 1997:279). The increasingly open denial of sovereign equality has, in the last few years, had major consequences for both the form and content of international law. The human rights-based critique of sovereign equality argues that the post-1945 UN system has to be radically reformed to prioritise the equality of human rights subjects over the equal rights of sovereign states.

Today, international advocates for human rights argue that trad-itional mechanisms of interstate regulation stand in the way of human rights regulation. Geoffrey Robertson questions the core foundation of international law: 'the legal theory that human rights can be subjugated to "state rights" is being recognised as a dangerous fiction' (1999:84). The established prodecure for making inter-national treaties, based on state consent, is held to be 'anachronistic, to the extent that [the treaty] is an emanation of agreements between sovereign states' (G. Robertson, 1999:82). Robertson believes that this framework should be abandoned under the pressure of 'millions of ordinary men and women, and of the non-governmental organizations which many of them support' determined to act against human rights abuses:

These people do not talk about *jus cogens* and *erga omnes*: they believe in the simple language of the Universal Declaration, and they are not bound by Article 2(7) of the UN Charter to avert their eyes from repression in foreign countries ... These citizens, of global society rather than nation state, cannot understand why human rights should not rule. (1999:82)

Human rights commentators question the constraints of Cold War institutional arrangements on activism to protect the universal interests of human rights. As Max Boot asks: 'But why should great powers limit their freedom of action by giving bureaucrats from not-so-great powers control over their military interventions?' (2000a) The demand that 'justice' should be done has led many commentators to assert a right to forcible humanitarian intervention, independently of UN Security Council support; the *devoir d'ingérence* (Bettati and Kouchner, 1987). The old principle of sovereign equality is a barrier to acting on the new 'principle' of the right to intervention. According to Michael Ignatieff: 'principle commits us to intervene and yet forbids the imperial ruthlessness required to make intervention succeed' (1998:94).

This new human rights principle, derived from the needs of the universal human rights victim, imposes a duty on outside bodies to act if the nation state, of which they are a citizen, fails to or is unable to. The advocates of this approach condemn the consensus politics of the United Nations and argue that 'international justice' and human rights can only be upheld by the leading Western powers taking a more direct lead in international affairs. For example, Robertson asserts that 'UNanimity cannot be the only test of legitimacy'; 'humanitarian intervention cannot be the prerogative of the UN' because it cannot be relied upon to act, and therefore the right of humanitarian intervention should stand independently (1999:72; 382). For Martin Shaw, 'it is unavoidable that global state action will be undertaken largely by states, *ad hoc* coalitions of states and more permanent regional groupings of states' (1994:186).

The UN Secretary-General, Kofi Annan, has agreed with the concept of the 'duty to interfere', but has tried to limit this to humanitarian aid organisations, rather than states (1998:3). However, the growing acceptance of the principle of an overriding right to intervene has meant that the UN has inevitably been forced onto the defensive. This was highlighted by the international institution that stands to gain most from a new approach. The independent right to interfere was outlined as Nato's new 'strategic concept', at the Alliance's Fiftieth Anniversary Summit in Washington in late April 1999. The US Deputy Secretary of State, Strobe Talbott, explained:

> [W]e must be careful not to subordinate Nato to any other international body or compromise the integrity of its command structure. We will try to act in concert with other organizations, and with respect for their principles and purposes. But the Alliance must reserve the right and freedom to act when its members, by consensus, deem it necessary. (Cited in Simma, 1999:15)

In fact, George Robertson, Secretary-General of Nato, has argued that the organisation needs an enhanced military capability precisely to take on 'non-Article 5 crisis management operations', actions not related to Nato members' self-defence and therefore neither defined nor limited in geographical scope by the Nato Charter (Littman, 1999:vii). Nato's lead is being followed by the European Union's common security and defence policy, which is concerned less with collective defence than developing the capacity for human rights intervention abroad in situations where Nato declines to get involved (Ulbrich, 2000).

It would appear that 'justice' determined by the new framework will be less universal than that of the UN-policed international society. Ironically, the new more 'global' forms of justice and rights protection involve law-making and law-enforcement, legitimised from an increasingly partial, and explicitly Western, perspective. David Held, for example, argues:

> In the first instance, cosmopolitan democratic law could be promulgated and defended by those democratic states and civil societies that are able to muster the necessary political judgement and to learn how political practices and institutions must change and adapt in the new regional and global circumstances. (1995: 232)

Shaw explains that behind the language of global 'civil society' lies the reality of legitimisation through 'economic, political and military resources' which gives the Western powers a new 'duty' or 'right' to assert 'global leadership':

This perspective can only be centred on a new unity of purpose among Western peoples and governments, since only the West has the economic, political and military resources and the democratic and multinational institutions and culture necessary to undertake it. The West has a historic responsibility to take on this global leadership. (1994:180–1)

This is precisely the perspective of the *Guardian*'s editorial piece, cited earlier in this chapter, which argues that the wealthy and powerful have a duty to 'do what they can where they can'. Geoffrey Robertson, has argued for precisely this radical solution, calling for the replacement of the UN by a 'democratic "coalition of the willing"':

[A]n organisation comprising only countries which are prepared to guarantee fundamental freedoms through representative government, independent national courts and by pledging to support an independent justice system ... Might it now be worth constituting a world government of 'parliamentary peoples' which would safeguard human rights by being premised upon them, a kind of global Nato, no longer lumbered with backward or barbaric states. (2000:447)

The duty to intervene can only ever fall on the most powerful states whatever the utopian rhetoric of the 'cosmopolitan civil society' theorists (considered in Chapter 4). This duty of the mighty derives from a very different basis than the one which legitimises UN intervention, and one that cannot be derived from any UN mandate or international law. The Independent International Commission on Kosovo (IICK), for example, stated that 'not only is the interventionary claim important, but also the question of political will, perseverance, and capabilities' (IICK, 2001:169). The question of will and capacity are commonly highlighted as key to legitimacy. As Ramesh Thakur, Vice-Rector of the United Nations University in Tokyo, argues, if there is no normative consensus on intervention there has to be 'realistic assessments of our capacity to coerce recalcitrant players' (2001:43). This approach sets up the scenario where intervention is the prerogative of the powerful against the weak. This point was emphasised in the discussion over the legality of the Nato war against the Federal Republic of Yugoslavia. Leading Nato states were in favour of a bombing campaign, but concerned that Russia and China would block authorisation through a Security Council veto. Although they could have taken the question to the General Assembly, under the 'Uniting for Peace' procedure, this move was rebuffed by the UK government because it was uncertain that the Nato powers would have achieved the necessary mandate (UKFAC, 2000c:par. 128). The British government also challenged the authority of the International Court of Justice to make a decision on the legality of the conflict. Government officials were against giving the ICJ the opportunity to 'arrest the development' of international law and 'unwilling to allow the "capricious" use of the court by the Yugoslavs' (UKFAC, 2000c:par. 136).

The report of the Independent International Commission on Kosovo acknowledged the gap between international law and Western intervention and suggested 'the need to close the gap between legality and legitimacy' (IICK, 2001:10). However, rather than proposing to extend international law, the Commission sought to justify a new idea of 'legitimacy', one which went beyond formal legality. They described their doctrinal proposal for humanitarian intervention as 'situated in a gray zone of ambiguity between an extension of international law and a proposal for an international moral consensus', concluding that 'this gray zone goes beyond strict ideas of legality to incorporate more flexible views of *legitimacy*' (IICK, 2001:164).

This commission was followed by the International Commission on Intervention and State Sovereignty which held further discussions on the question throughout 2001. These discussions indicate that legal ambiguity is central to the current 'developments' in international law. In a typical panel, Adam Roberts noted that it would be a mistake to 'focus mainly on general doctrinal matters' regarding law or a right to humanitarian intervention:

> The justification for a particular military action, if it is deemed to stand or fall by reference to the question of whether there is a general legal right of intervention, is likely to be in even more difficulty than it would be if legal considerations were balanced in a more *ad hoc* manner. (2001:2)

He recognised that in the current international context where 'there is no chance of getting general agreement among states about the types of circumstances in which intervention may be justified', it was necessary to counterpoise 'powerful legal and moral considerations' (2001:3; 13). The attempt to resolve the clash between the partial demands of Western powers and the universal form of law means that the advocates of extending international law assert the necessity of legal ambiguity:

> It may be for the best that the question of a right of humanitarian intervention, despite its undoubted importance ... remains shrouded in legal ambiguity. While there is no chance of a so-called right of humanitarian intervention being agreed by a significant number of states ... answers to the question of whether in a particular instance humanitarian intervention is viewed as legal or illegal are likely to depend not just on the circumstances of the case ... but also the perspectives and interests of the states and individuals addressing the matter: in other words, they are not likely to be uniform. (Roberts, 2001:113–14)

Whether a military intervention is 'legal' is held to be a matter of 'the perspectives and interests' of those involved. This viewpoint, which seems certain to be adopted by the Commission, is an open argument for law-making by an elite group of Western powers sitting in judgement over their own actions.

It is no coincidence that supporters of 'global civil society' and 'international justice' argue for a less universal and more partial form of law than the UN interstate one. Despite the human rights critique of the unreality of the nation-state, there is no other institution which is politically accountable or legitimate as a source of international law. As one commentator notes: 'The global community is no more an imagined community than the State. We just may be at a point where the overwhelming number of people within this imagined community have not actually taken that step of imagination yet.' (Mills, 1997:284)

While no international or global community exists beyond the imagination of the human rights advocates, the rights discourse is legitimising the destruction of the framework that does exist. As Professor Simma notes, the UN Charter is 'not just one multilateral treaty among others, but an instrument of singular legal weight, something akin to a "constitution" of the international community' (UKFAC, 2000c:par. 126). Norman Lewis emphasises that any attempt to establish a legally constituted international system could only be successfully done on the basis of socially-constituted legal subjects, not abstract moral codes (1998:88). The traditional legal criteria for statehood are neutral and value free: that an entity must possess territory, a permanent population, have an effective government and the capacity to enter into international relations (Montevideo Convention). International law is the form through which states relate to each other as recognised equals. John Vincent usefully described this:

> If states have rights in international law, the bearers of the correlative duties are, in the standard formulation, other states. This reciprocal relationship is taken to provide the sanction in international law, as well as a description of the system ... In general, I observe your territorial integrity because in doing so I reinforce a system in which you are expected to observe mine. (1992:258)

Human rights advocates sometimes argue that the formal equality of the UN interstate system is not democratic. Geoffrey Robertson writes, for example, that 'the General Assembly is hopelessly unrepresentative' as there is one vote for Antigua with a population of 60,000 and one for India, with a population of 936 million (1999:82). Undoubtedly, the conception of formal state equality is less democratic than the universal equality of involvement in decision-making for individuals under a global state government with representatives chosen by a politically-integrated global electorate. However, there is no indication that we are moving towards a global state of this nature, and no support among human rights advocates for any moves towards greater global political equality (for example, CGG, 1995:xvi; Kaldor, 1999b:148).

There is no conceptual difficulty with postulating that abstract rights expressing the highest needs and interests of humanity must override the sectional interest of nation states. The problem is in turning abstract rights into rights that can be exercised or enforced in an accountable manner (Buzan and Held, 2000). With no alternative, politically accountable framework the agreements voluntarily made between sovereign states express a democratic content that is far higher than the NGO and 'international civil society' alternatives. While many human rights advocates assert that committees of NGOs are more representative of collective humanity than committees of state representatives, it is states not NGOs which have some formal relationship of accountability to the population they claim to represent.

The upholding or promotion of human rights represents a major shift away from the UN Charter framework of international regulatory mechanisms, precisely because it replaces an enforceable equal standard of state sovereignty with an abstract universality that can never be realised within the confines of contemporary society. Human rights, within these parameters can, unfortunately, be nothing more than an empty concept whose function is, at best, the legitimisation and perpetuation of the existing mechanisms of international regulation, and, at worst, the legitimisation of a new more divisive international framework based on economic and military power.

The modern system of law (whether international or domestic) depends in two vital respects on the concept of formal equality between its subjects. At the most basic level, that of derivation, all international institutions, including the UN, OSCE and Nato, derive their authority from interstate agreements. International law derives its legitimacy from the voluntary assent of nation-states, which are to be bound by it. Without a notion of consent, the distinction between law (based on formal equality) and repression (based on force and arbitrary power) disappears (Dicey, 1959:202–3; Heartfield, 1996). International law, as expressed in the resolutions of the United Nations, explicitly relies on this conception. Sovereign equality is also essential for the application of international law. Law cannot exist without equality of application, without formal equality under the law. If states were not treated as equals, then the universal quality of law would be eroded. Rights of weaker states could be infringed on the basis that the law does not fully apply in their cases, or more powerful states would claim immunities from prosecution due to their 'special case' situation.

This extension of 'international justice' is, in fact, the abolition of international law. There can be no international law without equal sovereignty, no system of rights without equality between rights-bearing subjects. Without sovereign equality, and the resolution of differences through mechanisms of the UN, different states would be free to declare their own particular interests as law, leading to the end of certainty and consensus about international law. Because international law cannot be based on the new conception of 'international justice', the gulf between state practice and the UN Charter is growing (Shaw, 1994:174).

Leading advocates of 'international justice' challenge the concept of international law itself. For example, Roy Gutman and David Rieff, the editors of *Crimes of War: What the Public Should Know*

(1999), allege that international law is 'frustratingly counterintuitive' and cannot address 'which side was right and which side was wrong' (1999:11). For this reason, Albrecht Schnabel and Ramesh Thakur, editors of the United Nations University study *Kosovo and the Challenge of Humanitarian Intervention*, argue for the *ad hoc* and arbitrary application of international human rights protections:

> A code of rules governing intervention would be likely in the early 21st Century to limit rather than help effective and responsible action on the part of the international community ... Any attempt to get general agreements would be counter-productive ... It may be inevitable, possibly even preferable, for responses to inter-national crises to unfold selectively. (2000)

The US-led military interventions against Serbia and Afghanistan highlighted the transition of international law from 'hard law' to 'soft law'. The US government and Nato did not seek to justify their war against the Federal Republic of Yugolslavia on legal grounds (Wedgewood, 1999:829; Charney, 1999:836; Franck, 1999:859). It is not clear what the legal justification could be for the US-led military action against Afghanistan. Although two UN Security Council res-olutions were passed, in the wake of the terrorist attacks on Manhattan and Washington, neither of them could be construed as authorising military force (Mandel, 2001). The claim of acting in self-defence, under Article 51 of the UN Charter, is unlikely to apply as it is only available in response to the actions of states. However, Marc Weller argues that the Security Council's recognition of the massive nature of the assault on the United States indicates the possibility of 'an advance in international law' to treat this as analogous to a state attack (Steele, 2001). There is also the problem that self-defence in international law, as in domestic law, must be based on necessity which is 'instant, overwhelming, leaving no choice of means, and no moment for deliberation' (G. Robertson, 2001a; Holbrook, 2001, Mandel, 2001). The interval of time between the attack and the response, during which the Security Council had considered the matter, would invalidate the claim of self-defence. Leading inter-national lawyer Francis Boyle argues that 'retaliation is never self-defence' and that the US government has justified the war against Afghanistan neither by fact, the provision of any evidence linking the World Trade Center and Pentagon attacks to Osama bin Laden, nor by law, which clearly states that the US, like all other states should pursue a peaceful resolution of disputes (2001). The lack of questioning of the legality of the military action indicates that the law is no longer a serious consideration for the world's remaining superpower (Egelko, 2001). Theorists like Nigel Dower have asserted that a moral view of international relations means that 'one cannot simply support the law', opposition to evil must be the higher duty (1997:107). Rights interventionists, like Richard Falk, argue that the ethical imperative has 'superseded legalistic restraints'. International law has to move with the times and assume more of an *ad hoc* character: 'Otherwise, the self-marginalization of international law and international lawyers is assured in contemporary situations involving claims to use force, consigning their vocational fate to the demeaning roles of "apologist" or "utopian".' (Falk, 1999a:853)

Those who upheld international law against Nato's bombing campaign over Kosovo were indeed condemned as 'apologists' for genocidal policies or as out of touch 'utopians'. The UK House of Commons Foreign Affairs Committee confirmed Falk's view that the ethical imperative must come before the law, concluding that although the war was 'of dubious legality' it was, however, 'justified on moral grounds' (UKFAC, 2000c:par. 138). This finding was later supported by the report of the UN's Independent International Commission on Kosovo, which concluded that 'the intervention was legitimate, but not legal' (IICK, 2000:289).

INSTITUTIONALISING LEGAL INEQUALITY

The above arguments suggest that while the advocates of rights interventionism argue new institutional developments are an extension of international law, they can more accurately be seen to mark the end of law-bound international relations, as the formal equality of the legal subject is degraded. New institutional forms of international law are reflecting the end of its universal character and are more directly reflecting power relations. Prior to the 1990s international law was primarily consensual. The *ad hoc* extensions of traditional practices all involve a more confrontational approach. A more hierarchical and 'profoundly coercive' form of law is increasingly developing (Arbour, 1997:531). The new aspect of coercion has been introduced through the prioritisation of international law without a universal basis. This means that as the new forms of international law develop, there is a growing legal inequality between the more powerful states and the rest. Where international law is formally subordinate to domestic law in Western states, the opposite relationship is developing in the non-Western regions.

International Tribunals

Until the establishment of a series of UN tribunals in the early 1990s, sovereign equality of states meant that states and not individuals held rights under international treaties. This was confirmed in the *Eichmann* case in Israel in 1962 and the *Noriega* case in the United States in 1990 (Nariman, 1997:545). On 25 May 1993, UN Security Council Resolution 827 created the International Criminal Tribunal for the former Yugoslavia, for the prosecution of war crimes, crimes against humanity, and genocide. The Hague court overturned the past legal standing of international treaties in the *Tadić* case. *Tadić* held that the state's sovereign power to establish its own courts for punishment of crimes committed within its own territory must give way in the face of offences that 'do not affect the interest of one State alone but shock the conscience of mankind' (cited in Nariman, 1997:546). An *ad hoc* UN tribunal now had jurisdiction and authority to adjudicate offences committed by a citizen of a state, even though the offences were general criminal offences, like murder and rape, committed within the territory of the state (Nariman, 1997:546). The *ad hoc* tribunals being created by the UN with strong US support, for the first time gave international law primacy over domestic jurisdictions (Arbour, 1997:534). As Jim Hoagland noted, in the *Washington Post*: 'the new tribunals are exercising that most guarded of national powers, criminal jurisdiction, on an international basis' (2000b).

The *ad hoc* development of international law means that the law and its application differs according to the political standing of a particular country or state within the human rights hierarchy. The legal effect of an action is no longer judged on the basis of the action itself. The unequal application of juridical equality reflects the changing view of political equality in the international sphere. There are few modern precedents for these developments due to the formal institutionalisation of political and legal equality in international relations through the UN framework. For many rights-interventionists the template is that of the post-Second World War settlement where the Nuremberg trials legally distinguished between the two sides of the slaughter. The Nuremberg judgments are celebrated by today's rights internationalists for 'the erosion of national sovereignty' (H. T. King, 1999:61). It is interesting that this erosion of national sovereignty did not take a universal form. More to the point, the sovereignty held to have been eroded was that of the already defeated and occupied powers, Germany and Japan. As Jeremy Rabkin argues, national sovereignty was not in fact undermined by the Nuremberg trials (1999). The political sovereignty of these states had been annulled prior to Nuremberg by their unconditional surrender to the Allied powers. The tribunals were military courts, established by military victors. There was no pretence at legal equality between prosecutors and defendants. The only debate between the Allies was a strategic one of show trial or summary execution.

The creation of the ICTY provides a striking case study of the current institutionalisation of legal and political inequality in the international sphere. The Tribunal was established in response to the ongoing conflict in Bosnia and the powers of the UN court reflected the loss of sovereignty of the region, demonstrated in the creation of a Bosnian state through the US-imposed Dayton peace agreement. The people of Bosnia had no opportunity to assent to the new state created in their name by the international community and elected representatives were subordinate to international officials and a internationally-appointed High Representative (Chandler, 2000a). The assumption behind the Tribunal, and the imposed international protectorate, was that elected representatives and people in the region were not capable of coming to terms with the war without international regulation. For human rights advocates, like Lawrence Weschler, the Hague process was necessary to bring civilised values to the moral 'swampland' which was Bosnia: 'each of these individual prosecutions was like a single mound, a terp cast out upon the moral swampland of the war's aftermath' (1999:19).

There have been three interrelated problems with the approach of the International Tribunal: the absence of due legal process and questions of prosecutorial bias; the influence exerted on the legal process by leading Western powers; and the denigration of democracy in the region covered by the Tribunal's shifting mandate. These aspects all relate to the absence of universality in its approach.

First, because, like Nuremberg, the Tribunal was established on an *ad hoc* basis to try certain crimes with a preconceived aim, there was little pretence that defendants' rights would be safeguarded. This is indicated in the opening sentence of its statute, which states the aim of the Tribunal is the 'Prosecution of Persons Responsible for Serious Violations of International Humanitarian Law', people 'responsible', not people 'accused' of serious violations (Astier, 2000). There has been little pretence of judicial impartiality. The first President of the Tribunal publicly declared that the Bosnian Serb leaders, Karadzic and Mladic, were 'war criminals', a presumption of guilt which would have disqualified him in domestic legal systems (G. Robertson, 1999:279). ICTY Prosecutor Judge Louise Arbour similarly presumed guilt before trial, as indicated in her view that people linked with those accused by her court 'will be tainted by their association with an indicted war criminal' (cited in Skoco and Woodger, 2000:36). The issue of public indictments is condemned by Geoffrey Robertson QC:

> What is this, other than a public trial in absentia, of suspects who may in due course be arrested and put properly on trial, but by a court which has already found 'reasonable grounds for believing' in their guilt? This finding, of course, reverses the presumption of innocence promised by Article 21(3) of the Statute. (1999:283; see also Black, 1999b).

The court's implicit rejection of 'innocence until proven guilty' is reproduced in media coverage, which has similarly rejected the presumption of innocence, with even the higher quality press tending to use the phrase 'indicted war criminal'. As Henri Astier notes: 'A trainee on a local newspaper who referred to someone charged with selling crack cocaine as an "indicted drug dealer" would get a rap over the knuckles from his editor and a stern lecture on the presumption of innocence.' (2000)

Once the accused is in court, lawyers for the defence have complained about the prosecutorial bias whereby the defence have much more limited opportunities for gathering evidence than the prosecution, who have access to the resources of the UN (D'Amato, 2000). The Office of the Prosecutor is a fully-fledged branch of the Tribunal with its own budget, about 40 per cent of the $100 million the ICTY receives from the UN annually. The defence receives only a small fraction of this and does not have a separate office or budget (Astier, 2000). The emphasis is on prosecution rather than fact-finding. The Tribunal is not concerned with the context of the conflict or even the conflict as a whole, merely with the gathering of evidence to justify the indictments. As Carla del Ponte, the Tribunal's chief prosecutor told the UN Security Council: 'Our task is not to prepare a complete list of war casualties. Our primary task is to gather evidence relevant to criminal charges.' (Steele, 2000a)

Louise Arbour has claimed that the Tribunal was 'subject to extremely stringent rules of evidence with respect to the admissibility and the credibility of the product that we will tender in court' and that there were safeguards against 'unsubstantiated, unverifiable, uncorroborated allegations' (cited in Black and Herman, 2000). These claims do not appear to stand up. John Laughland, in *The Times*, described the ICTY as 'a rogue court with rigged rules' (1999a). As Christopher Black and Edward Herman note:

> The Tribunal violates virtually every standard of due process; it fails to separate prosecution and judge; it does not accord the right to bail or a speedy trial; it has no clear definition of burden of proof required for a conviction; it has no independent appeal body; it violates the principle that a defendant may not be tried twice for the same crime ... suspects can be held for 90 days without trial; under Rule 92 confessions are presumed to be free and voluntary unless the contrary is established by the prisoner; witnesses can testify anonymously, and ... Common Law rules against hearsay are not observed. (2000)

One of the most problematic aspects is the lack of any genuine appeals procedure, whereby (as in Soviet law) in front of the same court appellants risk getting an increased sentence, as well as new charges levelled against them, if they challenge the initial verdict (Stone, 2000). As many commentators have noted, the Tribunal is operating against the rules of Western jurisprudence, denying those accused of war crimes some of the basic protections enjoyed in the common law tradition. Élise Groulx, President of the International Criminal Defence Attorneys Association, argues that the Tribunal's hybrid mixture of the common law 'adversarial' system and the civil law 'inquisitorial' tradition of Continental Europe is geared towards securing convictions (Astier, 2000). John Laughland quotes Louise Arbour saying: 'The law, to me, should be creative and used to make things tight.' (1999a)

Second, because non-consensual 'international justice' is operating without an international state, the Tribunal lacks any independence from the major world powers, particularly the United States. Many leading commentators have noted that the ICTY appears biased, with prosecutorial decisions based on the needs of major Western powers, rather than the available evidence. Doubts about the Tribunal's political impartiality have been raised by the apparent close co-operation between prosecutors and Western governments. Article 16 of the Tribunal's Charter states that the Prosecutor shall act independently and shall not seek or receive instruction from any government. This section has been regularly breached. As Black and Herman note, Nato sources have regularly made claims suggesting their authority over the Tribunal. Former British foreign secretary Robin Cook, at a joint press conference with Louise Arbour, stated that 'we are going to focus on war crimes being committed in Kosovo and our determination to bring those responsible to justice' as if he and Arbour were part of the same team, deciding who would be held responsible for violations of international law, and ruling himself out from potential charges (Black and Herman, 2000). Prior to this, on 31 March, only days after the bombing had commenced, and two days after Cook had promised Arbour supporting information for criminal charges, she announced the indictment of Arkan, that had been kept secret since 1997. She also appeared in public during the Kosovo war, and held high-profile meetings with Nato state leaders including Robin Cook and Madeleine Albright.

The closeness of this relationship between Nato, and US policymakers in particular, and the ICTY has been a constant factor in the development of the *ad hoc* Tribunal. Its funding by, and interlocking functional relationship with, the top Nato powers have made the Tribunal appear to be an instrument of Nato policy. Black and Herman note that although Article 32 of its Charter declares that the Tribunal's expenses shall be provided in the general budget of the United Nations, this proviso has been regularly violated (2000). In 1994–1995 the US government provided it with $700,000 in cash and $2.3 million in equipment, despite failing to meet its obligations to the UN running costs that would have allowed the UN to fund what is, at least formally, its own tribunal (Black and Herman, 2000).

Tribunal judge Gabrielle Kirk McDonald has referred to former US secretary of state Madeleine Albright as the 'mother of the Tribunal' (Black, 1999b). Judge Arbour informed President Clinton personally of the indictment of Milosevic two days before informing the rest of the world, and the Prosecutor openly met with the Secretary-General of Nato and its supreme commander to 'establish contacts and begin discussing modalities of co-operation and assistance' (Black and Herman, 2000). There have been numerous other meetings between the Prosecutor and Nato officials, and Nato has been given the function of arresting suspects and collecting data. The relationship of dependency between the Tribunal and leading Nato powers clearly leaves open to question its claims to neutrality. As Michael Ignatieff notes, Chief Prosecutor Louise Arbour necessarily had an ambiguous relationship with Nato:

> Officially, of course, it [Nato] has nothing to do with her office. Practically, of course, Arbour is dependent on Nato governments for everything from the helicopters that fly her to the sites in Kosovo to the secret intelligence she needed in order to indict Milosevic. (2000b:119)

The failure of the Tribunal to take seriously accusations against the Nato powers has particularly provoked criticism. Robert Hayden, Christopher Black and Edward Herman, for example, note the indictment of Serb leader Milan Martic for the use of cluster bombs on the Croatian capital city, Zagreb, in May 1995, in which seven civilians were killed and damage was done to a home for the elderly and to a children's hospital. However, the evidence would indicate that the Nato use of cluster bombs in the May 1999 attack on Nis, which killed 15 people and damaged the main hospital, would be equally criminal as both cities were targeted intentionally (Hayden, 2000; Black and Herman, 2000). Similarly, Canadian lawyer Michael Mandel argues that Nato leaders deliberately and illegally made military targets of city bridges, factories, marketplaces, residential neighbourhoods and TV studios with slight or no military value, with the knowledge that hundreds of civilian deaths would be caused (2000).

A Human Rights Watch report on Nato action in Yugoslavia argued that the war signalled a 'disturbing disregard for the principles of humanitarianism', with the use of cluster bombs described as grave 'violations of humanitarian law' (Mandel, 2000; Hayden, 2000). The only reason for the lack of investigation into Nato actions would appear to be the close links between the two institutions. Jamie Shea, Nato spokesperson during the conflict, argued at a press conference on 17 May 1999 that prosecutions of Nato were impossible because 'Nato is the friend of the Tribunal. Nato countries are those that have provided the finances to set up the Tribunal.' (Cited in Hayden, 2000) This was supported by Robin Cook, who stated: 'If I may say so ... this is not a court set up to bring to book Prime Ministers of the United Kingdom or Presidents of the United States.' (Cited in Holbrook, 2000) The close relationship between a warring party and the international law-makers is clearly one open to abuse.

Michael Mandel points to the thin line where the ICTY stands accused of 'legitimating Nato's violent lawlessness against people unlucky enough to be ruled by "indicted war criminals" as opposed to the un-indicted kind that govern the Nato countries'. He suggests that the legitimisation of illegal acts is actually the very purpose for which the US sponsored the tribunal in the first place (2000). As Black and Herman note, the ICTY prosecutors not only failed to object to and prosecute Nato leaders for war crimes, but by indicting Milosevic on May 27 they gave Nato a moral cover for escalating attacks on a civilian population. They state that: 'Arbour and the Tribunal thus present us with an amazing spectacle of an institution supposedly organised to contain, prevent and prosecute war crimes actually knowingly facilitating them.' (2000)

These concerns would appear to be confirmed by the comments of Michael Scharf, Attorney-Advisor with the US State Department. He drafted the Security Council resolution establishing the Tribunal under Madeleine Albright's instructions and described the motivation behind it in the *Washington Post*:

> [T]he Tribunal was widely perceived within the government as little more than a public relations device and as a potentially useful policy tool ... Indictments also would serve to isolate offending leaders diplomatically, strengthen the hand of their domestic rivals and fortify the international political will to employ economic sanctions or use force. (Cited in Mandel, 2000)

Third, the Tribunal, while being dependent on Western powers for its operation and direction, and to some extent the extension of US sovereign power in the region, has operated to restrict the sovereign rights of states in the Balkans and the political rights of the citizens of former Yugoslavia. The *ad hoc* Tribunal has played an increasingly invasive role in the political process in the region. Initially, the Tribunal indictments of Bosnian Serb leaders Radovan Karadzic and Ratko Mladic prevented them from taking part in the peace negotiations. This was followed by the ban on the elected Bosnian Serb President taking part in the Bosnian elections. The ability of the Tribunal to define the terms of its own legitimacy, and award itself new powers, has involved the extension of its mandate to influence the political process in both Croatia and Serbia. This extension of the Tribunal's remit led to the indictment of the elected Yugoslav President, Slobodan Milosevic, along with indications that an indictment was also being prepared for the late Croatian president Franjo Tudjman.

There seems little doubt that the future will see growing pressure for the development of arbitrary 'international justice' through *ad hoc* international courts for selected regions. The Washington-based Human Rights Alliance of over 100 NGOs, with US and UK government support, is calling for an international tribunal for Iraqi leader Saddam Hussein. There have been discussions in Congress on indicting Cuban leader Fidel Castro for 'crimes against humanity' and the United States government has been pressing for the estab-lishment of international tribunals for Cambodia and Sierra Leone (Brown, 2000). The Sierra Leone proposals, drafted by the US ambassador to the UN, Richard Holbrooke, have been used to pressurise the presidents of Liberia and Burkina Faso, Charles Taylor and Blaise Compaore, to co-operate with policy in the region under the threat of indictment (Lynch, 2000; Harden, 2000). As John Laughland notes, the willingness of *ad hoc* tribunals to take over criminal law as well as indict elected heads of state means that countries at the sharp end of 'international justice', 'will not only be deprived of their ability to make their own laws. They may be deprived of the right to chose their own government.' (1999b)

International Criminal Court

In June 1998 the treaty for the International Criminal Court was signed in Rome. The proposed international court is likely to be established in the near future; the treaty will come into force once it has been ratified by 60 states. Despite the positive publicity the court has already received from the human rights movement, it can only magnify the dangers of the *ad hoc* tribunals. The standard of justice that will be delivered has already been widely questioned, as the odds will be stacked high against defendants with the court structured to enable close co-operation between the judges and pros-ecution at the expense of impartiality and even-handed justice (G. Robertson, 1999:308). The dependence of the court on the support of the major powers indicates that those brought to account for 'international crimes' will be little different than under the present *ad hoc* system. Like its *ad hoc* predecessors, it will be little more than the backdrop for show trials against 'countries like Rwanda and former Yugoslavia where none of the combatants have superpower support' (G. Robertson, 1999:304).

The human rights NGOs have been heavily involved in these international institutional developments. Amnesty International and Human Rights Watch led the lobbying of nearly 200 NGOs with delegates involved at the 1998 Rome Conference. The main message of the NGO reports was summed up by Human Rights Watch: 'Delegates are urged to ensure that the Rules do not add to the burdens of the Prosecutor, create additional procedural steps or further limit the Court's jurisdiction.' (Cited in Astier, 2000) Even legal commentators supportive of the new court were taken aback by the desire of these groups to abandon judicial neutrality in the search for 'justice'. Geoffrey Robertson QC notes 'what was truly ironic was their zeal for a court so tough that it would actually violate the basic human rights of its defendants' (1999:302). Amnesty International, an NGO that established its reputation by prioritising the rights of defendants, has even called for the abolition of traditional defences, such as duress, necessity and even self-defence, for those accused of crimes against humanity (G. Robertson, 1999:319). The rapidity with which established human rights NGOs, such as Amnesty, which previously defended the rights of all defendants, have taken up the agenda of international institutions, illustrates the shift away from universalist approaches to 'justice' today.

There has been much discussion about United States opposition to the establishment of the ICC, amid concerns that US military officers and diplomats may be charged under its rules (Black, 1999a). It seems likely that US reluctance to support the new court will wane in the future as the experience of the *ad hoc* tribunals indicates that prosecutorial independence from the UN Security Council (and US veto) will have little impact on the ability of the major Western powers to shape the development of the court. After President Clinton signed the treaty just before leaving office, leading international lawyers suggested that the US military were the 'least likely to be hauled before the court' and, in fact, would be the 'major beneficiary' of the ICC (Ricks, 2001). In the absence of any collective body which can enforce its rulings, it is clear that the ICC will be as reliant on the United States and other Western powers as the earlier UN tribunals.

National Courts

The inequalities of international law, reflected in the growth of *ad hoc* international tribunals, are becoming institutionalised in the domestic arena as well. Until the late 1990s the domestic courts could not be involved in human rights disputes with foreign governments, which were considered to be immune from their jurisdiction, except for acts leading to deaths or damages on territory over which there was national sovereignty (Karagiannakis, 1998:32). In a leading 1984 US case, *Princz* v. *Federal Republic of Germany*, a Nazi slave labour compensation case for a US citizen against the German government, Judge Robert Bork explained why international human rights issues should not be ruled on by domestic courts:

> [If] we impute to the Congress an intention that the federal courts assume jurisdiction over the countless human rights cases that might well be brought by the victims of all the ruthless military juntas, presidents-for-life, and the murderous dictators of the world, from Idi Amin to Mao Zedong. Such an expansive reading ... would likely place an enormous strain not only upon our courts but ... upon our country's diplomatic relations with a number of foreign nations. In many if not in most cases the outlaw regime would no longer be in power and our Government could have normal relations with the government of the day – unless disrupted by our courts, that is. (Cited in Karagiannakis, 1998:39)

In a dissenting opinion, Judge Wald held that the abuse of human rights went against the 'collective will of the international community' and that this justified the exercise of universal jurisdiction (Karagiannakis, 1998:37). This dissenting opinion has since won support from legal commentators keen to encourage the activism of US courts in relation to international law, rather than handing the question over 'to a politically self-interested Congress' (Karagiannakis, 1998:42). The case for universal jurisdiction for domestic courts was strengthened greatly by the UK Law Lords' ruling in March 1999 that former Chilean president Augusto Pinochet could not rely on any immunity as a former head of state. Accordingly, he could be extradited following a request from a Spanish prosecutor.

On the basis of newly declared powers of universal jurisdiction in the sphere of human rights, US judges in domestic courts have awarded millions of dollars in civil damages to victims of abuses in such places as Guatemala, Haiti, Ethiopia, Rwanda, Indonesia and the Philippines. In August 2000, in the first of two civil law cases filed in a New York court against former Bosnian Serb leader Radovan

Karadzic, a federal jury awarded $745 million to a group of Bosnian Muslim and Croat women in a genocide suit. The lawsuit was filed by attorney Catherine MacKinnon with backing from the National Organization for Women's Legal Defense and Education Fund and other organisations (Barrett, 2000). There was no defence case, no defence attorneys and no defendant, just a grainy snapshot of Karadzic taped to a chair by the plaintiff's attorneys (Miller and Haughney, 2000). The District Court Judge Peter Leisure entered a default judgment against Karadzic and ruled that, therefore, it was only up to the jury to decide the level of damages to be awarded (Neumeister, 2000). Later the same month, a law suit was filed in New York against Li Peng, the leader of the Chinese parliament at the time of the Tiananmen Square massacre, by the US NGO Center for Constitutional Rights (Wong, 2000).

The drive behind these trials, as Atlanta Defence Attorney John Matteson states, has been attempts by human rights activists to stretch the law to promote their political agenda: 'This all sounds noble, this all sounds great, but it is an absolute travesty ... It's a political deal. It's a show trial. And judges don't want to take the chance that it looks like they're siding with international terrorists.' (Cited in Miller and Haughney, 2000) This was confirmed in September 2000 when a second New York civil judgment against Karadzic ordered him to pay no less than $4.5 billion in damages. After the symbolic verdict, both the jury foreman and the judge took the unusual step of making statements to express their outrage over the conduct of the Bosnian Serbs (Rhode, 2000).

It is not just in Western courts that human rights activists are encouraging domestic claims for universal jurisdiction. Human Rights Watch and the Harvard Law School jointly organised and funded the indictment of Hissene Habre, former president of Chad, by a Senegalese court. This was regardless of the fact that the Chad government had not requested his extradition and was concerned that his prosecution would aggravate regional and ethnic tensions in the country (Bosco, 2000). Some US commentators are concerned that these national trials will open a Pandora's box, with American states officials being sued for damages in every other country in the world (*Washington Post*, 2000). However, few states are likely to wish to sour diplomatic and economic relations with major Western powers, nor are they likely to be able to assert their claims. As David Bosco notes: 'In international law, like cases are decidedly not treated in a like manner ... In many cases and for many years to come, *ad hoc* justice will be the only brand of justice.' (2000)

UNIVERSAL JUSTICE?

While the universal basis of law ratified by the UN Charter is unlikely to be replaced by any other coherent framework, international law is either ignored on the basis of 'might is right' or is developed in an *ad hoc* and partial way through specific tribunals for specific 'human rights abusers'. Michael Posner, head of the Lawyers' Committee for Human Rights, is right to assert:

> The rules of the game are changing. We are creating new rules of the road for international justice ... Whether it is Pinochet, the Hague Tribunal [for the former Yugoslavia], the Rwanda Tribunal, the [planned] International Criminal Court, or [a domestic] civil action, it's all of one piece. (Cited in Gutman, 2000b)

The two bases of modern law considered earlier in the chapter, equality of derivation and equality of application, are undermined through this process of extending 'international justice'.

Unequal Application

'International justice' and the human rights-based approach are a reflection of the dismissal of sovereign political equality. The inequalities of international law are increasingly institutionalising international political inequality. The desire to establish these new tribunals or universal jurisdiction for domestic courts institution-alises the shift in legal and political relations between the West and less powerful states. The idea that non-Western peoples and states cannot be trusted at the most basic level of the administration of law and government is increasingly articulated by Western policy-makers and NGOs. The legitimisation of universal jurisdiction lies in this deep mistrust. Human rights professor Diane Orlicher, for example, argues that the UK House of Lords' interference with Chilean sover-eignty was legitimate:

> The argument that outsiders should respect the choices made by 'Chilean Society' misses a crucial point: The victims of [the] torture chambers and the survivors of those whom he disappeared did not choose to consign his crimes to legal oblivion. (Cited in Bosco, 2000)

Universal jurisdiction on behalf of victims means that the decisions of the Chilean people on the path of democratic transition are considered to be illegitimate. NGOs and international lawyers feel free to be able to dictate to foreign governments how justice should be determined in their own societies. This shift is reflected in British government consideration of calls for universal jurisdiction in cases of serious crimes such as murder, if it is felt that the relevant national authorities are not responding adequately (Branigan, 2001a). Universal jurisdiction is a blank cheque for Western governments and NGOs to assume the right to meddle in affairs of which they know little, as long as they are publicly declaring that they are 'on the side of justice'. The basis of this claim is that the non-Western state cannot be trusted with its own administration of justice. As Reed Brody of Human Rights Watch states:

> In an ideal world ... Pinochet is tried in Chile, Habre is tried in Chad, and Milosevic is tried in Serbia, but given that most mass atrocities are committed in the name of the state, it's going to be rare that the state itself is in the position to conduct a prosecution. So then you go to the international stage. (Cited in Bosco, 2000)

The extensions to international justice can not be universally applied. Universal jurisdiction and *ad hoc* tribunals only operate to give powerful states greater international leverage over the less powerful. While the human rights lawyers suggest that the Taliban's refusal to take action against bin Laden 'provides a mandate for the US and its allies to breach Afghanistan's sovereignty' it would obviously be impossible for states without 'global reach' to act in the same way (G. Robertson, 2001b). Once non-Western states are seen as incapable of administering justice, the most basic right of sovereignty, self-rule, is put to question and neocolonial relationships legitimised. The dangers of this were highlighted clearly in April 2000 when a Brussels magistrate issued an arrest warrant for a leading member of the government of a former Belgian colony. Claiming universal jurisdiction for crimes against humanity, the Belgian authorities sought the arrest of Abdoulaye Yerodia Ndombasi, the Congolese Foreign Minister, for inflammatory speeches made to the national media which allegedly led to the deaths of ethnic Tutsis (Socolovsky, 2000).

Unequal Derivation

The central contradiction of the new international order of human-rights based 'justice' is that it is impossible to maintain a consensual basis of law against the human rights discourse, making it impossible to construct a stable system of international regulation. As the House of Commons Foreign Affairs Committee notes:

> These legal questions are not arcane. There is a need for a system of law governing the conduct of states, just as the internal affairs of states should be governed by the rule of law. An agreed system of law is particularly important where the use of force is concerned. It is in the national interest of the United Kingdom that an international order based on law should exist, and that individual states, or groups of states, should not be able to interpret the law perversely in their immediate interest. When the law is clear, there can be a consensus; when there is ambiguity, international stability and the mechanisms of collective security set up through the United Nations are threatened. (UKFAC, 2000c:par. 125)

The problem that the advocates of 'international justice' have to grapple with is that without sovereign equality there can be no international law. The position at the moment seems to be that the United States government believes that the US military should not be limited by its Nato allies and that Nato should not be constrained by the views of non-Nato states, but this position has not been forwarded as part of any new system of international regulation (Sciolino and Myers, 2001). It seems that the only principle of the new post-UN order is that intervention may be used to coercively enforce 'international justice' if the United States thinks that this would be a good idea (O'Connell, 2000:87). This certainly appeared to be the case when President Bush asserted his self-appointment as the leader of 'a fight to save the civilised world', demanding that Osama bin Laden be taken 'dead or alive' and later authorising the CIA to assassinate him and his supporters across the world (Gow, 2001). This was the pursuit of 'justice' through ignoring the judicial process and trampling international law.

The desire to intervene coercively in the cause of human rights is undermining the old international order but no universal framework of law is offered in its place. At present, there is an uneasy tension between 'yet unsystematized notions of international public order and the traditional precepts of international law' (Bianchi, 1999:271). Louis Henkin suggests a 'gentleman's agreement' between the major powers on acting outside the UN's Charter rather than a 'formal amendment' of the Charter (1999b:828). He cites the view of Professor Oscar Schachter that:

> [I]t is highly undesirable to have a new rule allowing humanitarian intervention, for that could provide a pretext for abusive intervention. It would be better to acquiesce in a violation that is considered necessary and desirable in the particular circumstances than to adopt a principle that would open a wide gap in the barrier against unilateral force. (1999b:826)

This seems to be the perspective that has been adopted. There is no international support for a formal annulment of UN Charter law or for a universal doctrine of 'humanitarian intervention' (Charney, 1999:837; O'Connell, 2000:81). The desire of Western states to enforce international regulation on their own terms, without a UN Security Council resolution, but without opening up this right to universal and equal application means that international law can no longer be the framework for 'international justice'. This solution is advocated by Michael Glennon, Legal Counsel to the Senate Foreign Relations Committee, who argues: 'International justice can in fact be pursued *ad hoc*, without a fully functioning legal system.' (1999) International law is no longer accepted as a legitimate curb on the use of force by Western powers, while coercive intervention by Western powers against other states is increasingly legitimised through the framework of 'international justice'. As several commentators have noted, 'just war' interventionists are 'not overtly concerned with legality' (Woollacott, 2001). The gap between 'justice' and what is 'legal' has led to the degradation of international law rather than to its development. Christine Chinkin writes:

> The West assumes that its wealth, power and assurance bestow a normative authority that discounts alternative views ... [I]t is hard to envisage that other states would be able to undertake such a campaign, either unilaterally or together, against the wishes of other members of the Security Council and without being challenged by them. (1999:847)

As the Foreign Affairs Committee concludes: 'if there is no prospect of a new treaty text, then this will have to remain a fig leaf of legal respectability for actions which are generally thought to be morally entirely justified' (UKFAC, 2000c:par. 142). This was confirmed in May 2000 by the Nato Secretary-General, Lord Robertson, who argued that the Western powers were engaged in an ongoing process of 'balancing law, morality and the use of force' (George Robertson, 2000). This balancing of law against other concerns was highlighted in the response to the September 2001 attacks on the World Trade Center and the Pentagon, when there was little public concern expressed by US and British leaders as to the legality of military intervention and the overthrow of the Afghan authorities (Rozenberg, 2001; Goldstone, 2001). International law is no longer a determining factor for Western powers. Once law is weighed against morality, the 'higher law' derives from Western powers only (Zizek, 2000:56).

CONCLUSION

The developments in international law since 1990 have been greeted by the human rights community as universalising and extending the law, providing greater protections for the least powerful. This chapter has attempted to explain that, in fact, the reverse is true. Attempts to strengthen international law, without the development of any global authority able to stand above powerful nation-state interests, have instead reinforced the political and economic inequalities in the world. Removing the rights of non-Western states to formal equality in international law has not led to a redistribution of power away from the powerful to the weak, but reinforced existing social and economic inequalities, institutionalising them in law and politics. Despite their rhetorical critiques of the old Westphalian order, the advocates of 'international justice' have done much to resurrect it. As we have seen in the Middle East, Africa, the Balkans and Afghanistan, the development of new international jurisdictions has heralded a return to the system of open Great Power domination over states which are too weak to prevent external claims against them. As Simon Jenkins notes:

Augusto Pinochet of Chile is seized from the authority of his own people for inquisition by Chile's former ruler, Spain. President Saddam Hussein is being bombed by Iraq's one-time overlord, Britain ... Post-colonial warlords are summoned from

Africa to stand trial for 'war crimes' in once-imperial European capitals. (1999a)

What is different in the twenty-first century is that this open domination is not legitimised by a conservative elite, on the basis of racial superiority and an imperial mission, but by a liberal elite, on the basis of ethical superiority and a human rights mission.

6 War: The Lesser of Two Evils?

No genuine leader is blind to the fact that war is evil, that unpredictable and atrocious violence will result. But here, our leaders have concluded that war remains the lesser evil ... We agree. – *Guardian* editorial, 15 May 1999.

Since the end of the Cold War the place of military intervention (war) in international relations has been transformed. This can be indicated on two levels. First, at the level of state and international institutional practice, military intervention is becoming central to policy-making. The UN is in the process of restructuring its military operations to be ready to be on a permanent war footing of 'continuing preparedness' (UN, 2000c:30) while the Nato Secretary-General, Lord Robertson, has warned that: 'The time for the peace dividend is over because there is no permanent peace in Europe or elsewhere.' (AFP, 1999) Second, at the level of public activism, peace movements in the West, opposed to military interventions and concerned with disarmament, have been displaced by NGOs and professional associations concerned with peace education and conflict resolution programmes in other countries (Aspeslagh and Burns, 1996:32–3). Rearmament and military activism by major Western states meets with little opposition at home. Leading members of the former peace movement in the UK, like former Labour leader Michael Foot, came out strongly in favour of Nato assaults on the Federal Republic of Yugoslavia (Foot, 1999). Opposition to the Afghanistan war was largely based on strategy and tactics rather than the war aims of the Western powers, including the overthrow of the Afghan regime. The limited nature of the 'to pause or not to pause' bombing debate was illustrated by high-profile UK rebel Labour MP Paul Marsden's support for military action, including sending in the SAS, if the UN took over from the United States (Marsden, 2001; White, 2001).

The transformation of the public and political perception of military action is reflected in the fact that the social democratic Left have been more in favour of military engagements by Western forces over the last ten years than the conservative Right. In its first

18 months, the UK Labour government dropped more bombs than the previous Conservative administration managed in 18 years (Pilger, 1999). The leaders of the United States, United Kingdom and Germany, prosecuting the Kosovo war, were all from social democratic backgrounds; German Defence Minister, Joschka Fischer, successfully overturning Green Party policy and constitutional barriers to German militarism abroad. The new wars of today also have the support of a wide range of human rights NGOs like MSF, Amnesty International and Human Rights Watch.

This chapter considers how war has been redefined through the ethical agenda of human rights, creating a dichotomy in which the barbaric aspects of warfare are seen to reside in the cultural backwardness of the non-Western world, while an idealised version of 'just' and 'humanitarian' war is used to categorise the military action of Western states. This chapter assesses human rights arguments that military intervention should be applied in situations of internal conflict and that peace should no longer be upheld as the central goal of the UN, and considers the impact of the human rights discourse in conflict and peacekeeping situations. It suggests that the privileging of human rights concerns creates an international order in which conflict is more likely and in which peace negotiations may be undermined.

THE CHALLENGE TO THE UN ORDER

As considered in Chapter 5, calls for international law to become more people-centred and less focused on protecting states bring into question the existing rules regulating the use of force in international relations. The legitimate use of force in domestic jurisdictions depends on the concentration of legalised force in a single authority and the criminalisation of the individual exercise of violence, with very limited exceptions. In the same way, international society was constituted through the development of the norm of non-intervention, the restriction of force outside the authority of the UN:

> The essential point is that whereas the right to wage war *inheres in each state individually* within the international anarchy, the non-intervention norm is *constitutive of the collectivity* of the international society of states. That is, without a non-intervention norm, there could not be such an international society. (Ramsbotham and Woodhouse, 1996:35)

The creation of international society, through the peace settlements at the end of the First and Second World Wars, marked the end of the Westphalian system of Great Power domination through military intervention and the reliance on force. Until this point, the right of the most powerful states to use force in international affairs (wage war) was considered the key to sovereignty (Ramsbotham and Woodhouse, 1996:38; Held, 1995:87). As the distinguished international scholar Louis Henkin notes, the transformative nature of this move should not be underestimated: 'We may not appreciate how remarkable that was, that transformative development in the middle of the twentieth century: "sovereign states" gave up their "sovereign" right to go to war.' (1999:1) This point is well made against the critics of the UN system who assert that the international order failed to 'break fundamentally with the logic of Westphalia' (for example, Held, 1995:88). This break was strikingly confirmed in 1949, in the International Court of Justice ruling in the *Corfu Channel* case. As Michael Byers notes, the court, in ruling against the UK governments' intervention to clear mines from Albanian territorial waters, specifically warned that the breach of UN principles of non-intervention would advantage the interests of the most powerful states. The judgement reads:

> The court can only regard the alleged right of intervention as a policy of force, such as has, in the past, given rise to the most serious abuses and such as cannot, whatever be the present defects in international organisation, find a place in international law. Intervention is perhaps still less admissible in the particular form it would take here, for, from the nature of things, it would be reserved to the most powerful states. (Byers, 1999:18)

The UN Charter, for the first time established an international legal framework that outlawed war. The only exceptions being those of (limited) self-defence or by UN Security Council agreement on a threat to international peace and security. Article 2(4) states: 'All members shall refrain in their international relations from the threat or use of force against the territorial integrity or political independence of any state, or in any manner inconsistent with the purposes of the United Nations.' As James Mayall notes, the great achievement of the UN Charter was that the sovereign's right to go to war, for reasons other than self-defence, was 'unambiguously outlawed': 'The move to establish a new security order ... represented the first serious attempt to ensure that force would only be employed to uphold rather than undermine international peace and security.' (2000:70–1) Louis Henkin writes that the UN Charter: 'declares peace as the supreme value, to secure not merely state autonomy, but fundamental order for all. It declares peace to be more compelling than inter-state justice, more compelling even than human rights or other human values.' (1995:113) The basic principles of the legal regime relating to the use of force were reaffirmed in the UN General Assembly Resolution on the Definition of Aggression of 14 December 1974 (Resolution 3314 (XXIX)). Article 5 provides that: 'No consideration of whatever nature, whether political, economic, military or otherwise, may serve as a justification for aggression.' (Cited in Littman, 1999:34)

During the 1990s, many commentators argued that there should be a right to wage war to prevent states from abusing the human rights of vulnerable citizens. For some commentators this right was implicit in the UN Charter, for others, the existence of this right could be established under customary international law, independently of Security Council mechanisms. These discussions were crystallised when the Nato bombing of the Federal Republic of Yugoslavia openly challenged the UN Charter regime, which formally barred unilateral declarations of war.

International Law

It has been difficult for human rights advocates to establish a case for international military intervention for human rights ends under international law. The UN Charter's primary purpose was 'to save succeeding generations from the scourge of war' by maintaining international peace and security (Charney, 1999:835; Falk, 1999a:855). Apart from a limited right of self-defence against armed intervention, the one exception to the ban on military force, outlined in Chapter VII of the Charter, is explicitly for the purpose of countering a threat to international peace and security, under UN Security Council authorisation (Chinkin, 1998). The status of the UN Charter clearly places peace as central to the UN system (Cassese, 1999:24). Professor Oscar Schachter's authoritative *International Law in Theory and Practice* states:

> Neither human rights, democracy or self-determination are acceptable legal grounds for waging war, nor for that matter, are traditional just war causes or righting wrongs. This conclusion is

not only in accord with the UN Charter as it was originally understood; it is also in keeping with the interpretation adopted by the great majority of States at the present time. (1991:128)

Despite the wealth of evidence to the contrary, in the late 1990s some human rights advocates sought to rewrite history to deny that peace was ever the primary aim of the UN Charter. Thomas Buergenthal, for example, argued that the UN was, in fact, designed to prevent a repeat of Hitler's rise to power through permitting international intervention in domestic affairs to deal with human rights issues. The only problem being that the UN Charter contained no provisions to support this because all the major powers were against international interference in their own domestic affairs (Buergenthal, 1997: 706). This, of course, begged the question of evidence to support the assertion that the UN was designed for such interventionist purposes. The editors of *Human Rights in Global Politics* went further, to assert that international regulation of the domestic sphere, to prevent totalitarianism, was actually recognised by the UN Charter and Universal Declaration:

As a consequence of the experiences of totalitarianism, governments recognised that there was a need to challenge the Westphalian model of unlimited sovereignty. In these emerging human rights norms, there was a clear consensus that states must be made accountable for their behaviour. (Dunne and Wheeler, 1999:1)

These leading advocates of a new interventionist order have no qualms about rewriting history in two fundamental respects. First, to see the UN system as designed to deal with states' internal domestic affairs rather than the danger of war between states. Second, to reinterpret the restriction of sovereignty, from one imposed on the Great Powers, who sought to intervene in the internal affairs of other states, into a licence for Western powers to intervene in the domestic affairs of other states, on the basis of human rights abuses. Today, every human rights commentator seems able to come up with contradictions in the wording of the Charter which indicate that there are fewer limits to waging war in a 'just cause'. Mostly, these interpretations involve the crudest of selective readings. Mitchell Meyers, for example, notes that Articles 55 and 56 require every UN member state to insure the 'universal respect for, and observance of, human rights and fundamental freedoms'. Therefore, this legal scholar upholds that:

> [T]he United States and other states, have a treaty obligation to intervene unilaterally when violations of international human rights law occur. Not only is this argument a defense for United States unilateral intervention, it also presents such intervention as a binding obligation. (1997:912)

The advocates of human rights intervention aspire to a new interventionist order in which the guarantees and protections for smaller states, institutionalised after the Second World War, are overturned. Some commentators, like Ruth Wedgewood, reverse the meaning of the UN Charter completely, to suggest that Article 51, the right of self-defence, could be interpreted to mean the self-defence of a population under assault from their own government, rather than defence of a state from external intervention (1999:833; see also Roberts, 1993:435). However, the Article itself makes clear that self-defence concerns an 'armed attack' which is against a member state. Geoffrey Robertson provides a typical example of this approach, in his contention that Woodrow Wilson's and Lenin's principle of popular sovereignty should, in fact, be read as a licence for international interference:

> It is open to future courts with judges independent of states ... to give the right of peoples to self-determination some meaning beyond the historic process of decolonialization ... In due course the charter principle of self-determination of peoples came quite illogically to denote some right of governments to avoid interference from other states ... [now it] can revert back to its true meaning, namely a right conferred on peoples against their own governments. (1999:143)

Similarly, Kurt Mills argues that African states have 'perverted the concept of self-determination' by divorcing the term 'peoples' from an 'ethnic or cultural meaning' thereby 'condemning populations to human rights abuse within so-called 'quasi-States' (1997:280). Richard Falk asserts that Milosevic's fundamental denial of human rights included the right to self-determination of 'a people' (1999a:849). Daniel Thurer argues that the international community has 'to cope with the dilemma of choosing between two fundamental principles of legitimacy in international law: on the one hand, the sovereignty and equality of States and, on the other, the right of peoples to self-determination' (1999). This right apparently authorises intervention 'with the object of restoring the State authority needed for the proper functioning of international law' (Thurer, 1999). When the right to self-determination of peoples was universally established in 1945 it was not understood to undermine sovereignty but to support it, as a UN human rights commissioner stated in discussion on the question in 1992:

> The right to self-determination had always been taken by the United Nations to apply to non-self governing territories and not to integral parts of sovereign and independent states ... the application of the right ... to constituent units of sovereign States could not but undermine the principle of territorial integrity of sovereign States and was thus a threat to democracy everywhere. (Cited in Pupavac, 2000a)

The Charter and the *travaux préparatoires* make clear that there was no intention of allowing any of the loopholes subsequently 'discovered' by the rights interventionists, who seek to assert that human rights-based intervention was always intended but that the state system had let down the ambitions of the Charter's drafters (see Buergenthal, 1997:706). The phrases 'territorial integrity' and 'inconsistent with the purposes of the Charter' were added to Article 2(4) to close potential loopholes on the use of force rather than open up new ones (Charney, 1999:835).

Customary Law

Many advocates of human rights-based military intervention argue that a new right has developed in customary international law. Even if the UN Charter has been breached this is not illegal because international law has developed since 1945. Karagiannakis' informative study highlights that the human rights provisions under UN treaties provide no obligation for states to act on breaches committed in other countries (1998:17). He makes the point that the ratification of international human rights treaties cannot imply a waiver of sovereignty for breaches as this was not stated in the treaties themselves. Because of the lack of international law supporting a right of human rights intervention he is forced to appeal to customary right, relying on the Universal Declaration of Human Rights. He admits the Declaration was 'not an international agreement' but argues, instead, that it should be held to be of higher status than a binding agreement because he believes that it was 'an authoritative statement on the content of custom' (1998:35). Naturally, the privileging of 'customary law' over international treaty opens many more avenues of interpretation.

Supporting the customary law approach, Ruth Wedgewood, for example, suggests that 'humanitarian reasons have served as justification' for the Vietnamese invasion of Kampuchea in 1979, which resulted in the overthrow of the Pol Pot regime, the Tanzanian invasion of Uganda in 1979, which overthrew Idi Amin's regime, and India's invasion of East Pakistan in 1971, to support Bangladeshi independence (1999:833). Rights interventionists are as cavalier with the history of the success of the humanitarian intervention arguments in the past as they are with the original purposes of the UN Charter. In the cases alleged to be justifiable on humanitarian grounds, such as those cited above, the invasions were justified at the time on the traditional grounds of self-defence, and were roundly condemned by international society (Roberts, 1993:434; Chinkin, 1998:110). In fact, it is doubtful whether these interventions could even be retrospectively seen as human rights-based. There was a strong 'national interest' involved in these actions, as the Indian government had clear objectives in intervening against East Pakistan, Vietnamese occupation not only removed Pol Pot but installed a puppet regime of its choice, and the Tanzanian invasion was a result of Ugandan troops crossing into Tanzanian territory (Forsythe, 1989:32–3).

In 1983 the United States invaded Grenada without Security Council authorisation. Geoffrey Robertson retrospectively justifies this as an humanitarian intervention, but notes that, at the time, the US claimed that it was a response to a communist threat and also that it was almost universally condemned as a breach of international law and state sovereignty (1999:60). In fact, the UN General Assembly condemned the action as unlawful by a vote of 108 to nine, with 27 abstentions. The United States was forced to veto a UN Security Council resolution finding the invasion in violation of international law (O'Connell, 2000:61).

In 1985, the International Court of Justice, in the *Nicaragua* case, found no really persuasive examples in state practice of human rights intervention and stated that in the absence of justification under the

UN Charter 'the use of force could not be the appropriate method to monitor or ensure respect' for human rights:

> [W]hile the United States might form its own appraisal of the situation as to respect for human rights in Nicaragua, the use of force could not be the appropriate method to monitor or ensure such respect. With regard to the steps actually taken, the protection of human rights, a strictly humanitarian objective, cannot be compatible with the mining of ports, the destruction of oil installations, or again with the training, arming and equipping of the Contras. The court concludes that the argument derived from the preservation of human rights in Nicaragua cannot afford a legal justification for the conduct of the United States. (Cited in Littman, 1999:4)

The following year, the UK Foreign Office summed up the accepted international law with regard to humanitarian intervention:

> [T]he overwhelming majority of contemporary legal opinion comes down against the existence of a right of humanitarian intervention, for three main reasons: first, the UN Charter and the corpus of modern international law do not seem to specifically incorporate such a right; secondly, State practice in the past two centuries, and especially since 1945, at best provides only a handful of genuine cases of humanitarian intervention, and, on most assessments, none at all; and finally, on prudential grounds, that the scope for abusing such a right argues strongly against its creation ... In essence, therefore, the case against making humanitarian intervention an exception to the principle of non-intervention is that its doubtful benefits would be heavily outweighed by its costs in terms of respect for international law. (Cited in Simma, 1999:5)

Despite the support for human rights in the abstract, state practice remained against justifying coercive military action for human rights ends. In fact, prior to the late 1990s there was no formal support for the undermining of the UN mechanisms, which accorded international peace with the highest priority in the interstate system. As Jonathan Charney points out, in the absence of intervening states claiming justification on the grounds of a right to humanitarian intervention, these actions can hardly serve as *opinio juris* in support of such a right (1999:836). Mark Littman QC notes that 'reliable authority covering a period of 30 years has failed to recognise a principle of humanitarian intervention' (1999:34). Some advocates of a customary right, for example, Professor Greenwood, have conceded that this is based on state practice which has only evolved since the end of the Cold War (UKFAC, 2000c:par. 131). However, the dominant legal opinion is that customary law has not been clearly established in the last ten years, especially as there is no clear consensus of international support for such practice (UKFAC, 2000c:par. 132; Littman, 1999:34–7).

REDEFINING WAR AND PEACE

'Negative Peace'

Today, human rights advocates declare that they desire 'peace' as much as the founders of the UN Charter system. The difference is that their definition of peace has changed substantially. They are not in favour of 'negative peace', defined as the absence of armed conflict, but 'positive peace', defined as the realisation of human rights protections (Cassese, 1999:27). The UN has ratified this rights-based approach, redefining peace to mean 'more than just the absence of war' (UN, 2000c:3). The privileging of a wide range of human rights goals over peace, through the redefinition of 'peace', reflects a fundamental reordering of international priorities.

The later sections of this chapter will focus on the consequences of this people-centred shift in the narrow sphere of conflict resolution and peacekeeping, but it should be borne in mind that the ethical discourse of human rights can justify a much broader right to military intervention than solely in conflict situations. If international agreements on everything from the environment to children's rights are seen as binding individual states under customary or moral human rights commitments, then the possibilities for military intervention on the basis of human rights protection are practically unlimited (see Observer, 1999b; G. Robertson, 1999:145–52).

Nigel Dower argues that international order and the preservation of peace are only of value as long as 'they are an effective means for realising universal moral values' (Dower, 1997:108). In fact, 'the scourge of war' is no longer seen as the worst outcome of international policy. As Rein Müllerson states:

[T]he ultimate aim of the human rights movement in the world is not to be an instrument for peace and stability but to promote and protect human rights and fundamental freedoms ... This means that states may have to be ready to risk a certain deterioration of inter-state relations. (1997:5)

Human rights interventionists often see non-military aid as a way of avoiding sending in the troops to right human wrongs. As touched upon in Chapter 2, the critique of humanitarian assistance is often couched in terms of this being a 'fig leaf' for an unwillingness to commit to military action (Bloomer, 1999:20). A 1997 ActionAid UK briefing paper argues that NGOs and UN forces should 'not just dish out relief in proportion to needs, but also dish out criticism (advocacy) or military bombardment in proportion to human rights wrong doing' (cited in Weiss, 1999:8). NGO campaigns such as 'No Peace Without Justice' vocally articulate this position, condemning conflict resolution based on neutral arbitration or negotiated settlements, which do not prioritise human rights concerns. Oxfam's 1998 submission to the UK Select Committee on Defence argued for much greater military commitment abroad: 'we have developed quite firm views on what does and does not constitute an appropriate role for the military ... Oxfam's starting point is that Britain should have a substantial role to play.' (UKSCD, 1998:par. 91) As Thomas Weiss notes: '[N]ongovernmental organizations (NGOs) at times have been among the most numerous and vociferous proponents of military intervention, a position quite inconceivable a decade ago.' (1999:2)

When Western states intervene militarily in Africa, the Middle East or the Balkans, this is no longer seen as war-making but as humanitarian action to protect human rights (see Chapter 2). The European Union's common security and defence policy, Nato's new remits and the UN's new approach to military action all eschew the idea that their beefed-up military programmes are about waging war. These institutions all prefer to use the language of responding to humanitarian crises or human rights abuses. This is ethical 'crisis management' not warfare (Ulbrich, 2000). It is on the alleged basis of these new human rights needs that the liberal social democratic interventionists have taken over from the conservative Right as the biggest advocates of increased military spending (Gray, 2000; Lloyd, 1999; AFP, 1999).

The advocates of coercive interventionism have no qualms about questioning any reluctance to use force on the part of Western governments. Their response has been a consistent one of calling for more military intervention to protect human rights in Africa or the Balkans. Liberal broadsheets, like the *Guardian*, *Independent* and *Observer*, have been more than willing to editorialise on the need for a firmer approach. With editorials like 'We Must Find the Stomach for Years of War over Kosovo' and 'There is No Alternative to This War' the liberal press have outdone the tabloids in patriotic jingoism (*Independent*, 1999; *Observer*, 1999a). For these crusading 'lap-top bombardiers' even months of bombing in Kosovo was not enough. They consistently argued for ground troops and the resolve to spend more resources and effort in the struggle for human rights. Ardent interventionist Michael Ignatieff puts the case strongly:

> Had we been more ruthlessly imperial, we might have been a trifle more effective. If General Schwarzkopf had allowed himself to become the General MacArthur of a conquered Iraq, the Iraqi opposition abroad might now be rebuilding the country; if the Marines were still patrolling the streets of Mogadishu, the prospects of moving Somalia forward ... might be somewhat brighter; and if NATO had defended the Bosnian government with air strikes against the Serbian insurrection in April 1992 ... [I]f after the Dayton peace accords of 1995, Western governments had simply taken over the administration of Bosnia ... Bosnia might have been reconstructed on a more secure foundation. (1998:94)

Positive War

For much of the twentieth century, war was seen as the product of power relations at the international level. This perspective had been challenged in the 1920s and 1930s with the rise of social psychology approaches in the United States and Europe. This psychological or cultural portrayal of conflict emphasised the barbarism of warfare disassociated from any political aims, in an attempt to undermine the legitimacy of armed struggle against colonial rule. In the aftermath of the Second World War, the social psychology approach was marginalised. In the Cold War era, the dominant theoretical framework of realism returned to an analysis of war which focused on state competition within a framework of Great Power rivalries (Donnelly, 2000). However, since the end of the Cold War, structural explanations for conflict have again gone into decline and war is much less likely to be understood within an international framework of power politics.

War has come to be redefined through the discourse of human rights and ethical intervention as either an attack on vulnerable people, that is, human rights abuse, or as an attempt to protect the human rights of the vulnerable. The redefinition of war and military intervention has made one kind of conflict irrational, 'degenerate' and uncivilised and another moral and ethical (see Kaldor, 1999b:2). War is equated with human rights abuses when the conflict occurs between or within non-Western states. In this case, it is seen as having little to do with economic and social struggles, but is an expression of the cultural and civilisational failings of the people of the region.

Civil and interstate conflicts of the 1990s were not held to be indicative of post-Cold War realignments of power in Africa and the Balkans but proof that 'man's capacity for evil knows no limits' (Annan, 1997b:365). This understanding of conflict as a product of particular cultures or mental states, denotes a retreat from the political and a return to a much more psychological understanding of war in non-Western societies (Pupavac, 2000b). Daniel Goldhagen, for example, writes that Serbia 'clearly consists of individuals with damaged faculties of moral judgement and has sunk into a moral abyss' (1999). Many human rights advocates stress the irrational and uncontrollable nature of these conflicts:

These internal conflicts are characterized by a highly unpredictable and explosive dynamic of their own, as well as by a radicalization of violence, the irrationality of which stands in stark contrast to the politically guided and systematically escalated use of military force for which the mechanisms and instruments laid down in the UN Charter ... were designed. (Thurer, 1999)

As leading human rights journalist Roy Gutman asserts: 'The Bosnian conflict was, in retrospect, an enormous crime against humanity, masquerading as a war' (2000a). It seems there can be no rational explanation for conflict in these less civilised societies, where the human rights commentators present killing people as the aim of war itself. Martin Shaw, for example, uses the Nuremberg distinctions to draw out the qualitative difference between war fought by the Allies and the 'genocide' being perpetrated by the Germans and Japanese. The 'extermination of Germans and Japanese was not, for the Allies, an end in itself' but the by-product of protecting vulnerable people, whereas for the Germans and by implication the Japanese, the aim of their policies was genocide, the destruction of social groups as an end in itself (Shaw, 2000).

For the people of non-Western states it is apparently 'less a noble clash of soldiers than the slaughter of civilians with machetes or firing squads, the mass rape of women in special camps, the cowardly execution of non-combatants' (Cassese, 1998:5). As a human rights campaigners' handbook *Crimes of War: What the Public Should Know* asserts in its introduction:

> Wars [involving non-Western states] today increasingly are fought not between armies where officers are bound by notions of honour but by fighters ... who are not soldiers in the conventional sense of the word. The goal of these conflicts is often ethnic cleansing – ... not the victory of one army over another. (Gutman and Rieff, 1999:10)

No longer connected with international relations of power, it appears that conflict has a dynamic of its own. Martin Shaw makes the point that for non-Western societies 'genocide may be discerned, therefore, in relatively limited mass killing' (2000). He argues that 'the concept of "genocidal massacre" should be proposed to cover smaller incidents, which are often a prelude to a larger-scale genocide' (2000). The use of the emotive term 'genocide' to describe these conflicts establishes them as qualitatively different from the slaughter of wars in which Western states were involved. Unlike war, which appears relatively more civilised in comparison, 'genocide' is regarded as either inherently atavistic and irrational or as morally evil.

In international attempts to protect human rights in societies where there is an irrational culture of human rights abuse, war is seen as the lesser of two evils. The same logic was at play in the argument that the deaths caused by the terrorist attack on the World Trade Center could not be compared with the terror wreaked by US carpet bombing, cluster bombing and AC130 gunships in Afghanistan. Jack Straw and Tony Blair regularly stating that, regardless of the death toll through bombing and malnutrition, the West's moral stance was the defining difference: 'We do all we can to limit civilian casualties, unlike Osama bin Laden and al-Qaida who did all they could to cause as many casualties as possible.' (Blair, 2001c) In order to enforce this moral distinction between the two sides of the conflict, the British media were warned not to equate deaths from terrorist attacks with those from Allied carpet bombing and CNN journalists were instructed that it was 'perverse to focus too much on the casualties or hardship in Afghanistan' (Wells, 2001; *Times*, 2001). While the Taliban were accused of manipulating statistics of civilian casualties as part of a 'propaganda war', few commentators questioned the US and British authorities use of estimates of 5–6,000 Manhattan deaths, which were around twice the likely figure (Farrell, 2001; Ellison, 2001; Baxter, 2001). Today, war is seen to be a civilising force, killing people only as an unintended consequence of restoring human rights and a framework for protecting the vulnerable. In this case, even the military techniques deployed by the Western powers are held to be civilising. Gutman and Rieff argue that after the embarrassing colonial period, 'in well-off Western countries, the canons of international humanitarian law took hold', they even cite as evidence the US-led carpet bombing of Iraq during the Gulf War, praising the United States government's 'attempt to adhere scrupulously to these [humanitarian] norms' (1999:8). Similar praise was applied to the US planners in the Kosovo and Afghanistan conflicts, who were held to have 'occupied the moral high ground' because they allegedly strove to comply with the Geneva Convention and avoid civilian casualties (UKFAC, 2000c:par. 157). In both these conflicts, civilian deaths were seen either as inevitable 'collateral damage' or as in some way justified by the actions of the civilians themselves unfortunate enough to be in the vicinity of US targets. The US Defense Secretary, Donald Rumsfeld, argued that many of the civilian victims, in destroyed Afghan villages 'were not cooking cookies', intimating that they were guilty of more than being in the wrong place at the wrong time (Borger, 2001).

THE 'PEOPLE-CENTRED' APPROACH TO PEACE

The Secretary-General's Millennium Report *We the Peoples* opened the formal process of revising the UN's approach to peace operations after criticism of UN failures in Rwanda, Bosnia and Sierra Leone in the 1990s and Nato action over Kosovo which bypassed Security Council controls (UN, 2000b). The Millennium Report develops the conception of people-centred approaches to questions of war and military intervention, and notes in its introduction: 'No shift in the way we think or act can be more critical than this: we must put people at the centre of everything we do.' (UN, 2000b:7) The report states that a 'new understanding of the concept of security is evolving' (UN, 2000b:43). International security during the Cold War was 'synonymous with the defence of territory from external attack' and was bound up with the principle of state sovereignty and its corollary of non-intervention. In the new millennium the conception of international security is different: 'the requirements of security today have come to embrace the protection of communities and individuals from internal violence' (UN, 2000b:43). Far from upholding sovereignty and the principle of non-intervention, the demands of international security are deemed to necessitate a fundamental rethinking of the UN's strategy. The Secretary-General describes this new strategy as a 'more human-centred approach to security' in distinction to the previous 'state-centred' approach (UN, 2000b:43). This report was followed at the end of August by the Brahimi UN Panel Report with more detailed proposals for reform, which were ratified at the UN Millennium Summit in New York in September 2000.

The people-centred approach directly challenges the doctrine of state sovereignty at the centre of the UN-order. Instead of the nation-state at the centre of policy priorities it is the people of the state, particularly those most in need. This framework follows the approach of human rights advocates, who argue for an explicitly people-centred approach, making the subject of international policy the universal citizen, not the political citizen defined by the nation-state. People's human rights are seen to be particularly vulnerable in conflict situations. As the Millennium Report observes, despite international resolutions, 'the brutalization of civilians, particularly women and children, continues in armed conflicts':

> Women have become especially vulnerable to violence and sexual exploitation, while children are easy prey for forced labour and are often coerced into becoming fighters ... In the most extreme cases, the innocent become the principal targets of ethnic cleansers and *genocidaires*. (UN, 2000b:46)

The emphasis on the rights of vulnerable people rather than the rights of states is explained as necessary because many non-Western states can no longer be assumed to be able, or willing, to safeguard the rights of their citizens. As the Millennium Report argues: 'states are sometimes the principal perpetrators of violence against the very citizens that humanitarian law requires them to protect' (UN, 2000b:46). Given the changed Western perception of the non-

Western state, the advocates of human rights assert that the international community must have the power to step in to protect the rights of the vulnerable.

The concept of empowering vulnerable people extends to the post-conflict situation and the prioritisation of conflict prevention and peacebuilding: 'strategies of prevention must address the root causes of conflicts, not simply their violent symptoms' (UN, 2000b:44–5). The Secretary-General suggests that the 'root causes' of international conflict are no longer to be located in the geo-political competition of major states but rather in the internal political and social arrangements of much less influential powers:

> The majority of wars today are wars among the poor. Why is this the case? ... In many poor countries at war, the condition of poverty is coupled with sharp ethnic or religious cleavages. Almost invariably, the rights of subordinate groups are insufficiently respected, the institutions of government are insufficiently inclusive and the allocation of society's resources favours the dominant faction over others. (UN, 2000b:45)

The new context of international security concerns considers smaller and economically less developed states to be the most likely to be prone to conflict due to problems of poverty, ethnic and cultural division and political exclusion. It is these states that will be increasingly subject to new peacekeeping approaches and are the focal point of ongoing policy discussions, which attempt to establish a new balance between the rights of state sovereignty and the protection of human rights. The events of 11 September 2001 were, therefore, seen to lie in the frailties of the Afghan state. Javier Solana, the EU security chief, warning that: 'Conflicts now are ... connected to states that have failed economically and politically, where those in power have no democratic mandate.' (Phillips, 2001) This new people-centred approach, concerned with how small states treat their most vulnerable citizens, is a very different one from that taken by the UN since the Second World War. As Paul Taylor notes: 'the earlier relationship between intervention and sovereignty would be reversed: weight would increasingly be placed on the question of the justice of the state's claim to sovereignty rather than upon the nature of the justification for intervention' (1999:559).

The people-centred rights discourse, through the understanding of conflict in the non-Western world as a question of human rights abuse, has mounted a strong attack on the rights of self-government and political autonomy in post-conflict regions. It also brings into question the concept of conflict resolution based on international diplomacy and a negotiated settlement rather than the force of arms. Following the human rights approach, the UN is increasingly concerned with protecting the vulnerable in regions of conflict rather than merely ending conflict itself. This has led to a rethinking of the UN's peacekeeping role. 'Traditional peacekeeping' deployment, which 'was straightforward: war, ceasefire, invitation to monitor ceasefire compliance' is now condemned because it 'treats the symptoms rather than sources of conflict' (UN, 2000c:3). The discourse of human rights legitimises an extended international role in conflict situations. International intervention is now argued to be necessary at every stage of the peace process, including overseeing the initial peace agreement, imposing its terms, and long-term regulation to ensure a human rights framework which can prevent future conflict.

Peacemaking?

The involvement of the UN and government envoys in attempting to bring conflict to a halt through diplomacy and mediation is increasingly viewed with suspicion. The tendency to view conflict in terms of human rights abuser and victim clearly encourages intervention to support the claims of one side rather than intervention to negotiate a settlement. The UN was heavily criticised in the late 1990s for failing to safeguard human rights due to its prioritisation of finding a negotiated peace. Some commentators have called for the UN to prioritise human rights abuses and demand a rejection of the previous principle of seeking a negotiated settlement between parties to a dispute. 'To do otherwise would turn the [international community] into just another political actor, rather than an impartial force in favour of human rights principles.' (Gaer, 1997:8) Human rights interventionists, like Michael Ignatieff, argue that the UN can no longer have a role in human rights-guided peacemaking, because the outlook of the institution is too imbued with its neutral past: 'peacekeepers by definition are impartial without being fair; it is not their task to make moral distinctions between aggressor and victim' (1998:103). Richard Falk, similarly, asserts that the UN was ill-suited to make a decision as to the proper course of action over Kosovo because it was unsure which policy to follow 'whether that of neutrality and impartiality, or of supporting the victimized ethnic group' (1999:850).

Geoffrey Robertson makes the case that the problem with the UN is its 'diplomatic mindset', which leads to attempts to negotiate rather than take sides with military force (1999:71). Max Boot, the features editor of the *Wall Street Journal*, also considers the politics of diplomacy to be at the core of the United Nations' failure:

> UN administrators ... think that no problem in the world is too intractable to be solved by negotiation. These mandarins fail to grasp that men with guns do not respect men with nothing but flapping gums ... Just as the US Marine Corps breeds warriors, so the UN's culture breeds conciliators. (2000a)

The international commentators' call for human rights enforcement rather than diplomacy is a call for military action to impose a settlement, to be prioritised over peacemaking. For these advocates of international human rights, the moral goals can only be muted by political compromises. Boot, for example, is astonished that, after a breakdown in a deal for the UN inspection of Iraqi weapons, the Secretary-General, Kofi Annan, still could state: 'I'm not convinced that massive force is the answer. Bombing is a blunt instrument.' (2000a)

The human rights approach, which seeks to impose a settlement, has clashed with the UN's role in attempting to negotiate a solution. If human rights are ethical imperatives, they cannot be negotiated. This clash between the demands of traditional peacemaking and human rights activism was highlighted within the UN peacemaking mechanisms in Bosnia. In August 1992, the International Conference on the Former Yugoslavia (ICFY) was established to co-ordinate international pressure for a negotiated peace between the Bosnian factions. At the same time, the UN Commission on Human Rights appointed a Special Rapporteur to report on the human rights situation. The ICFY Co-Chairpeople met with the Special Rapporteur intending him to bring valuable insights into framing the peace proposals, concerning the rights of nationalities and minorities, and hoping that he would spearhead a brainstorming process on this topic. When the meeting began, the Special Rapporteur focused on two issues: the implementation of the no-fly zone and the prospects of Nato becoming involved on the ground (Anonymous, 1996:254). The agenda for a negotiated peace and the agenda for taking sides in the war were diametrically opposed and the dialogue between the Special Rapporteur and the Co-Chairpeople ended.

In the Yugoslav conflict, the clash between human rights and peace was evident as every peace agreement was judged from the perspective of whether it 'rewarded aggression' or 'ethnic cleansing'. In Bosnia, as in every other conflict, there was a fundamental tension between a negotiated peace and the human rights demand of a return to what was perceived to be the pre-war status quo. The presumption of the human rights campaigners, that the outcome of any settlement should be the establishment of a unitary Bosnian state, meant parties to the conflict were prevented from reaching an agreement amongst themselves. In spring 1992, the leaders of the three Bosnian parties chose to make provision for a federal republic of three constituent nations for the three constituent peoples: Croats, Muslims and Serbs. However, the agreement was strongly criticised by human rights commentators who declared that the ethnic division of Bosnia could not be accepted (although they supported the break-up of multi-ethnic Yugoslavia) and the United States encouraged the Muslim leadership to reject the agreement (L.J. Cohen, 1995:243; Petras and Vieux, 1996:16–17). Again, in spring 1993, the Vance–Owen Peace Plan and then the Owen–Stoltenberg Plan came under heavy criticism from human rights advocates who argued that the international community was condoning aggression and ethnic cleansing, and that this was a return to Munich, with the negotiators Cyrus Vance and David Owen being condemned as latter-day Chamberlains (Anonymous, 1996:252–3). The Bosnian-Muslim leadership rejected a deal, hoping that the United States would intervene militarily in its favour, under pressure from the human rights campaigners, and the war continued for a further two-and-a-half years.

When the United States stepped in to impose a settlement from the summer of 1994, it renounced the approach of a negotiated agreement between the three parties, instead providing support for a Croat-Muslim federation and attempting to impose a resolution against Serb objections. This ensured that the war continued for another year-and-a-half before Nato bombing, international sanctions and US support for Muslim and Croat forces forced the Serbs to accept the imposed terms. As noted in the *Human Rights Quarterly*:

> Targeting violators of human rights and bringing them to justice is essential. Accusation, however, comes more easily than making peace. The quest for justice for yesterday's victims of atrocities

should not be pursued in such a manner that it makes today's living the dead of tomorrow. That, for the human rights community, is one of the lessons from the former Yugoslavia. Thousands of people are dead who should have been alive – because moralists were in quest of the perfect peace. Unfortunately, a perfect peace can rarely be attained in the aftermath of bloody conflict. The pursuit of peace is one thing. Making peace is another. (Anonymous, 1996:258)

In fact, this lesson was not learnt. The human rights criticism of the international attempts to negotiate peace in Bosnia, Kosovo, Sierra Leone, and elsewhere, is often based on the fact that there were negotiations at all. It is argued that if the UN was serious about protecting the vulnerable and upholding human rights, it should have had the political will to impose a solution. Many rights advocates have argued that even the Dayton agreement, imposed through US military force at the end of 1995, was not perfect enough. For Francis Boyle, and other commentators, the creation of an international protectorate which denied Bosnians a say, not just in the peace settlement but also in the running of the state, was still not interventionist enough to protect human rights (1996:515).

The apparent unwillingness to apply military force early enough was often condemned: 'Again and again, threats were followed by inaction, pinprick strikes, and an inability to follow up.' (Gaer, 1997:4) Hugo Young argued in the *Guardian* that the 'allies' should not commit themselves to a negotiated settlement on Kosovo as this 'for all Clinton's sound-bite pieties, will be a deal and not a victory' (1999a). The liberal critics of limited human rights intervention, like the influential media NGO Radio Free Europe/Radio Liberty (RFE/RL), stated that the war over Kosovo was disappointing because it resulted in a 'Saddam Hussein peace', leaving Milosevic in power and failing to continue the war to take over the running of Serbia (RFE/RL, 2000b). A negotiated settlement was far from the mind of Daniel Goldhagen, for whom the only solution for Serbia was war for unconditional surrender:

As with Germany and Japan, the defeat, occupation and reshaping of the political institutions and prevailing mentality in Serbia is morally and, in the long run, practically necessary. With an ally-occupied Serbia ... peace and eventually prosperity could come to the region. (1999)

This strategy may be an encouraging one for the Nato strategists, but promises little hope of a sustainable settlement for the citizens of states held to deserve bombing to the point of unconditional surrender. As Sir Michael Rose stated during the Kosovo war: 'Bombs never have and never can solve complex political or humanitarian problems of the world. History shows us no successful examples in such circumstances and I am afraid that it will be the same story now.' (Cited in Littman, 1999:iv) Several commentators have noted that the Nato states were willing to go to war rather than be seen to compromise the moral high ground by seeking a negotiated solution. Richard Falk notes: 'The recourse to war by Nato in these circumstances seems to have cast aside the legal, moral and political commitment to make recourse to war a *last resort*.' (1999:855) As Jeffrey Garten observes in *Foreign Policy*, the human rights advocates, by prioritising human rights over other foreign policy concerns, are in effect 'saying that diplomacy does not matter ... [and] giving up the tools of negotiation and persuasion' (1996).

The problem with the human rights approach of military coercion is that peace negotiations depend on local accountability and flexibility. There needs to be room for give and take on behalf of the parties to the conflict. Raising a broad range of additional issues or threatening to take military action against one side in the conflict can only limit the possibilities of a peaceful solution (Anonymous, 1996:256; D'Amato, 1994). Aryeh Neier argues that the human rights movement 'needs to develop the argument that the promotion of human rights should not be weighed against competing concerns' (1996). Similarly, Geoffrey Robertson asserts: 'a human rights offensive admits of no half-measures'; 'crimes against humanity are, by definition, unforgivable'; 'justice, in respect of crimes against humanity, is non-negotiable' (1999:73; 260; 268).

Military human rights interventions to ensure the provision of internationally imposed people-centred protections, provide room neither for any compromise or negotiation nor for a democratic say in the outcome for people of the region. It is difficult for human rights interventionists to accept peace deals around the negotiating table. Any compromise between the parties is often labelled as 'appeasement' or condemned for condoning the gains of 'ethnic cleansing' (see, for example, Garton Ash, 1999; Goldhagen, 1999). The removal of peace processes from a process of negotiation to the imposition of human rights claims, regardless of context, can only lead to conflict rather than peace, as can be seen from the breakdown of the Rambouillet talks over Kosovo (Chomsky, 2000). As Susan Woodward informed the UK House of Commons Foreign Affairs Committee, 'the way [Rambouillet] was structured meant that it would fail' because the focus on human rights meant denying that 'this was a genuine conflict over territory ... and both sides had arguments on their side, and this was not simply a matter of imposing an agreement on one that had violated ... international law' (UKFAC, 2000c:par. 56).

The human rights community is rarely challenged over their belief that external military intervention and the undermining or removal of regional political leaders in the cause of externally-imposing people-centred protections, can achieve a more sustainable solution than one negotiated by, and accountable to, the people of the region. Adam Roberts highlights the dangers of externally undermining the existing political framework:

> In reality, in situations of conflict, states not only remain powerful, but are also often essential to securing a peaceful settlement. After a conflict a new local balance has to emerge, in which states and political forces in the area, including the belligerents themselves, are likely to play a key role. States should not necessarily be seen as operating on a lower moral plane than other actors. Governments seeking to address conflicts may make decisions on the basis of legitimate interests and moral principles which deserve respect even if they sometimes clash with humanitarian principles. (1999:15)

The experience of the 1990s demonstrates the instability produced by undermining the traditional basis of the international order. The process in which Western powers are becoming the final political arbiter rather than the sovereign state has meant that the internationalisation of human rights questions has become highly politicised. This process has enabled opposition/separatist groups to appeal to external institutions, weakening state legitimacy and encouraging conflict rather than compromise. The UN Secretary-General has acknowledged the potential problems inherent in this interventionist framework, which 'might encourage secessionist movements deliberately to provoke governments ... in order to trigger external interventions' (UN, 2000b:48). Michael Ignatieff usefully points up the vicious circle where weak states are further weakened by human rights processes which see states as part of the problem not part of the solution:

> Note here the causative order ... Disintegration of the state comes first, nationalist paranoia comes next. Nationalist sentiment on the ground ... is a secondary consequence of political disintegration, a response to the collapse of state order and the interethnic accommodation that it made possible. (1998:45)

International human rights intervention may start from ostensibly neutral positions but can only further weaken regional mechanisms of conflict resolution increasing instability. The irony of the interventionist approach, which allegedly is concerned with the dangers of conflict in weaker states, is that internationalising the situation can easily encourage conflict through weakening local mechanisms of co-operation. Sovereignty is particularly important in parts of the world where states are weaker. For example, the Organisation of African Unity's insistence on non-intervention was based on the fragility of African states and the artificiality of their borders, which meant that conflict in one state risked destabilising the region (Clapham, 1999:536). To conclude, from problems of inter-ethnic co-operation, that there should be less power in the hands of elected state and regional authorities, as liberal interventionists do, leads to policies which tend to exacerbate, rather than resolve, the crisis. The fragmentation of Yugoslavia is a tragic example of this process of external rights intervention creating a cycle of disintegration as Yugoslav leaders in a weaker position were encouraged to put their faith in international intervention rather than reach a negotiated solution (Chandler, 2000c). The double-edged nature of the people-centred approach in this area, reflects the potential dangers in politicising UN peace operations and the clear contrast between a people-centred approach which tends to internationalise conflict situations and the former Cold War approach which prioritised local or regional solutions based on consensus between the parties.

Peacekeeping?

In the past, the UN, which had been invited in by the parties, would have been forced to withdraw if renewed conflict broke out. Peacekeeping meant deploying monitors and lightly armed forces between ex-combatants once there was a peace to keep, not imposing peace on the parties. Today, this is no longer seen to be adequate to protect the vulnerable from the risks of conflict. The UK government argues that: 'we firmly believe that the doctrine of peacekeeping, which evolved in the 1950s in the context of interstate conflict, is no longer valid' (UKJCC, 2000:8). The consensus that UN peacekeeping mandates be extended to protecting civilians in armed conflicts, and the demand that UN troops or police 'who witness violence against civilians should be presumed to be authorized to stop it', establishes a very high threshold of expectation and necessitates the deployment of much larger military resources (UN, 2000c:11). The UN Brahimi Panel proposes that ensuring peace mandates are enforced 'means bigger forces, better equipped and more costly, but able to pose a credible deterrent threat, in contrast to the symbolic and non-threatening presence that characterizes traditional peacekeeping' (UN, 2000c:9). This transition was heralded in Kofi Annan's philosophical shift to a more coercive approach in the summer of 2000: '[T]he time has come for us to base our planning on worst-case scenarios: to be surprised by co-operation, if we get it. And to go in prepared for all eventualities, including full combat, if we don't.' (Cited in Hoagland, 2000a; see also UN, 2000c) The panel, therefore, suggests:

> Rules of engagement should not limit contingents to stroke-for-stroke responses but should allow ripostes sufficient to silence a source of deadly fire that is directed at United Nations troops or at people they are charged to protect and, in particularly dangerous circumstances, should not force United Nations contingents to cede the initiative to their attackers. (UN, 2000c:9)

Peacekeeping is also being transformed in another direction. Today, the UN argues that the traditional neutrality of the Blue Helmets should be abandoned:

> Impartiality for such operations must therefore mean adherence to the principles of the Charter and to the objectives of a mandate that is rooted in those principles. Such impartiality is not the same as neutrality or equal treatment of all parties in all cases for all time, which can amount to a policy of appeasement. In some cases, local parties consist not of moral equals but of obvious aggressors and victims, and peacekeepers may not only be operationally justified in using force but morally compelled to do so. (UN, 2000c:9)

For the Brahimi Panel, the former position of equal treatment of all parties 'can in the best case result in ineffectiveness and in the worst may amount to complicity with evil' (UN, 2000c:ix). This more direct and engaged military role for UN peacekeepers comes in response to human rights criticisms of the long established policy of neutral peacekeeping. Neutrality is now an embarrassment rather than an asset. In response to this international shift, the Swiss government, for example, is organising historical commissions and questioning its decision to remain neutral and outside international humanitarian intervention missions (Wartburg, 2000). Similarly, the governments of Sweden, Finland, Austria and Ireland have rejected neutrality for 'military nonalignment' and membership of Nato's Partnership for Peace (Ulbrich, 2000).

Neutral peacekeeping, which is derived from respect for the autonomy and self-government of UN member states, was seen by human rights advocates as irrevocably compromised by the failure of UN troops to safeguard the lives of those in Srebrenica when the town fell to Bosnian Serb forces:

> Until mandates to keep the peace are interpreted by the UN as mandates to fight the aggressor factions, if this is the only way the peace can be kept and genocide prevented, there will be many more Srebrenicas ... Or else there will be more unilateral humanitarian enforcement action, such as Nato's intervention in Serbia. (G. Robertson, 1999:72)

Since the fall of Srebrenica, in July 1995, the liberal interventionists have been keen to transform peacekeeping mandates into a show of massive military force. The UN's new approach takes on board the critique of human rights advocates, like Michael Ignatieff who condemned the UN's intervention in Sierra Leone in the *New York Times*:

> To keep the peace here is to ratify the conquests of evil. It is time to bury peacekeeping before it buries the UN ... Where peace has to be enforced rather than maintained, what's required are combat-capable warriors under robust rules of engagement, with armour, ammunition and intelligence capability and a single line of command to a national government or regional alliance ...the international community has to take sides and do so with crushing force. (2000a)

Rhetorically, Western leaders still uphold the UN Charter's primary aim of protecting humanity from 'the scourge of war' (UKJCC, 2000:3). Yet, military intervention is becoming far from an 'option of last resort'. The militarised peacekeeping mandates designed to be able to deploy overwhelming force will inevitably raise expectations and place UN credibility on the line more often. Despite the rhetorical repetition of the agreement to use force only as a last resort, as the UK government asserts 'the threat of it may be needed at an early stage in a conflict' (UKJCC, 2000:6). As could be seen in Kosovo, once the threat of force is used to apply pressure to the parties, the conflict is internationalised and there is pressure to apply force to maintain international credibility.

This militarisation of peacekeeping not only runs counter to the traditional role of the UN, but also heralds a fundamental institutional change legitimised by the demands posed by the transformation in UN peacekeeping towards greater military preparedness. As Michael T. Corgan, a former political and military planner for Nato, now an associate professor of international relations at Boston University, notes: 'We have to recognize that peacemaking essentially involves war. You must be able to convincingly threaten full combat even if it doesn't come to that, and you incur many of the costs of a war.' (Cited in Radin, 2000) The Brahimi Panel recognises 'that the United Nations does not wage war' (UN, 2000c:10). This means that peacekeeping enforcement will be increasingly shifted from UN control to that of Nato or other 'coalitions of the willing' (UN, 2000c:10). This shift could be seen in the disagreements between the British Government and the UN over military intervention in the former British colony of Sierra Leone in Autumn 2000. Britain pushed for more militarised 'peacekeeping' and, keeping separate control over its military forces, was keen to support the government against the Revolutionary United Front (RUF) rebels. This strategy undermined the UN Mission's attempt to negotiate a settlement between the two sides. As a senior diplomat commented: 'We have two missions with fundamentally incompatible goals ... One wants to fight, the other wants to continue to treat the RUF as a force that can be dealt with rationally and brought to the table.' (Farah, 2000)

The question of the suitability of many UN member states for taking on the military tasks involved in the new peace operations is raised in the UK Government Joint Consultative Committee Paper on UN Reform, which argues:

[T]he UN's reaction to human rights abuses or conflict situations has sometimes been slow, inconsistent and ill co-ordinated ... Those nations with the capacity to support peacekeeping or other operations, whether it be financially, logistically or through the provision of high quality forces and equipment, need to respond swiftly and effectively. (UKJCC, 2000:3)

The Brahimi Report suggests an exclusive membership for 'coalitions of the willing': 'caution seems appropriate, because military resources and capability are unevenly distributed around the world, and troops in the most crisis-prone areas are often less prepared for the demands of modern peacekeeping than is the case elsewhere' (UN, 2000c:10). The shift towards a greater stake in peace operations for select 'coalitions of the willing' reflects the increasing willingness of Western states to undertake peacekeeping tasks independently of the UN. The decline of the UN as the central peacekeeping institution is underlined by the fact that 77 per cent of UN troops are currently contributed by developing countries, and no developed country contributes troops to the most difficult UN missions in Sierra Leone or the Democratic Republic of the Congo, while the major powers, like the United States, the United Kingdom, France and Germany, contribute sizeable forces to Nato-led operations (UN, 2000c:18).

Commentators, like Mary Kaldor, emphasise that 'peacekeeping could be reconceptualized as cosmopolitan law-enforcement' (1999b:10–11). However, as can be seen from the foregoing section, this is a mistake on two counts. First, the peacemaking and peace-keeping components are becoming more militarised and more coercive, making them less like domestic policing arrangements. Second, and more importantly, they will be increasingly dictated by self-selected 'coalitions of the willing' rather than the UN Security Council. As David Rieff notes, this conflation of military coercion with international police law-enforcement is 'morally as well as intellectually noxious':

But however understandable the motivations, and however good the intentions of those who advocate it, humanitarian intervention is not, cannot be and should not be presented as a species of crime-stopping. It is warmaking ... If there were a world government, the notion of humanitarian intervention as crime prevention might have some basis in reality. But there is no such thing. (2000b)

THE 'GUERNICA PARADOX'

Geoffrey Robertson sharply posed the question of waging war for human rights:

> And so, on the cusp of the millennium, the Western Alliance had to wrestle with what might be termed the Guernica paradox: When can it be right to unleash terror on terrorists, to bomb for human rights, to kill to stop crimes against humanity? (2000:402)

What might have been a difficult ethical quandary in the past about the morality of violence is merely a rhetorical question for the human rights advocates of today. Robertson, responding in the wake of the September 2001 attacks on the World Trade Center and the Pentagon, argued that it did not matter whether US retaliation against Afghanistan could be legally justified under international law. This was because: 'A more modern and more permissive legal justification for an armed response is provided by the emerging human rights rule that requires international action to prevent and to punish "crimes against humanity".' (2001a)

Even before the 11 September events, many leading human rights advocates had taken up similar positions in favour of greater legal 'permissiveness' for action to prevent human rights abuses, arguing that the right of military intervention should not just apply when atrocities have happened or when negotiations have broken down. Martin Shaw believes that in the light of historical experiences, such as *Kristallnacht*, where relatively small numbers of deaths later led to larger-scale slaughter, it is possible that 'we can now read genocidal dangers ... even if full-scale genocide may still be some way off' (2000). Radio Free Europe/Radio Liberty assert that small-scale violence is not necessary for intervention, merely inflammatory rhetoric:

> Milosevic's aggressive intentions were clear from his rhetoric in the 1980s, just as Hitler's were in the 1930s ... but it was not until Kosova in 1999 that the Atlantic alliance showed that the lessons of the previous decade had been learned. (RFE/RL, 2000b)

Jonathan Charney considered that the Kosovo conflict could only be understood as an 'anticipatory humanitarian intervention' as the extent of the human rights violations prior to withdrawal of the

OSCE observer force 'was not massive and widespread' (1999:839). Richard Falk similarly argued that the Kosovo war was reasonable 'in light of earlier Serb tactics in Bosnia, as epitomized by concentration camps, numerous massacres and crimes against humanity' (1999a:849). The evidence was not necessary as 'it was reasonable to assume (and, to some, irresponsibly naïve not to assume) that, given the people involved, worse things were in store' (Reisman, 1999:860). Tim Judah informed the House of Commons Foreign Affairs Committee that 'at any time we could have had a new Srebrenica: how was one supposed to know that was not going to happen?' (UKFAC, 2000c:par. 123) As Mark Laity, acting Nato spokesperson, stated after the ICTY failed to find the evidence to substantiate Nato's claims of Serb genocide in Kosovo: 'The point is did we successfully pre-empt or not ... I think the evidence shows we did. We would rather be criticised for overestimating the numbers who died than for failing to pre-empt.' (Cited in Steele, 2000b)

Marc Weller observes that the doctrine of 'anticipatory' war, used to justify US and British air campaigns against Iraq in December 1998 and throughout 1999, 2000 and 2001, 'has extremely dangerous implications for international relations' (1999b:81). As one commentator in the *American Journal of International Law* noted:

> Such intervention ... is a particularly dangerous permutation of an already problematic concept ... If this action stands for the right of foreign states to intervene in the absence of proof that widespread grave violations of international human rights are being committed, it leaves the door open for hegemonic states to use force for purposes clearly incompatible with international law. (Charney, 1999:841)

Bernard Kouchner recognises the problem, but has little solution beyond trust in the US-led authorities (see also Bugnion, 2000:49; Mayall, 2000:70): 'Let me assure those who accuse the emergent humanitarian army of acting on the basis that "might makes right". On the contrary, we are trying to protect the weakest and disinherited, not the strong.' (1999) The question, of course, is who decides whom to protect and how? As the UN Secretary-General, Kofi Annan, warns:

> Can we really afford to let each State be the judge of its own right or duty to intervene in another State's internal conflict? If we do,

will we not be forced to legitimize Hitler's championship of the Sudeten Germans, or Soviet intervention in Afghanistan? (1998:3)

Former South African president Nelson Mandela, on a visit to the United Kingdom in April 2000, raised similar concerns about undermining the UN, seeing the human rights community's interventionist disregard for international conventions as the main threat to international peace: 'The message they're sending is that any country which fears a veto [from the UN] can take unilateral action. That means they're introducing chaos into international affairs – that any country can take a decision which it wants.' (Cited in Sampson, 2000) Weller notes that the acceptance of the unilateral use of force without UN sanction, can only 'fundamentally challenge the presently existing structures of the international order, rather than strengthening them' (1999b:96):

> To accept that forcible action which is not permissible in general international law can be taken outside of a Security Council mandate is to embrace anarchy and to return to an acceptance of war as a means of international, if not national, policy. (1999b:96–7)

As William Rees-Mogg describes in *The Times*, this doctrine has two leading characteristics:

> It extends the justification for war from self-defence to defence of human rights inside another state. It leaves the judgement to the individual nation or alliance, and does not refer it to the United Nations, or any other international body. It thereby removes both consensus and certainty from international law. (Cited in Mayall, 2000:70)

The more the concept of human rights militarism is allowed to gain legitimacy, the greater the inequalities become between the enforcing states and the rest of the world. It makes it easier for military action to be taken by Western powers and more difficult for less powerful states to challenge the legality of military intervention. Western powers will no longer have to respect sovereignty or be invited in by governments. As Tony Blair asserts: 'the most pressing foreign policy problem we face is to identify the circumstances in which we should get involved in other people's conflicts' (cited in

Cook and Campbell, 2000). The implicit assumption is that major powers, like the United States and United Kingdom, have the right to intervene limited only by their own consideration of whether it is appropriate or not.

The double standards involved in this process were highlighted when the US Ambassador to the UN, Richard Holbrooke, argued for the right of the United States to use pre-emptive force on the basis that 'war was still viewed by many as the best means to settle differences' (UN, 1999b). He was talking about minor non-Western states, of course, not the US's post-Cold War use of military force to settle its differences with Iraq throughout the 1990s, with Sudan in 1998, or against Afghanistan in 1998 and 2001, against Bosnian Serbs in 1994–95 and against the Federal Republic of Yugoslavia in 1999. While the international community takes no action against the ongoing US bombing of Iraq without Security Council backing (Norton-Taylor, 2000b) and has not responded to Sudan's request for an investigation into the US bombing of a pharmaceutical factory in Khartoum, in violation of the UN Charter, focus is being shifted to the 'potential problems' in selected pariah states.

It is difficult to underestimate the divisive nature of the two-tier system developing as international institutions expand their remits of interference in the affairs of smaller non-Western states. The UN's Millennium Report, for example, argues that poor countries are particularly prone to war, and need to be actively 'named and shamed' to prevent conflict arising (2000b:45–6). The United States, refusing to ratify the Comprehensive Test Ban Treaty but then insisting there should be a campaign against the stockpiling of small arms, sums up the one-sidedness of the new human rights order. While there is progressively less restriction on the military interventions of major powers, weapons obtainable by smaller states are becoming the focus of increasing regulation, leading to the recategorisation of small arms as 'weapons of mass destruction' (UN, 2000c:52; UN, 1999b).

The morality of 'anticipatory' or 'pre-emptive' war-making is carried to its logical extreme by Bernard Kouchner, the founder of the Nobel Peace Prize-winning NGO Médecins sans Frontières:

> Now it is necessary to take the further step of using the right to intervention as a preventive measure to stop wars before they start and to stop murderers before they kill ... We knew what was likely to happen in Somalia, Bosnia-Herzegovina and Kosovo long before they exploded into war. But we didn't act. If these experiences

have taught us anything, it is that the time for a decisive evolution in international consciousness has arrived. (1999)

Armed with the ability 'to identify the early stages of genocide' and to judge 'murderers before they kill', it would seem highly likely that the demand for military-led rights interventions will rely more on prejudice than any objective 'justice'. As considered above, legal and institutional international restrictions on war in the cause of human rights are being annulled under pressure for a more flexible framework legitimising the use of unilateral force. Once the law of the Charter is trumped by the morality of human rights there can be little formal protection for smaller states against military aggression. As the former UN Secretary-General Javier Pérez de Cuéllar noted in 1991: 'We are clearly witnessing what is probably an irresistible shift ... towards the belief that the defence of the oppressed in the name of morality should prevail over frontiers and legal documents.' (Cited in Roberts, 1993:437) The UK Foreign Affairs Committee found that the Nato bombing campaign was not legal under the UN Charter or customary international law. Nevertheless, they concluded that the bombing of Yugoslavia in 1999 was 'justified on moral grounds' (UKFAC, 2000c:par. 138). War that is moral can know no legal bounds. As Kofi Annan has declared, 'no legal principle ... can shield crimes against humanity' (cited in UKJCC, 2000). This is why, in support of the Nato action, the *Guardian* could editorialise that 'morality can sometimes be ahead of the law' (2000b).

Vaclav Havel, in a speech to the Canadian parliament a month-and-a-half into the bombing campaign against the Federal Republic of Yugoslavia, clearly explained that international law was now a secondary factor:

This war places human rights above the rights of the state ... although it has no direct mandate from the UN, it did not happen as an act of aggression or out of disrespect for international law. It happened, on the contrary, out of respect for a law that ranks higher than the law which protects the sovereignty of states. The alliance has acted out of respect for human rights, as both conscience and international documents dictate. (Cited in G. Robertson, 1999:73)

The term for the type of 'higher law' which justifies waging war, in spite of international law, is the law of the jungle, or a return to the pre-UN forms of 'anarchic' international society, in which the use of force was unregulated. As the Nato Secretary-General, Lord Robertson, explained, human rights morality gives the Western powers a blank cheque because 'the only immorality is not to do what one has to do, when one has to do it' (George Robertson, 2000). The right to go to war is once again reverting to the Great Powers, particularly the United States. While some human rights advocates may be rightly concerned that 'blank cheques should not be handed out to vigilante states', other commentators argue that this is precisely the situation we are in today (G. Robertson, 1999:382).

CONCLUSION

The new ethical agenda of human rights interventionism has re-habilitated the moral ideals of an inherent duty placed upon the 'civilised' and economically developed nations to intervene in smaller countries' affairs. In this context, today's human rights academics at the UN University's Peace and Governance Programme are happy to condone the 'good international citizens' who are 'tempted to go it alone' waging war for human rights, with or without international sanction (Schnabel and Thakur, 2000; Linklater, 2000). This rehabilitation of imperial duty conflicts with an international framework which still formally reflects the discrediting of these elitist ideals in the aftermath of the Second World War.

The new world of human rights-based militarism is very different from the world of 1945 when the ideology of race and empire was discredited and the Great Powers were on the defensive. As Geoffrey Robertson states:

> The past has been a matter of pleading with tyrants, writing letters and sending missions to *beg* them not to act cruelly ... Human rights discourse will in the future be less pious and less 'politically correct'. We will call a savage a savage, whether or not he or she is black. There will be less mealy-mouthedness about behaviour which cries out for condemnation. (1999:386)

The flexible definitions of human rights, the denial of sovereign equality and lack of formal protections under international law mean that there are few restrictions on strident condemnation turning into sanctions, bombing and military protectorates

(Chomsky, 1999:155). Benjamin Schwarz rightly warned, at the April 2000 roundtable on intervention organised by the *Atlantic*:

> If we choose to be morality's avenging angel in places like Kosovo, we may at first be pleased to see ourselves, like Kurtz in *Heart of Darkness*, as 'an emissary of pity and progress'. But as warriors for right, faced with those we have demonized, we may well succumb to Kurtz's conclusions as well: 'Exterminate the brutes'. (2000)

As Michael Ignatieff notes: 'What is to prevent moral abstractions like human rights from inducing an absolutist frame of mind which, in defining all human rights violators as barbarians, legitimizes barbarism?' (2000b:213) The human rights discourse makes it difficult to place limits on the use of force by major powers allegedly acting on behalf of the vulnerable of the world. This is a genuine problem, however, for Ignatieff it is merely a rhetorical point. The 'absolutist frame of mind' can only be cohered by his support for moves to abolish the current international framework, in which UN controls and the need for international political consensus heavily restrict the use of force.

This chapter has suggested that any serious consideration of the international order should see that tearing up the UN restrictions on the right of major powers to use unilateral force, can only guarantee the legitimisation of barbarism in the human rights cause. The outcome of this process will be the return to 'might is right', reversing the gains of the postcolonial era. This is highlighted in the mandates of the UN tribunals and the ICC (Black, 1999b). Prior to the Second World War there was only limited restriction on the sovereign right of Great Powers to wage a war of aggression. Under the UN system, waging aggressive war was unlawful and the 'conspiracy to launch aggressive war' was the central charge put against the Nazi leadership at the Nuremberg Tribunal (Rabkin, 1999). Today, the new international courts can no longer prosecute states that wage a war of aggression. The new international agenda directly reflects the new-found confidence of the West. While the international courts have new powers to prosecute the governments of peripheral states for domestic abuses of power, they have lost the capacity to hold the major states to account for the 'crime of war'.

7   The Retreat from Political Equality

> The sad but important point is this: the meddling Western 'outsiders' ... are *far better* representatives of the genuine interests of the Croatian, Serbian, and Bosnian peoples and states than their patriotic leaders. – Bogdan Denitch, *Ethnic Nationalism: the Tragic Death of Yugoslavia* (1996), p. 210.

Politics as a differentiated area of human activity arose alongside the development of the conception of political equality. Politics originated in the limited sphere of equality of slave-owning Athenian democracy and of mercantile wealth within the Italian city states of the Renaissance (Rosenberg, 1994:Ch. 3). The general separation of politics from the direct domination of economic relations and the creation of formal political and legal equality was only possible with economic and social development. As Ellen Meiskins Wood notes, under feudalism, 'where juridical and political difference is the substance of property relations, there can be no such thing as formal democracy' (1991:175). It was only under certain economic and social circumstances that 'the idea of "liberal democracy" became thinkable' (Wood, 1995:234).

With social and economic development in seventeenth-century Europe, the ideas of the Enlightenment and the French and American Revolutions generalised the conception of political equality. The political sphere expanded in the nineteenth and twentieth centuries with the end of servitude in Russia and the emancipation of slaves in the United States, the granting of property rights to women, and the extension of suffrage independently from distinctions of social class, race and gender. The public political sphere is inherently egalitarian, institutionally separate from the social inequality of the private world of the family or the market place. Today, a historically unique process is unfolding of the rolling back of the political domain, with social and economic power being exercised more overtly, narrowing the framework of formal equality.

The ethical discourse of human rights reflects the declining importance attached to representation in the political sphere and explicitly questions the underpinnings of popular democracy and the conception of political equality. The human rights advocates directly criticise domestic and international institutional arrangements, which are legitimised on the basis of legal and political equality. In the international arena, the consequences of the human rights discourse are more pronounced. There are two reasons for this. First, the acceptance of a political domain separate from the direct domination of economic wealth and social power has been more overtly disputed in the field of international relations than in domestic politics. This dispute has reflected the attenuated struggle over decolonisation since the 1930s, and, since 1990 has been reasserted through the focus on democratic consolidation in the newly independent states of the former Soviet bloc. Second, the framework of formal equality in the international sphere has always been less institutionalised than in the domestic setting. As noted in Chapter 5, it was only in 1945 that an interstate framework based on political equality was reluctantly introduced, even then this framework covered only limited mutual concerns of international security. There was no interstate body able to directly regulate international society or take on the determining role that the domestic state plays in managing a country's affairs.

This chapter seeks to clarify the consequences of the prioritisation of human rights values by consideration of the questions raised by the denigration of the concept of political equality for the working of political institutions in non-Western states, the management of the international sphere and finally in the domestic sphere of Western states themselves.

NON-WESTERN STATES

At first glance the human rights critique of the political domain of the non-Western state is a radical one. For human rights campaigners, like Geoffrey Robertson, the political elites of 'many, if not most countries in the world' are the 'stumbling block' in the advance of civil rights and a 'complete impasse' to securing economic and social rights for their citizens (1999:147). The principles of state sovereignty and democracy are held to afford 'protection to rulers who loot or otherwise misappropriate vast sums of private money' (1999:147). Political elites are alleged to be able to abuse with impunity, making international human rights protections necessary to ensure they 'behave with a minimum of civility towards their own people' (1999: 373). For human rights activists, human rights are a necessity 'to hold political leaders responsible for the great evils they visit upon humankind' (G. Robertson, 1999:375). They also enable new structures of rule. Richard Falk, for example, writes that:

> When the state fails to provide governance, other political actors are needed to protect a vulnerable citizenry from the perils of chaos and civil strife, as well as from unrelated forces of ethnic and religious extremism. This is particularly true in much of Africa, where the intermediate structures of civil society are very weak, offering little protection in the event that government institutions collapse. (2000:68)

The human rights critique of non-Western elites has a radical edge because it is often couched in terms of defending the rights of the people in these regions. A typical example of this was the high-profile defence of the rights of the people of Afghanistan prior to international intervention, Tony Blair declaring that the people were not enemies but victims of the government (Wintour and White, 2001). This was reinforced three weeks into the bombing, UK Foreign Secretary Jack Straw arguing that: 'If we are to feed and shelter them, and later to help them to build a nation for themselves, we first have to get rid of the main obstacle to their self-fulfilment ... removing the Taliban regime.' (2001a) However, the rights with which the human rights advocates are concerned are not those of the political sphere. Criticism of non-Western elites does not conclude with a call for greater democracy in these regions. Instead, the international advocates of 'civil society', like Mary Kaldor, are more likely to argue that representative institutions should be bypassed entirely: 'What is needed is an alliance between local defenders of civility and transnational institutions which would guide a strategy.' (1999b:10)

The reason for the lack of attention to political rights is that the criticism of elites is usually a subtle way of introducing a broader critique of political responsibility, which encompasses the whole of the political arena. The critique of the political sphere in non-Western states is highlighted by the growing number of commentators who openly argue that elections are problematic. In the peace-building and developmental literature, the political sphere is regularly seen as one that should be deprioritised. Michael Pugh argues that 'the introduction of elections and associated adversarial politics can heighten tensions between groups and communities rather than dampen them' (1995:323). As Roland Paris suggests:

> Instead of promoting democratic elections ... peacebuilders could encourage rival parties to share power in a nondemocratic regime, thereby avoiding the problems associated with political liberalisation ... [M]any students of development have argued that democracy is an unaffordable luxury for most developing countries, where the need for effective government may outweigh the need for accountable government. (1997:79)

Nils Rosemann argues that the problem today is not unelected dictators backed by one or other of the Cold War superpowers but the elected politicians: '[T]he Cold War is over, gone are the Titos and Stalins (with some exceptions). Today we are dealing with Milosevics, Putins or Fujimoris – all more or less freely elected statesmen – who committed crimes against humanity.' (2000) Daniel Goldhagen asserts that: 'The majority of the Serbian people, by supporting or condoning Milosevic's eliminationist politics, have rendered themselves both legally and morally incompetent to conduct their own affairs and a presumptive ongoing danger to others.' (1999)

For *The Economist*: 'It is not just unlucky coincidence that Africa has had such a poor crop of leaders. Leaders emerge from a society, and they remain part of it.' (2000b) The problem is not just the alleged corruption of a tiny elite but African society, which condones elite behaviour and, therefore, is held to be ill-suited to democracy: 'Their loyalties are regional or tribal, and they support the president because he is the big chief. "I will vote for you when you are president," challengers are sometimes told.' (2000b) According to *The Economist*, extending democracy in African society would lead to little improvement for the 'hopeless' continent (2000a).

Once military action had been declared, Western politicians and media commentators expressed similar views about the validity of democracy and self-government in Afghanistan. John Simpson, the BBC's World Affairs Editor, arguing that the problems of the region were due to too little, rather than too much, external involvement in the country's affairs, asserted: 'The Afghans' own devices are what have ruined this country, turning its towns and villages into a vast killing field.' (2001) Tony Blair stated in a World Service broadcast to the region that the West would have to guide the political process in the country: 'We are not going to walk away again. We made that mistake in the past.' Senate foreign relations committee chairperson Joe Biden shared that view, stating that: 'If we had not lost interest, perhaps Afghanistan would not have turned into a swamp of terrorism.' (Wintour, 2001a) Clare Short has also argued that the problem is the Afghan people themselves, stating that: 'you can't force Afghans to do anything. They are very independent minded. Afghanistan is a nightmare, full stop.' (Kite, 2001) With this perspective to the fore, the British government appointed an open advocate of the 'new age of empire', Robert Cooper, as special adviser on Afghanistan (Cooper, 2001).

This view of ordinary people as incapable of democracy has only been expressed clearly by liberal academics, journalists and NGO advocates since the end of the 1980s. As David Beetham notes: 'anti-democrats or reluctant democrats [tended] to present their reservations as disputes about how the term should be defined' (1999:29; see further Chandler, 2000a:Ch. 1). In the 1990s, liberal academics have expressed their doubts about representative democracy much more openly. One indicator of this shift is the growing popularity of elite theorists such as Arend Lijphart, who argues that, in a socially divided society, majoritarian democracy should be replaced by elite consociationalism (1984). The dangers of democracy in ethnically or tribally fragmented societies are clearly stated by British academic James Mayall:

> Whenever powerful and unassimilated national communities must coexist within a single polity, they are likely to use the institutions of democracy to gain preferential access to state power ... at the expense of their ethnic rivals. The competition to establish their respective national rights is likely to prove sufficiently ferocious to ensure that any commitment to uphold the merely human rights of all citizens will remain theoretical. (1991:423–4)

Professor Rei Shiratori, adviser to the Washington-based International Foundation for Electoral Systems and other international bodies engaged in democratisation, asserts that elite theory is increasingly relevant because 'ordinary people can only react, they cannot act' and cannot resolve political problems (2000). Professor Shiratori is by no means unique in his opinion that political engagement requires skills beyond the average person's capacity.

The view of ordinary people presented by liberal academics is shared by the radical NGOs. A recent addition to the RFE/RL weekly reports on Central and Eastern Europe entitled *(Un)Civil Societies* sums up this more overtly elitist view of non-Western societies (RFE/RL, 2000a). At a seminar on democracy and human rights held in Bosnia in July 2000, NGO representatives argued that Bosnian people should be considered as politically incapable. Alenka Savic from the highly regarded Bosnian Women's Initiative programme asserted that women's support for nationalist parties indicated they were easily manipulated, which meant that her NGO could make progress by manipulating women in the direction of civil society. When questioned over her view of women's incapacity to think independently, she replied: 'People think they have an opinion but they haven't – they share the opinion of their society, of the media, of their environment. Bosnian women are not used to thinking independently, they haven't learnt that.' (2000) While the Women's Initiative had little respect for the views of Bosnian women, the NGOs involved in youth work expressed little respect for the adult generation as a whole, arguing that Bosnia could not be trusted with self-government until the current generation had no political influence. Even young people couldn't be trusted with politics at this stage and were advised to stick to following music like that of U2 and discussing art and cinema (Nezic, 2000).

Once the responsibility of governments and their electorates is held up for question the human rights campaigners are happy to suggest alternative forms of regulation for the non-Western state. The acceptance of human rights regulation implicitly concedes that government legitimacy should no longer be solely derived from the consent of its own population or the will of the electorate. As Dower notes:

> If nations do commit themselves to human rights conventions, then they are at least implicitly committing themselves to the moral logic of human rights talk, that is, to a criterion for evaluating the internal and international behaviour of nation-states, which is independent of the particular interests of nation-states themselves. (1997:95)

The accountability of government or the 'evaluation of internal and international behaviour' no longer lies with the electorate but with the international institutions or states responsible for overseeing human rights conventions. Any method of evaluation independent of 'the particular interests of nation-states' is also, of course, independent of the expressed interests of the electorate in that particular state.

The critique of sovereign equality in the international arena and emphasis on the need for human rights regulation, has done much to undermine the legitimacy of the non-Western state. The political sphere is becoming increasingly marginalised as democratic government is being redefined as human rights governance. The UN resolutions of the Economic and Social Council reflect this shift away from representative democracy. The UN's *Promotion of the Right to Democracy* resolution, of April 1999, highlighted 'the indissoluble links between the principles enshrined in the Universal Declaration of Human Rights and the foundation of any democratic society' (UN, 1999a). In April 2000, the much lengthier *Promoting and Consolidating Democracy* resolution emphasised 'the indissoluble link between human rights as enshrined in the Universal Declaration of Human Rights and in the international human rights treaties and the foundation of any democratic society' (UN, 2000a). The conflation of democracy with human rights institutionalises the shift in the derivation of legitimacy of the non-Western state, essentially reflecting the return of Westphalian ideas of Great Power regulation based on the legitimacy of economic and military power. Once legitimacy is judged externally, the room for self-determination and political autonomy is established by international institutional regulation (P. Taylor, 1999:557–63). This is reflected in the UN document, which focuses on the administrative, economic, social and cultural regulations deemed necessary by the external body. This perspective of an openly expressed lack of trust in the political sphere of non-Western nation-states is a relatively recent development. Justin Rosenberg makes the point that today's view of the non-Western state allows less room for self-determination than that of the classic imperialism of writers like John Stuart Mill in the nineteenth century (1999).

Human Rights Conditionality

Today, human rights concerns are central to most international treaties and held to justify a wide range of conditions, which have to be met for membership of the European Union and other international bodies. At the same time, an increasing variety of human rights conditions have been integrated into interstate agreements on aid and trade and for economic development aid from international institutions. The comprehensive nature of human rights allows conditionality to cover nearly every aspect of government policy once economic and social development are included under the human rights rubric. This can involve subjecting economic and social policies to 'independent external evaluation' and the development of a set of conditions, such as the reduction of military budgets, taking steps to combat political corruption, or spending more on education and welfare (Felice, 1998). This trend towards external accountability could in effect spell the end of independent economic and social policy-making in the less developed world, subjecting areas of traditional domestic policy decision-making to international bodies (G. Robertson: 1999:149). Nigel Dower argues that:

> [I]f any country manifestly fails to realise the basic rights of people of a political, civil or economic nature, through deliberate policies of oppression, unequal treatment or discrimination, then actions can be legitimately taken to put pressure on such a country to mend its ways. (1997:105)

As considered in Chapter 2, unconditional humanitarian aid is perceived to be problematic today because non-Western states are increasingly seen to be unable to rule themselves. Radical critics condemn aid programmes as supporting governments more than the poor, and see aid as increasing corruption. For Geoffrey Robertson, international aid, which is conditional on human rights policies, can hardly be seen as 'human rights imperialism' rather, it is a 'sensible step in global governance' as it is based on empowering the people that are worst affected by poverty: 'transforming them from passive recipients of aid into plaintiffs who had obtained their due by asserting before the international community their human right to a remedy for the hopelessness of their collective life' (1999:150).

Moves in this direction can already be seen in the 'holistic approach' to development taken in the Comprehensive Development Framework presently being implemented in several African states, which the World Bank launched in 1999 as an alternative to the failed policies of structural adjustment (Pender, 2000). As Gordon Crawford notes, bilateral and multilateral aid from the private sector, governments, the World Bank and the IMF is becoming conditional on agreed reform packages which leave developing countries with

less and less influence over policy decisions (1996:36–7). Bradlow
and Grossman state that the impact of greater human rights conditionality means that power and influence is exercised more unevenly
in international affairs because it is the poorer and weaker states that
are most dependent on the financing services of these institutions
(1995:427–8).

The introduction of human rights concerns into the policy-
making powers of international financial institutions, such as the
World Bank and the IMF has created a new range of *ad hoc* powers.
These institutions operate independently from the United Nations
and, in effect, have the power of independent decision-making on
all financial issues. The inclusion of human rights concerns under
the financial mandate has, essentially, given greater unaccountable
powers to these leading international institutions. For example, the
Articles of Agreement of the International Bank for Reconstruction
and Development (part of the World Bank Group) preclude it from
intervening in the 'political affairs' of its member states, requiring it
only to take 'economic considerations' into account in decision-
making. It is entirely up to the bank to interpret which human rights
issues impact on economic development and, therefore, are not
purely 'political'. In this context, it has made loans conditional on
the suppression of female genital mutilation but not, for example, on
the prevention of torture. As Bradlow and Grossman note, the
inclusion of human rights in the mandates of these institutions
introduces a completely *ad hoc* factor which gives these institutions
arbitrary powers over domestic affairs: 'The arbitrary nature of this
situation becomes clear when one takes into account the connection
between freedom of the press and hunger, and between freedoms of
speech and association, transparent and accountable governance,
and economic development.' (1995:431–2)

With the development of human rights conditionality clauses in
international agreements between major economic powers and other
states, existing relations of formal equality between states in the West
and the developing world are brought into question. Political equality
and independent policy-making capacities are being undermined by
Western paternalism in the cause of human rights. Nigel Dower
suggests that criticisms of external interference in the promotion of
human rights tend to 'overwork' the appeal to democracy:

No theory of democracy says that no-one either inside or outside
a community, may for moral reasons, seek to influence the way

democratic preferences turn out. But at a more fundamental level, it seems to me that there is a false contrast being drawn between what a fundamental morality demands and what a genuinely democratic procedure would select as basic rights to be protected. (1997:106)

The conflation of external human rights regulation with democratic outcomes legitimises the elitist perspective that external institutions are better suited to making policy decisions than non-Western governments and their electorates.

Direct Protectorates

The extension of the logic of conditionality can be seen in the developing UN agenda of civil administration over post-conflict states. Until the end of the Cold War, UN peace operations had no direct mandates to reshape the political sphere. Over the last decade, the UN's peace operations have increasingly extended to the political sphere under the rubric of 'peacebuilding', building the 'foundations of something that is more than just the absence of war' (UN, 2000c:3). This new programme is part of a people-centred framework in which the human rights component of a peace operation is seen as critical to its long-term effectiveness (UN, 2000c:7). The August 2000 Brahimi Panel Report defines peacebuilding as including, but not limited to: rebuilding civil society; strengthening the rule of law, through police restructuring and judicial and penal reform; improving the human rights situation by monitoring, educating and investigating abuses; democratic development including election and media regulation; tackling corruption; HIV/AIDS education and control; and promoting conflict resolution and reconciliation (UN, 2000c:3).

Regarding the rule of law, the UN panel emphasised the importance of the international reform and restructuring of the penal and judicial system in post-conflict societies, and the need to involve international judicial experts, penal experts and human rights specialists. The panel also suggested a 'doctrinal shift' in the role of civilian police in post-conflict operations (UN, 2000c:7). In the past, their role was a monitoring one, documenting behaviour and, by their presence, attempting to discourage unacceptable behaviour. This was now seen as a 'somewhat narrow perspective'. Instead, the panel report proposed that the UN police should reform, retrain and restructure local police forces and have the capacity to take over their role if necessary, responding to civil disorder.

The panel also emphasised the danger of seeing post-conflict elections as marking the end of the period of international administration. It warned that 'elections merely ratify a tyranny of the majority' until democratisation and civil society-building processes have been completed and a 'culture of respect for human rights' has been established (UN, 2000c:7). Because of the perceived lack of legitimacy of post-conflict governments, elected or not, the panel suggested that the economic reconstruction programme should be kept under UN control, with no direct aid or investment, as the UN 'should be considered the focal point for peacebuilding activities by the donor community' (UN, 2000c:8). The panel further recommended that 'quick impact projects' were established, to overcome hostility to the UN's regulation of economic reconstruction and 'help establish the credibility of a new mission' (UN, 2000c:7).

The logical conclusion of the focus on extending peacebuilding regulation in post-conflict societies is the extension of the mandates of the 'transitional' civil administrations headed by the UN. The first fully developed peacebuilding mandate of this sort was established in 1995, when the UN effectively took over the civil administration of Bosnia. This was originally a one-year mandate, but was extended indefinitely after two years (Chandler, 2000a:158). This was followed in 1999, by indefinite formal mandates of civil administration over Kosovo and then East Timor and the UN may have a major role in Afghanistan (Wintour, 2001a). These missions have revealed that the 'nation-building' or peacebuilding project is highly likely to be a long-term one during which state sovereignty is effectively surrendered by the post-conflict state (Dempsey and Fontaine, 2001). As the Brahimi Panel noted, the UN has been given responsibility for micro-managing these societies: making and enforcing the law, establishing customs services, collecting business and personal taxes, attracting foreign investment, adjudicating property disputes, reconstructing and operating public utilities, creating a banking system and running the schools (UN, 2000c:13).

The panel suggested that the UN Security Council should establish a centre of responsibility for the tasks of transitional administration to manage future direct mandates. It also suggested that the UN draw up a 'justice package' with an interim legal code to avoid the difficulties of establishing 'applicable law'. This would solve the problems of Kosovo where the UN was formally working under federal

Yugoslav law but allowed their appointed judges to overrule it while Nato troops and UN police initially worked according to their own conflicting national laws (Chandler, 2000a:210).

Once the non-Western state is no longer seen as a political equal the trend is for greater levels of external regulation, as can be seen by the establishment of international protectorates in Bosnia, Kosovo and East Timor. As Michael Ignatieff notes: 'The United Nations once oversaw discrete development projects. Now it takes over the political and administrative infrastructure of entire nations and rebuilds them from scratch.' (1998:79) The advocates of human rights, of course, dispute any connection between their perspective of long-term management as a transition to self-government and that of Great Power domination in the past. As Bernard Kouchner asserts:

> The charge of 'human rights imperialism' against local cultural norms is also not a valid argument against the right to intervene. Everywhere, human rights are human rights. Freedom is freedom. Suffering is suffering ... When a patient is suffering and desires care, he or she has the right to receive it. This principle also holds for human rights. (1999)

The problem with the 'freedoms' campaigned for, by the first internationally appointed colonial governor of Kosovo, is that they are won through the radical restriction of the political sphere. The protectorate solution is a logical outcome of the human rights discourse but clearly demonstrates the limits of this perspective, which holds that external regulation can manage society better than democratic involvement in decision-making. The result is that under the new international protectorates, the human rights subjects have little possibility of taking ownership of political issues (Waal, 1997a:221). As Christine Chinkin notes, regarding Kosovo: 'The internationalization of the internal dispute by the commission of human rights abuses and the military action has displaced the agency of the local players and made them passive objects of international proposals.' (1999:845) The consequence of international regulation under the rubric of human rights protection is not merely the formal removal of democratic accountability. The central problem with regulation in East Timor, Bosnia and Kosovo has been that the political sphere has been colonised by external regulation with negative consequences for any self-sustaining solution. If there is ever a UN administration established in Afghanistan it is unlikely that it would have any better results (*Economist*, 2001; Roy, 2001).

In all the UN administrations, the vast network of human rights protections leaves little space for any local accountability. As Seth Mydans noted in the *New York Times*, one critical problem with the UN protectorate's nation-building attempts, involving an overhaul of every aspect of East Timorese society, has been that 'relatively few local people are being given important roles in the planning and running of the reconstruction effort' (2000). While UN bureaucrats took on the roles of district administrators, the leading political group in East Timor, the National Council for Timorese Resistance (CNRT), was ignored by the UN and refused office space in the capital Dili (*Financial Times*, 1999). There were daily protests at the UN's high-handed rule over the territory. José Ramos Horta, CNRT Vice-President, complained: 'We saw time going by and no Timorese administration, no civil servants being recruited, no jobs being created.' (Cited in Aglionby, 2000)

The Bosnian example is probably the most revealing, as after six years of international rule the problems of external regulation are becoming clearer. The constantly expanding role of the multitude of international organisations has inevitably restricted the capacity of Bosnian people to discuss, develop and decide on vital questions of concern. At state level, the Bosnian Muslim, Croat and Serb representatives can discuss international policy proposals under the guidance of the Office of the High Representative, but at the most can make only minor amendments or delay the implementation of externally-prepared rules and regulations. Even this limited accountability has been diminished by the High Representative who has viewed democratic consensus-building in Bosnian state bodies such as the tripartite Presidency, Council of Ministers and State Parliament as an unnecessary delay to imposing international policy. Compared to the swift signature of the chief administrators' pen, the working out of democratic accountability through the joint institutions was seen as 'painfully cumbersome and ineffective' (OHR, 1997b). At the end of 1997, the 'cumbersome' need for Bosnian representatives to assent to international edicts was removed and the High Representative was empowered both to dismiss elected representatives who obstructed policy and to impose legislation directly. The international community thereby assumed complete legislative and executive power over the formally independent state.

The Dayton settlement for Bosnia, like the Rambouillet proposals for Kosovo, promised the decentralisation of political power and the creation of multi-ethnic administrations in order to cohere state institutions and provide security to ethnic minorities and safeguard their autonomy. However, the experience of Dayton suggests that the outcome of the framework imposed will inevitably belie any good intentions that lie behind it. Minority protections, promised to the three constituent peoples under Dayton, have not been delivered under the international administration. At state, entity, city and municipal levels, a clear pattern has emerged where elected majorities have been given little control over policy-making. However, this power has not been decentralised to give minority groups security and a stake in government but transferred to the international institutions and re-centralised in the hands of the High Representative. Today, the international community regulates Bosnian life down to the minutiae of local community service provision, employment practices, school admissions and sports (OHR, 1997d:par. 5.7). Multi-ethnic administrations exist on paper, but the fact that the consensus attained in these forums is an imposed one, not one autonomously negotiated, is important. Compliance with international edicts imposed by the threat of dismissals or economic sanctions does little to give either majorities or minorities a stake in the process, nor to encourage the emergence of a negotiated accountable solution that could be viable in the long term.

The institutions of Bosnian government are hollow structures, not designed to operate autonomously. The Bosnian state Council of Ministers with the nominal role of assenting to pre-prepared policy has few staff or resources and is aptly described by the Office of the High Representative as 'effectively, little more than an extended working group' (OHR, 1997a:par. 24). Muslim, Croat and Serb representatives have all argued for greater political autonomy in policy-making, and have attempted to uphold the rights protected in the 'letter' of the Dayton agreement against the *ad hoc* reinterpretation of international powers under the 'spirit of Dayton' (Woodger, 1997). As an adviser to former Bosnian President Alijah Izetbegovic noted, there is a contradiction between the stated aims of the international protectorate and its consequences: 'A protectorate solution is not good, because the international community would bring all the decisions which would decrease all the functions of Bosnia-Herzegovina institutions. The High Representative's mandate is actually an opposite one, to strengthen the Bosnia-Herzegovina institutions.' (OHR, 1997c)

The frailty of Bosnian institutions has perpetuated the fragmentation of political power and reliance on personal and local networks of support which were prevalent during the Bosnian war. Both Susan Woodward and Katherine Verdery provide useful analyses of the impact on Bosnian society of the external undermining of state and entity centres of power and security (Woodward, 1995:136–7; Verdery, 1996:82–3). The lack of cohering political structures has meant that Bosnian people are forced to rely on more narrow and parochial survival mechanisms, which has meant that ethnicity has maintained its wartime relevance as a political resource.

It would appear that the removal of mechanisms of political accountability has done little to broaden Bosnian people's political outlook. The removal of sites of accountable political power has, in fact, reinforced general insecurity and atomisation which has led to the institutionalisation of much narrower political relations in the search for individual links to those with influence and power. The narrowing of the political domain and reliance on individual survival strategies has assumed a generalised pattern across society. The 'new feudalism' noted by some commentators and the continued existence of weak para-state structures in Muslim and Croat areas of the Federation are symptomatic of the vacuum of integrative institutional power at state and entity level rather than some disintegrative dynamic (Deacon and Stubbs, 1998).

The Dayton process has institutionalised fears and insecurities through high-handed international rule disempowering Bosnian people and their representatives. With little influence over, or relationship to, the decision-making process there is concern that entity boundaries or rights to land, employment and housing can easily be brought into question. The extended mandates of the international institutions have undermined the power of the main political parties and their elected representatives but have not created the political basis of a unitary Bosnia, except in so far as it is one artificially imposed by, and dependent upon, the international community.

Under the human rights international protectorates there is a high level of external regulation but little democracy and no mechanisms through which the rights administrators can rebuild fragmented societies. While mainstream commentators conflate human rights with empowerment, self-determination and democracy, there are few critics who draw attention to the fact that the human rights discourse of moral and ethical policies is essentially an attack on the public political sphere and democratic practices. The result is a 'hypertrophied public realm' with the political arena reduced to a narrow one of international officialdom with extensive powers wielded in isolation from wider society, and an 'atrophied public realm' in the sense of a loss of citizenship with collective political society reduced to reliance on personal and parochial networks (see Weintraub, 1997; Garcelon 1997). In fact, the time scales for external administration have been extended as society becomes increasingly atomised (Chandler, 1998). In Bosnia, Kosovo and East Timor external regulation has been highly destructive of the political sphere as increasing levels of civil interaction have come under regulatory control.

There are good reasons for pessimism over any internationally-imposed regime selected to replace the Taliban. It may prove easy to impose a pro-Western administration on a shattered and war-torn country and to justify this as being for the good of the people there – in the form of a liberal 'transitional' regime. However, as demonstrated in similar experiments, if the imposed government has little support within the society itself it can become a paper institution, unable to bridge regional, political or ethnic divisions. This danger appears to be a likely prospect in view of the fact that many Western commentators and politicians argue that any future government should actively promote human rights. This perspective has been questioned as potentially alienating Afghan society; Michael Griffin, author of *Reaping the Whirlwind: The Taliban Movement in Afghanistan* (2001), asking: 'How popular would a democratic human rights-orientated post-Taliban government be, in the Islamic world where none of these things exists, and they are regarded as dangerous practices?' (Cited in Appleton, 2001) Even more worrying is Jack Straw's commitment to an *ad hoc* coalition of 20 countries 'with an interest in a stable Afghanistan' agreeing on the make-up of any future regime (2001a). The history of Afghanistan since the Soviet withdrawal in 1989 has proved the fragility of governments agreed between external powers, including Pakistan, the United States, Russia and Saudi Arabia. As Josie Appleton notes, these governments generally sat as isolated cliques in Kabul, while much of the country remained under the control of excluded factions (2001). It seems clear that the only solution to the Afghan crisis will be one that is accountable to the people of Afghanistan. Plans to impose a 'friendly' administration, which vets political parties and those the

West disapproves of, seem likely to lead to more civil conflict rather than less.

INTERNATIONAL SPHERE

For many commentators, the weakening of the concept of state sovereignty would indicate a more central role for the UN in international policy-making. There can be little doubt that the extension of human rights-based mandates to legitimise UN transitional administrations heralds a public retreat from the principles of self-determination and sovereignty. This shift is highlighted by the British government's suggestion that 'there is a strong case for reassessing the role of the Trusteeship Council', suspended since the last UN protectorate, Palau, was granted independence in 1994 (UKJCC, 2000:9). Nevertheless, the relationship between state sovereignty, particularly of smaller and more marginal states, and the world of UN decision-making control is far from a zero-sum one.

The international call for a focus on people-centred human rights approaches inevitably calls into question the role and standing of the UN itself. The human rights discourse goes beyond the questioning of sovereignty in non-Western states. Once sovereignty is seen as a negative aspect it is difficult to defend the central political institution of the post-war international order. As leading human rights advocate Geoffrey Robertson notes, it is not just the UN's peace operations that are problematic, but its whole organisational structure, based on post-Second World War ideas of state sovereignty and political equality, rather than people-centred human rights. For Robertson, the problems of international policy-making derive from the 'Machiavellian fiction that "peoples" and their government ("the State") are conceptually interchangeable' (1999:141). This 'fiction' is promoted by states themselves, 'their trade union' the General Assembly, UN diplomats and 'politically correct' ICJ judges (1999:141–3). For Robertson: 'Obeisance to member state sovereignty is the UN's systemic defect, and it accounts for the pathetic performance of the Human Rights Commission and that toothless tribunal the Human Rights Committee.' (1999:xix)

Far from legitimising the UN, the prioritisation of human rights can only lead to its discrediting, as it is still tainted by the political process of reaching interstate agreement. The human rights discourse distances itself from the political process based on achieving international consensus, arguing that policy should not be based on what states agree over but 'what they should do according to principles of fairness and justice' (G. Robertson, 1999:143). Max Boot argues that the respect for state sovereignty means the UN is hamstrung by political considerations, as the General Assembly has to treat all regimes as equal regardless of whether they are democratic or not. He argues that to avoid offending member states the institution is forced into a position of neutrality, despite the rights and wrongs of a situation (2000a). As Robertson argues, the need for interstate agreements 'devalues human rights by trusting governments with them', and current international mechanisms legitimise states and 'shore up state sovereignty – the traditional enemy of the human rights movement' (1999:151). Instead, he calls for 'a consensus of principles and not an accommodation with political power' (1999:xix).

The Critique of Politics

For the critics of the UN, the defining moment of their moral compromise with politics was the fall of Srebrenica, the Bosnian-Muslim safe-haven, in July 1995, to Serb forces which led to the alleged execution and death of thousands of Muslims. Srebrenica is held up by human rights advocates as the worst war crime in Europe since the fall of Hitler. UN troops were meant to be defending the town but instead stood back and watched as Serbs took Muslim men and boys away for questioning, opening themselves to the charge that they 'acquiesced in genocide' (G. Robertson, 1999:70). Srebrenica stands as a warning that human rights-based foreign policy needs to be separated from politics. International efforts to protect the vulnerable were held to be hampered by the 'Mogadishu factor', the politician's fear of bringing back body-bags. The UN troops were helplessly underrepresented, the 'safe areas' were being protected by 7,400 instead of the 34,000 initially called for. Dutch troops could have called for Nato to bomb the Serb advance, but again political concern about troops being taken hostage or killed meant that nothing was done.

Once morality has replaced politics as the guide for policy-making, politicians not only become redundant but are also actually a barrier to human rights promotion. The result of this attack on international politics has been calls for alternative institutions to fill the vacuum; institutions not legitimised by state representation but by their independence from nation-states, in the form of international lawyers or international NGOs. To be seen as a favoured body the only qualification appears to be a distancing from politics. Geoffrey

Robertson makes the point that, as government representatives, UN officials are bound to regard their role as 'political rather than judicial' (1999:42). Instead of governments making appointments to UN committees, Robertson suggests that NGOs should be involved in the process, to ensure that appointees are critical of governments (1999:43). Pursuing the defence of the innocent and taking sides against the aggressor is not the job of politicians.

As Robertson states: 'At the close of the twentieth century, international law remains subordinate and subservient to state power, which will tend to favour economic, political or military interests whenever they conflict with the interests of justice.' (1999:84) Because some states cannot be trusted to resolve questions without oppression even the central question of power, 'who constitutes the political community' should be left to 'impartial arbitration' by an international court. In Geoffrey Robertson's view, even the existence of states would be upon the sufferance of an international tribunal of judges:

> In an ideal world, such tribunals would have power to decide at what point minorities deserve representation in government or some measure of self-management or territorial autonomy within the framework of the wider state, or even when they should be permitted to secede. (1999:145)

The human rights advocates assert that their struggle to remove elected representation is a democratic one. That the 'great obstacle to peace is the immense concentration of power in the nation state ... and the task before us is to find ways to diffuse that power' (Nariman, 1997: 546). The only role for ordinary people in this scenario is to persuade their governments to cede away their power.

While the international lawyers argue that they should have the job of running the world, rather than political representatives, the NGO advocates naturally assert that they, in fact, should be having a central say in decision-making. Many commentators, who argue against the representation of non-Western governments in international forums, argue that NGOs from these states should be given a position 'at the centre of the rights debate' (Posner, 1997:630). There is an automatic assumption that nationally-based NGOs have a greater legitimacy than elected governments and that the non-political nature of NGOs makes them central to new institutional developments. Michael Posner, Executive Director of the Lawyers'

Committee for Human Rights, argues that: 'human rights NGOs will lead the way towards greater accountability by governments and enhanced institutional safeguards to prevent human rights crises in the future' (1997:630). This position, of making governments accountable to NGOs, advocated throughout the human rights lobby, expresses a view of accountability fundamentally hostile to representative democracy (Brett, 1998). As Susan Burgerman notes, there is an increasingly complex web of non-state actors who 'participate in other people's politics without resorting to the power base of either their own government or that of the target state' (1998:908).

Steve Charnovitz correctly asserts that the involvement of NGOs in policy-making cannot make nation-states more accountable. Many of the NGOs most active and influential on human rights issues, like Human Rights Watch, the International Crisis Group or the International Commission of Jurists have no mass membership and concentrate on elite advocates to enable them to gain admittance to government and international officials (Forsythe, 2000:167–8; Charnovitz, 1997:270; Waal, 1997b). As Jenny Bates at the Progressive Policy Institute states: 'NGOs are not elected and, unlike governments, need not answer to the broad public they claim to represent.' (Cited in Bosco, 2000) Charnovitz also makes the point that the establishment of NGO advisory committees actually gives nation-state governments greater control over decision-making as the real power belongs to the international officials who determine which NGOs to appoint (1997:283).

The Nato Solution

In their condemnation of the UN for its political consensus-building and calls for human rights protections to come before nation-state-based politics and international law, the human rights advocates have, in fact, facilitated the power of the nation-state. Not the non-Western nation-state, increasingly marginalised from international decision-making, but the Western states with the economic and military resources to lead the 'coalitions of the willing', which have increasingly taken on the authority to decide which human rights will be enforced and how. The sidelining of the UN in the US-led military intervention against Afghanistan indicated the new hierarchical international order. While the United States and Britain were happy to pay lip-service to the UN's role in regional aid co-ordination and promise it greater influence in the non-military aspects of the international fight against terrorism, there was little consideration of the UN maintaining its former role as authoriser of military force (MacAskill, 2001a; Perkins, 2001).

Ominously for the future of the UN, as the key institution in upholding international peace and security, the Brahimi Panel indicated that changes to the Security Council procedures were necessary to ensure more effective protections for human rights: 'The tradition of the recitation of statements, followed by a painstaking process of achieving consensus, places considerable emphasis on the diplomatic process over operational product.' (UN, 2000c:46) The panel argued that political consensus in the Security Council had been a barrier to effective mandates and action:

> As a political body, the Security Council focuses on consensus-building, even though it can take decisions with less than unanimity. But the compromises required to build consensus can be made at the expense of specificity, and the resulting ambiguity can have serious consequences in the field ... While it acknowledges the utility of political compromise in many cases, the panel comes down in this case on the side of clarity, especially for operations that will deploy into dangerous circumstances. (UN, 2000c:10)

The UK government is also in favour of change and has advocated the expansion of the Security Council to include Germany and Japan as well as additional members from Latin America, Africa and Asia, as new permanent members, and also the addition of another four non-permanent members, increasing the size of the Council from 15 to 24 (UKJCC, 2000:4). The United Kingdom argues that the expansion of the Security Council will increase its legitimacy and 'allow us the opportunity to reassess the circumstances under which a veto can be used' (UKJCC, 2000:4). Considering the UN Secretary-General's view that the Security Council has a 'moral duty' to act on behalf of the international community in the cause of human rights and that 'no legal principle' should stand in the way, it would seem likely that the use of veto powers will be restricted in the face of serious human rights concerns (UN, 2000b:48). Through the prioritisation of 'clarity' over 'consensus', where there is no unanimity in a crisis situation, as over Kosovo, reform looks set to legitimise unilateral action by 'coalitions of the willing', which would otherwise necessitate international consensus-building.

The reform of the Security Council and the likely abolition of the powers of veto, in situations held to be of serious human rights violation, suggest that the UN will no longer be bound to uphold an international consensus on intervention in the cause of human rights. The end of consensus means that dominant world powers, particularly the sole remaining superpower, the United States, will be increasingly able to dictate whether or not economic or military intervention is necessary. It, thus, seems likely that the UN will be further sidelined when it comes to questions of war or peace and that its formal role of being able to hold major world powers to account will be increasingly eroded.

This shift will reflect the declining political influence of non-Western states within the UN since the end of the Cold War. During the Cold War, US influence over the General Assembly was restricted by the strength of the non-aligned movement and the Soviet bloc. The veto was, therefore, defended by the United States as a barrier to UN censure. Today, removing the veto will weaken the other Security Council members rather than the United States. UN reform also institutionalises the changed balance of power between the UN and Nato. The transformation of the UN's peacekeeping role to that of the civilian rather than military tasks of peace operations will confirm the position of the UN as the handmaiden to Nato, the pre-eminent 'coalition of the willing', rather than the authorising authority. While Nato powers will have an increasingly free hand to define the limits of sovereignty in the non-Western world and intervene when they consider it necessary, the UN will have the task of cleaning up afterwards and have to take responsibility for the unrealistic expectations raised by the growing internationalisation of conflict situations.

The proposed end of the Security Council veto will mean that the UN will no longer have to forge an international consensus, which takes on board the concerns of smaller non-Western states, nor those of non-Western states on the Security Council, Russia and China. It is ironic that UN reforms are demanded by human rights advocates as a way to create a global community based on the universal rights of the individual, rather than states. In fact, the consequence of reform will be the demise of the one international institution that did represent the desire for a political expression of international needs, which went beyond nation-state interests. By institutionalising political inequality in the international sphere, international society is more fragmented than before with less formal mechanisms of protection for the weaker and more vulnerable against the strong and powerful.

DOMESTIC SPHERE

While few academic commentators are concerned with the divisive consequences of human rights interventionism in the Balkans, Africa or elsewhere, the corrosive effects of this discourse can also be seen in the Western domestic sphere. Western leaders have been able to achieve a level of leadership and coherence through standing above politics on the ethical high ground but the drawbacks, even for the political elites, are already becoming apparent.

Ethical policy can only detract from the sphere of politics. As Hugo Young notes in the *Guardian* 'ethically based interference in the affairs of foreign countries, especially big ones, is ... hard for ministers' (1999b). While ministers have the pressure of account-ability to constituents and businesses affected by trade or foreign investment concerns, it will always be difficult to take decisions damaging to those interests. *The Economist*, similarly, flags up the impossibility of government ministers promoting ethical foreign policy which is bound to clash with the promotion of trade and the British arms industry, a leading exporter. Despite former foreign secretary Robin Cook's willingness to do some 'short-term' damage to trade in the interests of ethical foreign policy, it was inevitable that the UK government would tread more carefully with important trading partners like Saudi Arabia, inevitably opening up the government to charges of hypocrisy (1997). Young makes the point, shared by many radical critics, that the reluctance of both Labour and Conservative governments to seize Pinochet, given the oppor-tunity, demonstrates that judges will always be far better defenders of human rights, essentially because of this lack of accountability.

John Gray suggests that the costs of sustaining a foreign policy based on human rights rather than self-interest may be too high for politicians or voters to accept:

> Public opinion has not yet understood that protecting human rights across all of Europe will use up much of the peace dividend that came with the end of the Cold War. Understandably, polit-icians are reluctant to press the point ... Yet if voters are not educated in the cost of peace in Europe it will not be secure. (2000)

For Geoffrey Robertson, the electorate in Western states cannot be trusted to ensure that human rights policies are enforced by governments, democracy is no guarantee of justice as 'votes are not informed by evidence or argument' (1999:132). Daniele Archibugi argues that 'the choices of a people, even when made democratically, might be biased by self-interest' (1998:211). Nicholas Wheeler also fears that governments' formal accountability to the electorate could be a barrier to ethical policy making and argues that 'it is crucial that policy-makers in the West are not constrained' by their domestic publics (2000:303). For this reason, he favours an independent UN rapid reaction force able to commit to military action without public discussion.

Not only does the human rights discourse suggest that Western governments should not rely on public opinion for foreign policy initiatives, the logic of the argument also reaches into the domestic sphere. Once it is accepted that government policy for 'higher values' abroad should not be tempered by the reluctance of the electorate, it makes little sense to argue that public accountability should be a barrier to government policy in the service of human rights at home.

As John Wadham the Director of Liberty, argued, in a debate on the Human Rights Act, introduced in the UK in October 2000, human rights are about 'putting a limitation on the power of democracy; putting a limitation on the power of the state'. For Wadham and other human rights advocates, democratic account-ability is seen to be of little importance. He argues 'that whoever you vote for the government gets in'; that human rights are a necessary 'restriction on the right of democratic countries to oppress their peoples' (2000). The distrust of government is not a distrust of elites, but of representative democracy: 'Elected parliaments in this country and around the world have shown that, on their own, they are not able to protect human rights properly. This is partly because most of them, including our own, are dominated by the government.' (Wadham and Lawrence, 2000) The objection is to the majority rule of democracy which Wadham alleges will inevitably lead to the denial of rights to minorities: 'In any mature democracy, minorities and human rights are best protected by the checks and balances in the constitution.' The 'checks and balances' proposed are ones free from any democratic influence. While being wary of elected polit-icians, Wadham is much more trusting of the judiciary: 'This country now has the best set of judges we have ever had and they can be trusted to protect our rights'. Nevertheless, even this can be improved upon: 'We need to remove the power to appoint our judges from the government ... and put it in the hands of an independent appointments committee.' (Wadham and Lawrence, 2000)

The consequences of this change indicate that the judiciary will be empowered rather than the people, but also that public debate over policy-making will be more restricted. There are problems with judges developing the law; the lack of accountability of judges is the reason why even in the new millennium the courts are generally held to be subservient to elected politicians. Former UK home secretary Michael Howard notes that it is misleading to argue that the Human Rights Act will 'protect individual rights from abuse'. First, it is not straightforward to balance the competing rights of individuals or those of the individual and the state. Second: 'The key question is whether such judgements should be made by politicians accountable to the electorate and subject to summary dismissal or by unaccountable judges who cannot be dismissed.' (2000)

The Human Rights Act brings an entirely new quality to the law. Law is no longer based on a rigid framework of protections of individual freedoms, but is to be interpreted as a means to a just or equitable end. As Lord Irvine, the Lord Chancellor, states, this 'will create a more explicitly moral approach to decisions and decision-making' (cited in Klug, 2000b:33). Rather than starting with the rights of the individual, each case is to be taken as a specific balancing of rights and freedoms. This means that previous case law is no longer seen to set a precedent (Travis and Dyer, 2000). Few lawyers realise the consequences of the human rights approach, as Francesca Klug notes: 'Well-meaning lawyers can make matters worse – particularly those who have yet to make the transition from a legal culture obsessed with the meaning of words to one which seeks the purpose of human rights values.' (2000a)

Klug and others describe the human rights framework as living under a 'higher law', which sets ethical guidelines for government policy (1997:149). The *Guardian* favourably notes that 'this act alters the very hard-wiring of our constitution; it marks a shift of power from the executive to the judiciary' (2000c). The judges will be drawn much more directly into the political process under new powers to consider the merits of administrative decisions under judicial review, not only whether such decisions conform to the proper procedures. Although the judges cannot strike down parliamentary legislation, they can make a 'declaration of incompatibility' (Bamforth, 1998; Addo, 1998; Ewing, 1999). This declaration then allows changes to be made bypassing parliament. Instead of holding a full debate in the House of Commons, the government will have the power to amend legislation by statutory instrument (*Economist*, 2000c).

Against human rights advocates, like John Wadham, other commentators have pointed out that the supporters of the Human Rights Act, who believe that an unaccountable judiciary will be more progressive than an elected government, may well be disappointed (N. Cohen, 2000). However, whatever the relative merits of the unaccountable judiciary versus the accountable politicians on specific policies, the cost of any shift in power is that there is less public involvement and debate on policy issues (Griffith, 1998:27). Even if the unaccountable judiciaries were more progressive than an elected government, judicial intervention would still mean the removal of policy questions from the public arena.

Francesca Klug feels that human rights values 'have the capacity to set the terms for most of the ethical debates of our age' (1997:149). The problem is that the ethical debates, whether they are over the limits to the right of free speech, rights to private schooling, government health priorities, or the separation of Siamese twins, will not take place in the public arena, where the decision-makers are held accountable, but in the courtroom or the ethics committee. Klug admits that even if improvements are made to healthcare or prison conditions these often remain 'unsung' because there is no broader public involvement (2001). Even the programmes of political parties stand to be vetted by the human rights enforcers. For example, in New Zealand, the Chief Human Rights Commissioner, established by the 1993 Human Rights Act, made a public statement that the Christian Coalition Party's policy of affirming marriage by targeting benefits on married couples with children was discriminatory (Rishworth, 1997). The more judicial involvement there is in the political sphere, the more public involvement in the decision-making process will be curtailed. Once questions, which are currently considered to be political, become recategorised as ethical or legal ones, they are no longer subject to public accountability.

The colonisation of the political sphere by law and ethics, facilitated by the discourse of human rights, is a high price to pay for ethical policy-making, one which, in the end, can only be counterproductive for society. Politics was about popular influence on priorities and needs decided by the competition for representation. Today, it is increasingly reduced to ethical priorities decided by the judiciary or some other unelected elite. The fact that unelected and unaccountable judges are held to make better policy in the field of human rights and ethical policy is not merely a matter of practical politics. Ethical decisions are by necessity undemocratic, not open to public debate and decision. Ethical policy cannot be decided by voting but only by select committees of the 'great and the good'. We are all likely to come across the increasingly ubiquitous 'ethics committees' in workplaces and colleges, but are unlikely to witness 'ethics elections'. The recasting of politics through the human rights approach is destructive of political society through inevitably reducing discussion to ethics and thereby to elite decision-making. As a *Catalyst* paper by Steve Platt notes, UK Labour government policy-making is increasingly being made by task forces of the 'great and the good' (1998).

CONCLUSION

As Tony Evans points out, democracy and human rights are today often mistakenly thought of as two sides of the same coin (1997:123). As this chapter has sought to illustrate, the assumptions of the human rights discourse, in fact, question the essence of democratic accountability. At the level of the non-Western state, the human rights approach facilitates external regulation by international institutions under the increasingly invasive policies of conditionality, which restrict democratic decision-making. In a growing number of states, subject to transitional UN mandates of civilian administration, the political sphere is entirely marginalised, institutionalising social fragmentation. In the international arena, the human rights approach has undermined the central political institution of international society, the United Nations, resulting in increasingly direct international regulation through 'coalitions of the willing' involving major Western powers, primarily the United States. In the domestic sphere, the focus on human rights has, similarly, narrowed public political debate through legitimising the developing decision-making role for the judiciary and unelected task forces and ethics committees.

The key argument forwarded by the human rights advocates is that international institutions, international and domestic courts, NGOs or ethics committees are better representatives of the people's needs than are elected governments. Governments and elected representatives are seen as suspect precisely because they are held to account by their constituencies and, therefore, are perceived to have 'particular' interests, as opposed to acting on ethical principle. This perspective is false on two central grounds. First, because it assumes that political decision-making can be detached from society and approached from the perspective of an *a priori* programme of technical governance and human rights administration by 'experts'. Second, because it assumes that political communities can be constructed, and held together, from above by external regulation. In fact, the consequences of human rights regulation demonstrate the inadequacy of this perspective. As considered further in the concluding chapter, there is no shortcut to constructing a political community; restricting freedom and autonomy can only institutionalise divisions and fragment society further.

8 Conclusion: Humanism or Human Rights?

> In the twentieth century, the idea of human universality rests less on hope than on fear, less on optimism about the human capacity for good than on dread of human capacity for evil, less on a vision of man as maker of his history than of man the wolf toward his own kind. – Michael Ignatieff, *The Warrior's Honor* (1998), p. 18.

Many, if not all, books on human rights focus on the most barbaric and degraded aspects of human interaction, from genocide and torture, to mass rape and ethnic cleansing. This book has followed a different approach. This is not because I don't believe that humanity is capable of great barbarity and destruction (nearly all the members of my mother's German Jewish family died in the Holocaust). This work has not focused on the detail of 'human wrongs' for two reasons. First, because the liberal preoccupation today with genocide, war crimes and barbarism has little to do with either the genocide and ethnic cleansing of the Holocaust, or with recent civil conflict in Africa and the Balkans. Second, because the key subject of concern has been the political approach which underlies the current preoccupation with man's inhumanity to man.

This book set out to question the ethical agenda of human rights intervention in an intellectual climate in which there is little discussion of the implications of the human rights critique of the political sphere and of democratic and egalitarian conceptions of political decision-making. The previous chapters sought to illustrate the dangers of an uncritical adoption of the human rights framework. Chapter 2 drew out the development of human rights-based concepts of regulation in more interventionist NGO approaches and the conflation of humanitarian aid with military intervention in the 'new humanitarian' framework. Chapter 3 considered the internationalisation of human rights foreign policy as a pragmatic or opportunist approach to problems of domestic political legitimacy. Chapter 4 highlighted the normative framework of the human rights discussion and indicated the elitist consequences of creating new rights, which can only be enforced by ruling authorities. Chapter 5 focused on the impact of the human rights discourse in undermining the legal equality of state sovereignty and legitimising the return of open Great Power domination. Chapter 6 emphasised the consequences of prioritising the human rights agenda over locally negotiated peace settlements, the trend towards military as opposed to diplomatic solutions and the dangers of internationalising conflicts. Chapter 7 illustrated the elitist consequences of the human rights critique of the political sphere for new forms of governance in non-Western states, for the UN international system and for domestic politics.

The following section seeks to provide an overview of the domestic dynamic behind the human rights consensus and consider why it cannot be more than a temporary solution to problems of the political domain. The later sections return to the core elements of the human rights thesis laid out in the introductory chapter, to draw out and restate the deeply problematic essence of the human rights discourse.

THE POISONED CHALICE OF HUMAN RIGHTS

In Chapter 3, the institutionalisation of a new ethical agenda in foreign policy and the shift towards a human rights approach to politics was seen to derive from domestic concerns rather than international ones. The search for rebuilding connections between the government and society has driven Western governments to attempt to define themselves through taking the moral high ground and this process has led to a more active foreign policy. Foreign policy has become increasingly important to the domestic agenda as an area in which governments and leading politicians are more likely to be able to present themselves as having a sense of purpose or 'mission'. Ethical foreign policy also enables Western leaders to appear to be directly representing the moral concerns of people regardless of political affiliation. This is possible because foreign intervention does not impact directly on the electorate's immediate concerns, avoiding the problem of direct accountability and creating a sense of national unity around a moral platform.

The capacity to generate a moral consensus around human rights appeals to pragmatic governments and is pursued almost by instinct through the knee-jerk response of making declarations of commitment to causes without necessarily thinking through the policy implications. This search for political common ground dovetails with the human rights campaigning of liberal journalists and international NGOs, who see government pragmatism as an official endorsement of their concerns. However, the domestic dynamic behind the shift towards a human rights focus goes beyond government opportunism. Domestic political considerations rather than universal altruism also drive the liberal human rights advocates, who see themselves as creating or leading a movement for ethical policy-making. Their concern with the lack of social engagement in domestic politics and increasing fragmentation of social ties has led them to seek to reform the electorate through moral education about responsibility and sacrifice. Where ruling elites focus on the problem of their isolation from society through the knee-jerk and opportunist policies of ethical foreign policy, the liberal academics address the same problem through a more ambitious solution of politically engineering the transformation of the passive (non-)voter into a morally responsible citizen.

The concern of many leading liberal commentators, like Mary Kaldor, Michael Ignatieff and David Rieff, is not so much with legitimising new forms of international regulation, but with the moral conception of society itself and the social and political engineering required to create responsible citizens. Mary Kaldor's focus is on creating spaces of civil society and mechanisms of providing international support for 'zones of civility' as a barrier to violence in the inner cities of Western Europe and North America as well as Africa and the Balkans (1999b:11). Ignatieff and Rieff more self-consciously address the moralisation of domestic politics. Rieff argues that what is important about the human rights movement 'is an idea, rather than a practice' (2000a). The idea is the one of moral inclusion and moral responsibility. The advocates of human rights intervention see this as a public demonstration of the government's seriousness in addressing the concerns of moral community. Rieff, for example, stresses the importance of a 'new synthesis of values and interests' in US foreign policy to involve the public in 'a truly democratic debate' about the 'kind of world the United States wants ... and what it is willing to sacrifice ... to achieve its goals' (1999b). For this reason, wars of human rights protection cannot be too easy or the public will not take them seriously and they will not forge a new sense of moral community.

This is the essence of Michael Ignatieff's argument in *Virtual War* (2000b). Ignatieff supports Western intervention but is concerned

that without real risks and real casualties war will not have a transformative effect on the domestic electorate, it will have no more
impact than a TV war movie:

> [Citizens of Nato countries] were mobilized, not as combatants
> but as spectators. The war was a spectacle: it aroused emotions in
> the intense but shallow way that sports do. The events were as
> remote from their essential concerns as a football game ...
> commitment is intense but also shallow. (2000b:3–4)

Explicitly, he makes the point that waging war for values or ethics
with impunity is not good enough domestically: 'But if impunity is
required before values are defended, what exactly are values worth?'
(2000b:5) Unlike wars fought in the past, Ignatieff feels that human
rights interventions, like that in Kosovo, have failed to mobilise
society and offer people 'a moment of ecstatic moral communion
with fellow citizens' (2000b:186). David Rieff agrees that fighting
wars without risk does not civilise or moralise domestic society,
condemning 'the indifference with which the American and Western
European public lethargically assented to the Kosovo war, always
providing, that is, that there were no casualties on our side' (2000c).
Nicholas Wheeler suggests that 'the duty of moral guardianship
requires state leaders to spend treasure and shed blood in the name
of human solidarity' (1997:12). As Mary Kaldor argues, the key goal
is not merely intervention to protect human rights but the creation
of a moral community, which depends on 'whether it is acceptable
to sacrifice national lives for the sake of people far away'
(1999b:130). For both Rieff and Ignatieff, the opportunistic use of
human rights interventions abroad by Western governments is inau-
thentic and insincere and unlikely to achieve long-term gains in
binding society together on the basis of moral values.

The human rights discourse of ethical politics, whether taken up
by political engineering liberal academics and journalists or by
pragmatic governments, has little to do with addressing real
problems in the non-Western world and much to do with responses
to the fragmentation of the political framework domestically. It is in
the search for solutions to domestic problems of moral community
and institutional legitimacy that the dynamic behind the human
rights movement and ethical foreign policy must be located. The
irony is that, in seeking to address the problems of the political

sphere in this way, the human rights discourse can only further undermine political collectivity and social cohesion.

In the short-term, the moralisation of domestic politics can help shore up the credibility of governments whose traditional political constituency of support no longer exists. However, as considered in the previous chapters, this is only done through exaggerating the problems of the political domain abroad. In order to highlight the urgency of the liberal message of concern with domestic fragmentation or to highlight the government's mission to save democracy and human rights, in Africa or the Balkans, the political sphere in non-Western states is portrayed in alarmist terms of collapse, incompetence and social breakdown. The alarmist analysis of non-Western states and exaggerated fears of social breakdown and preoccupation with genocide and barbarism are necessary because the real problem cannot be openly addressed. The more sensitive commentators are to the question of political dislocation domestically the less willing they are to openly confront it. Governments confront the problem of their lack of legitimacy by exaggerating the legitimacy problems of peripheral or pariah states. Liberal commentators work through their solutions of civilising the domestic electorate through moral education by exaggerating a concern for the education, democratisation and human rights awareness of the poor, abused and vulnerable in other parts of the world.

This process of addressing broader domestic concerns of social cohesion through minimising or deflecting the question could be seen in the discussion of the 'allegiance' of British Muslims during the war against Afghanistan. The British government's proposals for citizenship classes for new immigrants and the greatly exaggerated fears that British Muslims would support Osama bin Laden reflected the sensitivity of British authorities and media columnists to the loss of a collective vision or shared values holding British society together. This form of deflecting the question comfortingly presented the rest of British society as sharing a set of values around the conduct and aims of the war, at the same time as attempting to create a framework in which these assumed values could be articulated.

However, just as the debate on the loyalty of British Muslims further exposed the lack of shared values of 'Britishness', exaggerating the problems in the non-Western world is not and cannot be a long-term solution to the problems at home. In fact, the increasingly open cynicism with elections and governments abroad, and calls for a moral or ethical alternative, cannot strengthen or cohere government or society in the West. As considered in Chapter 7, the impact of the critique of the political sphere abroad has been to add to cynicism and disenchantment about politics and government. The more the emphasis is on morals and ethics as a way of escaping the problems of political coherence the more pressure there is on the political sphere and governments are increasingly forced on to the defensive. The Labour government's decision in September 2000 to back down on claims that ethical foreign policy could be consistently pursued demonstrates the short-term nature of the ethical solution and the dangers of failure being expressed in even less legitimacy for governing institutions (Dodd and MacAskill, 2000). The ideal of ethical foreign policy remains untarnished while the government appears compromised by its economic and trade concerns.

The human rights discourse will not be able to provide a political solution through the attempt to recast politics as non-political ethics. In fact, the retreat from politics and anti-political trajectory of the human rights discourse can only be destructive of the political sphere. This destructiveness can be demonstrated by returning to the three themes essential to the discourse, identified in the introductory chapter.

UNIVERSAL?

The universality of the human rights discourse is an idealistic one, more concerned with drawing out moral lessons than with transforming reality. The essence of human rights universalism is the construction of moral community. The aim is that of drawing out moral parables or lessons about the constancy of human nature rather than inspiring change on a global level. The universal 'human wrongs' at the centre of the discourse are essentially timeless wrongs, linked through the rubric of human rights abuse, which stand outside any social, economic or political context and could be applied to the ethnic cleansing of Native Americans in the nineteenth century, to the Nazi Holocaust or civil strife in Sierra Leone. As considered in Chapter 4, the view of human universality expressed by the discourse of human rights and human wrongs has more in common with religion than politics. The universality of human rights presupposes a victim in a fallen world, not a collective maker of history. This is a view of a passive collective human subject, the opposite of the active or creative subject of earlier secular universal approaches.

This human rights universalism is a narcissistic one, not concerned with external change to develop the rights and freedoms for people across the world, but with domestic angst about a fragmenting society. This is expressed well by Francesca Klug, Director of the Human Rights Act Research Unit, King's College, London, in the title of her book *Values for a Godless Age*, in which she argues: 'In a country where there is no one unifying religious or ethical worldview, human rights values have an as yet untapped potential to bind and cement a diverse society. (2000b:18) This is why Richard Rorty's perspective of promoting human rights through telling and retelling 'sentimental stories' is central to the human rights approach (1993:133). These sentimental stories seek to restore a bond of moral community by encouraging empathy with the vulnerable, in contrast to the fragmentary individualism of the modern age. Community is forged by giving 'recognition' to atrocities of the past, real or imagined (Burke, 2000). But along with sentimental stories the advocates of human rights also require demonstrations of community through public punishment of wrongdoing.

Agnes Heller, for example, argues that law should be no barrier to such public punishments of evil and human rights abuse. The punishment of evil is of prime importance for social consensus, 'but it is of secondary importance whether the surviving perpetrators of crimes are actually punished' (1993:172). For Heller 'we should tell and retell the story of those "carnal, bloody, and unnatural acts" ... perpetrated by the hand of evil, in the twentieth century' (1993:172–3). The universal human rights protections, involving 'naming and shaming' abusive states or bringing war criminals to trial, are not promoted merely for the benefit of vulnerable people in African or the Balkans. They provide a 'mission' for Western governments and also play an important role as a morality play to stress the need for moral community at home and provide the basis for moral citizenship education in inner-city schools.

As Michael Ignatieff astutely notes: 'Modern moral universalism is built upon the experience of a new kind of crime: the crime against humanity' (1998:19). Tom Campbell sees the creation of a moral community through the 'torture paradigm' which connects human rights with a social consensus on an unacceptable evil: 'The moral power of the human rights ideology derives from the consensus that there are certain things that people have done to each other in the course of human history which are atrocious and ought not to be repeated.' (1999:18) This attraction to abstract suffering humanity rather than real suffering humanity is reflected in, and confirmed by, the fact that the support for the discourse of human rights and ethical interventions abroad does not lie in the successful impact of human rights regulation in the international arena. There has been little concern expressed about the impact of human rights protectorates in Bosnia or Kosovo, or the long-term impact of Nato military action in Iraq or Serbia. In fact, the most striking aspect of the depth of feeling of human rights advocates and educationalists is the ease with which they shift from one issue to the next as the humanitarian bandwagon rolls on from Iraq to Somalia to Bosnia to Kosovo to East Timor to Sierra Leone to Afghanistan. The concern for particular human rights victims is not only fickle but also highly superficial. The key aspect these activists are concerned with is highlighting the barbarism of genocide and human wrongs and the need for moral lessons, they care little for an understanding of the problems in trouble-torn societies.

The superficiality of the universalism of human rights advocates was apparent in the expressions of concern over the Nato bombing campaign in Kosovo. The human rights camp was more critical of the fact that no Nato troops died in the conflict than the accidental 'collateral' killings of Serb and ethnic-Albanian civilians. The Nato powers could not be seen as morally just if it appeared that Nato strategy was prioritising the lives of Nato soldiers over Balkan civilians. The same sentiment made many human rights advocates wary of US reprisals against Afghanistan after the World Trade Center attack, because there was a danger of treating the people of Afghanistan as more expendable than Americans. This concern for universality of treatment is a degraded universalism. The concern is not for the real suffering and loss of life of either Nato pilots or Balkan refugees, nor of Manhattan office-workers or Afghan villagers, but for the preservation of an ideal universality of moral community demonstrated by sacrifice. This degraded and ideal universalism cares little for the real suffering caused by sanctions, civil conflict, acts of terror or aerial bombing. The suffering of people through war or oppression is appropriated as 'moral capital' to be used wisely by Western governments in the cause of moral cohesion (Shaw, 2001). In fact, the real suffering is seen as a necessary tableau on which to construct the ideal of moral community in the West.

EMPOWERING?

The key aspect of human rights doctrine, that leads to the celebration of empowerment, is its individual focus. Human rights are upheld as constituted independently of society itself. Claims based on human rights do not derive from social struggle or collective aspiration, but the desire of the individual. The human rights framework connects the atomised individual directly to the most powerful governing institutions at both international and domestic levels. The individual focus of empowerment has a broad resonance as it reflects the fact that people have been squeezed out of public life, as has been demonstrated by the declining numbers of people participating in political parties, trade unions, churches and all kinds of cultural organisations (Ryan, 2000). People's lives have, as a consequence, become much more individuated and privatised. However, this does not mean that we have a strengthened sense of ourselves. On the contrary, individuals have become less assertive about their own interests (Heartfield, 1996). Today's individualism is a weakened sense of self that is more cautious, vulnerable and self-effacing than before.

The attractiveness of human rights, and the reason the discourse fits the wider Third Way concerns of Western governments, is that in distinction to political rights, human rights are as much about duties as freedoms. This is a return to pre-Enlightenment ideas of rights. Conservative theorist Leo Strauss fully recognised that 'the pre-modern natural law doctrines taught the duties of man', whereas modern liberal rights theory 'regards the fundamental political fact of rights, as distinguished from duties, of man' (cited in Pennock, 1981:1). As Francesca Klug points out, the impact of the Human Rights Act in Britain should not be confused with the libertarianism of bills of rights of an earlier era. The focus on freedoms in the US Bill of Rights, in its uncompromising defence of gun ownership and unbridled free expression, is very different from the balance of duties and rights of modern rights regulation (1997). Far from increasing freedom, the emphasis on the protection of the individual and the balancing of rights and duties would mean that it would be a mistake to declare that the government has ceded power to the people through granting the protection of human rights (Klug, 2000a; see also 2000b:124).

The form of individual empowerment offered by the human rights framework can only be a vacuous and hollow one. If human beings are conceived merely as passive individuals or victims then the focus of the human rights discourse is to continually look beyond society for solutions. As considered in Chapter 7, the empowerment of the human rights framework leaves the question of social power untouched. The universal right is to have one's voice heard in a plea before judges or human rights advocates. These rights are protected, not through the political process of collective decision-making, but by legal edict. The defence of rights is disassociated from any collective rights exercised through the political process. Empowerment without political autonomy or collective engagement can only enforce the status quo. In the name of the human rights victim, it is the enlightened elites who are empowered with the final power of decision.

This is illustrated in the human rights approach of empowering individuals through the campaigning work of NGOs. Mary Kaldor, one of the most prominent advocates of NGO politics, argues that 'the role of NGOs is not to be representative but to raise awareness', adding that the 'appeal is to moral conscience', not to political majorities (2001). These 'moral' claims are then adjudicated by the authorities. Similarly, Johan Galtung gives support to this form of empowerment, which he terms 'democracy by articulation, not by representation' (2000:155). These new forms of NGO, civil society or 'Third Sector' involvement in non-representative 'democracy' seek to legitimise policy-making processes restricted to select elite advocates.

Geoffrey Robertson demonstrates the narrow institutionalisation of the political process in his discussion of the empowering nature of an international court which could deal with economic abuses of human rights:

> Should one be established, it would need the power to make the state of which its supplicants are nationals a party to the action, in order that its government could be given directions on how to change its present policies so as better to satisfy the basic needs of its citizens. Whether this would be hailed as a sensible step in global governance or as human rights imperialism is beside the point, since it would empower those most affected by poverty, transforming them from passive recipients of aid into plaintiffs who had obtained their due by asserting before the international community their human right to a remedy for the hopelessness of their collective life. (1999:150)

In this scenario, the individual is empowered, but not through the political process in which he or she can participate as an equal. In fact, equality and accountability are further eroded through international edicts on policy-making. The individual is empowered through the legal process, through assuming the status of plaintiff and having a direct connection to the adjudicative body. This illustrates how the implementation and enforcement of human rights, through the expansion of international and domestic law, reflects and institutionalises a diminished degree of political involvement. Obrad Savic, of the Belgrade Circle NGO, expresses this perspective clearly: 'Only in the courtroom and in the language of law are rights defended and represented as the achievable rights of individuals.' (1999a) This perspective inevitably leads to the dismissal of the political sphere:

> This new scene ... had to constantly cleanse itself of political pollution ... In the flaring conflicts on many political fronts ... the civic option cautiously stood on the sidelines. It quietly took a depoliticized position from which it did not wish to offer attractive programmes or engaging solutions. (1999b:335–40)

Instead of taking arguments about rights into the public political arena, the liberal elite's disillusionment with ordinary people and the political process leads them to focus more on the empowered individual, taking their case to the judge who will listen and decide. In reality, the individual is not empowered through playing the role of supplicant to the human rights judges and tribunals or international institutions. Far from challenging the individual isolation and passivity of our atomised societies, human rights regulation can only institutionalise these divisions.

Criticism of human rights regulation cannot stop at the critique of the consequences of particular forms of regulation which treat people as less capable of collective decision-making. It is also necessary to draw out that these critiques of democracy and egalitarianism can do little to empower the subject or challenge the trend towards social fragmentation. Social links cannot be rebuilt and injustice cannot be prevented or ameliorated by institutionalising the passivity and atomisation of the political individual. On the contrary, the less opportunities there are for collective engagement in the political process the more atomised society will become, as law is seen to replace politics as the vehicle for articulating needs in the public setting. The concerns over 'litigation society', as social clashes, from neighbour disputes to disagreements over school catchment areas, are taken up in the courts, are a reflection of the decline of the political sphere and the desire to rearticulate needs from an individual rather than a collective perspective. The advocates of human rights have not addressed the disillusionment and separation of people from politics, but through their critique of the principles of mass democracy have theorised this withdrawal and institutionalised the lack of public discussion and participation in policy-making.

HUMAN-CENTRED?

The human rights discourse is often proclaimed as a positive vision of the future. Any closer consideration of the motivation behind it reveals a rather different picture. Susan Mendus, for example, suggests that human rights should be supported 'as an expression, not of philosophical optimism, but of political pessimism':

> [T]hey imply no commitment to a thick theory of human nature, but serve rather as a warning against over-enthusiastic attempts to create solidarity. It may be said that the specification of those constraints will, in itself, imply a theory of human nature, and perhaps this is so. However, such a theory will be very 'thin' and will require only minimal agreement about what is evil, not any agreement about what constitutes 'the good for man' nor any commitment to the possibility of creating similarity or solidarity amongst diverse people. On this understanding, human rights are bulwarks against evil, borne out of an acknowledgement of difference, not harbingers of goods consequent upon a commitment to similarity, whether created or discovered. (1995:23)

The consensus on human rights is not based on a new-found optimism about the human subject, but the opposite. The President of the UN General Assembly argues that human rights regulation is necessary to tackle human rights abuses at source: 'The source lies ... in the hearts and minds of men, because those who ignore and flout the freedoms and rights of others are moved by hatred, selfishness, intolerance and prejudice.' (UN, 1998) For many commentators, '[i]t is evident, in the bloody twentieth century, that humans need to be restrained from their inner darkness' (Langlois, 1998:21). As Mendus notes, 'the political impetus for human rights comes from the recognition of evil as a permanent threat in the world' (1995:23–4). It is our new sensitivity to the degraded nature of humanity which is being celebrated as a positive step, not the capacity of collective humanity to achieve change and transform society.

The moral community constituted by the human rights discourse is a fearful and restrictive one. Most human rights books start with stories of genocide, mass rape, ethnic cleansing and torture, to emphasise the urgency of their cause. As Shute and Hurley state at the opening of their edited collection: 'You cannot just go back, whether comfortably or uncomfortably, to whatever you were doing; you feel that something must be done.' (1993:3) Oliver Ramsbotham and Tom Woodhouse's *Humanitarian Intervention in Contemporary Conflict* opens with a lengthy quote from Thomas Hobbes' *Leviathan*:

> Whatsoever therefore is consequent to a time of war, where every man is enemy to every man; the same is consequent to the time, wherein men live without other security ... In such condition, there is no place for industry ... no arts; no letters, no society; and which is worst of all, continual fear, and danger of violent death; and the life of man, solitary, poor, nasty, brutish, and short. (1996:vi)

Hobbes paints a fearful picture of society before the social contract, of a war of all against all, in which there are no social bonds. Of course, the view of humanity as pre-social individuals prior to the modern age was a myth. Nevertheless, this myth of non-socialised relations is a powerful one for human rights advocates, concerned with social fragmentation and the breakdown of political inclusion. The Second World War is never far from the thinking of human rights advocates. It is not the struggle against fascism that motivates them, as it did the Cold War Left, eager to rebuild a moral cause for uniting people and instigate collective change. For the advocates of human rights, it is the barbarity of the Nazi experience that holds their fascination. In the nightmare of the Holocaust they see a vision of moral breakdown. In the words of H. G. Wells' *On the Rights of Man*, a moral restatement of the Allied war aims, the Nazi experiences 'remind us all how little mankind has risen above the level of an exceptionally spiteful ape' (cited in G. Robertson, 1999:23).

Civil war and intercommunal strife are the leitmotifs for the 'human rights and human wrongs' distopian view of humanity. The barbarism of war is no longer presented as a result of social contradictions within society, which can no longer be contained. In the aftermath of the First World War, attention to a systemic understanding of the causes of war was shifted to scapegoating dominant elites, perceived to be fighting to preserve their wealth and status by sacrificing the lives of ordinary men and women, the 'cannon-fodder' of the trenches. In European and American literature, war was something imposed upon individuals by powerful social forces, so that 'most of them had been whirled into it like a cloud of dust and had simply found themselves caught up in the vast vortex, each one of them tossed about willy-nilly like a pea in a great sack' (Zweig, 1996:xi). In the debates following the Versailles settlement, the conflict was widely blamed on the militaristic outlook of the Prussian ruling aristocracy. Similarly, the horrors of the Second World War were widely blamed on the erratic mindset of Adolf Hitler.

In the years since the end of the Cold War, the academic fashion has swung in the opposite direction. War has been increasingly understood to be a product of the lack of civilisation of ordinary people. This is not to conceal the social roots of conflict, but to justify and represent humanity as much more incapable of political responsibility. Historians of the Second World War have increasingly focused on 'Hitler's Willing Executioners' (Goldhagen, 1996; Rees, 1997). For Francesca Klug: '[A]ll over supposedly democratic Europe, men and women ... collaborated in the deportation and even murder of millions of innocent men, women and children who had been their neighbours, colleagues or friends.' (2000b:96) In Africa and the Balkans, commentators have understood populations drawn into conflict as imbued with a 'culture of violence'. Human rights organisations have documented the drawing of populations into conflict or civil war as proof of widespread support for human rights abuses, rather than as indicative of the force of external pressures on weak states (see Chandler, 2000c).

As seen in Chapter 6, the understanding of war and conflict as moral and civilisational questions has led to the questioning of the capacity of people and their representatives in war-torn societies to be able to establish peace. Justifying universal human rights on the basis of universal wrongs challenges the justifications of self-government and autonomy on which democratic conceptions of rights depend. Both political rights and human rights are justified by distinct, though opposing, perceptions of the potential of the human subject. The human subject, which serves as justification for the human rights thesis, is a problem not a solution to the question of civilised government. The new 'human-centred' approach of the human rights framework replaces political or social analysis with a moral condemnation of humanity itself. In the words of Lévi-Strauss:

> Today, the greater peril for humanity does not come from the activities of a regime, a party, a group, or a class. It comes from humanity itself in its entirety; a humanity which reveals itself to be its own worst enemy and, alas, at the same time, also the worst enemy of the rest of creation. (Cited in Mészáros, 1989:54)

While 'humanity' may have taken central stage, the view of humanity is entirely negative. This is a direct critique of traditional justifications for state-based political and civil rights, which assume that human beings are capable of transforming society and of governing themselves.

It is this negative view of humanity which is the basis from which the egalitarian political gains of democracy and sovereignty are seen to be a fiction: 'The great play of sovereignty, with all its pomp and panoply, can now be seen for what it hides: a posturing troupe of human actors, who when off-stage are sometimes prone to rape the chorus.' (G. Robertson, 1999:347) This degraded view of the political sphere should not be seen as a 'West versus the Rest' discourse, exaggeratedly celebrating the virtues of domestic society (Hall, 1992). It is, in fact, a moral warning about the breakdown of community at home, as Daniel Thurer notes:

> We have to ask whether these cases ... are not the expression of a much deeper potential threat to our civilization. Faced with the collapse of law and order and political civilization, we are forced to ask whether such autistic aggression is a basic human instinct. (1999)

He concludes that our 'instinctual passions are stronger than reasonable interests' (1999). For many human rights commentators, the veneer of human civilisation is a thin one, both at home and abroad, easily exposed by the risk of collapse into genocide: '[P]utting out the inferno of genocide is in both the national and the global interest because failure to do so risks creating a contagion that will undermine the values of all civilized societies.' (Wheeler, 2000:303) The lesson of the newly commemorated Holocaust Memorial Day is not one of the unique historical circumstances of the Nazi experience but rather of the universal nature of the threat of genocide. The UK government's National Holocaust Memorial Day web-site recognises that:

> [T]he type of behaviour demonstrated in Nazi Germany was not a phenomenon limited either to Germany or to the mid-Twentieth Century ... Events in Cambodia, Bosnia Herzegovina, Rwanda and Kosovo, to name but a few, amply demonstrate the propensity of human beings to murder en masse. (HMD, 2001)

Will Hutton of the *Observer*, for example, highlighted twelfth- and thirteenth-century English policy towards the Jews, warning against British complacency: 'Tell your children that the English once mass-murdered Jews and made them wear Stars of David.' (2001) The lesson of the much hyped BBC series *Five Steps to Tyranny* which aired in December 2000 was that 'we are all capable of willingly committing atrocities' (Crossley, 2000). Colonel Bob Stewart, former commander of UN forces in Bosnia, suggested on the programme that 'given the right circumstances, similar human rights atrocities could be committed in Britain', while broadsheet features on the series concluded that 'everyday prejudice can quickly develop into full-blown oppression and even genocide' (Bright, 2000). It is for this reason that the British government claimed that the Holocaust Memorial Day was 'as much about the future as it is about the past' (HMD, 2001).

As the *Guardian* noted: 'This is not just about remembrance of the victims of a terrible atrocity; what lies behind [Holocaust Memorial Day] events is a hugely ambitious attempt to mould the country's political culture' (2001). The problem with the drive to forge a moral community at home through the focus on man's inhumanity to man is that it can only produce a disillusioned and negative view of our common humanity. This degraded view of humanity is perhaps summed up best by the leading advocate of human rights interventionism, Bernard Kouchner, who views 'man himself' as the 'worst enemy of humanitarianism' (1999).

CONCLUSION

The degraded vision of the social world, provided by the ethical discourse of human rights, serves, like any elite theory, to sustain the self-belief of the governing class (Malik, 1996:105). This book has sought to establish that while the framework of human rights can provide some short-term coherence for elites in major Western powers, this can only be a temporary device. The human rights discourse is good at destroying and undermining but cannot create stability or offer a constructive vision for the future.

The destructive dynamic of human rights interventionism is not because human rights policies are not fully applied or because international institutions are following some hidden Great Power agenda, but precisely because the human rights discourse itself is deeply corrosive of the political process. There is little positive vision on offer, merely the distrust of governments and people in non-Western society and cynicism about the actions of governments and international institutions in the West. It is a deeply negative perspective on human collective experience where governments can no longer be trusted not to engage in genocide against their own people and questions of state legitimacy and economic development and aid should be left to outside administrators rather than risk the ballot box.

If anything, the ethical discourse of human rights regulation is reminiscent of the *fin de siècle* pessimism at the close of the nineteenth century, when the attempt to regulate and cohere society was expressed in the elite ideology of race. Elite theory at the start of the last century was undermined through the rise of mass democracy and popular movements, which made overt elitism untenable. Today the return of elitism reflects the decline of mass politics and the retreat from the public sphere. The much emphasised universality of human rights is a hollow one that does not empower but denies people dignity and respect and degrades democracy. Instead of the 'new humanitarianism' we need a new humanism, a positive approach to problem solving that makes the most of people's capacity for autonomy and collective rational decision-making, a capacity denied by the proponents of ethical regulation from above.

9   Afterword

Writing three years after the publication of the first edition of *From Kosovo to Kabul,* the importance of the trends identified, outlining the rise of a corrosive ethical elitism, is undiminished. If anything, the discussion and critique which the book attempted to initiate are even more necessary in the aftermath of the 2003 war against Iraq, which highlighted the undermining of shared international legal norms and the problems of international interventions which are accountable to none but the intervening powers themselves. The war against Iraq and problems of post-conflict stability further assisted in the post-9/11 process of consolidating the interventionist framework of non-Western state-failure and Western state-building – bringing the regulatory discourse of human rights into the centre of justifications for post-9/11 security policies (see, for example, UN, 2004; SGESC, 2004; RAND, 2003).

Some authors have been keen to challenge the broad thesis presented in the previous chapters, which has detailed the destructive consequences of the human rights discourse in the international sphere, whether in the degradation of the universalist humanitarian framework, the undermining of UN Charter frameworks of international law and non-intervention, or the elitist attack on the principles of liberal democracy (for the most detailed critiques see, for example, Bellamy, 2002; Evans, 2005; and for a response Chandler, 2003a). However, these authors have essentially sought to defend the normative construction of the human rights discourse while disregarding the problems of transition from ideal norms to international practice – the subject of this book.

Rather than restate the arguments of the foregoing chapters, I intend instead to use this Afterword to take up some of the arguments of those who have been critical of humanitarian intervention and human rights justifications in the context of the shift towards US unilateralism and the war in Iraq. The essence of their critique is that talk of ethics and shared values is merely a smokescreen: international interventions can be fully explained through attention to the self-interested motives of power and economic gain. If this critique were correct, then the task would be to reveal the material interests driving conflict, not to focus on the framework of ethical justifications. I want to draw out below why popular scepticism regarding government claims of ethical, value-based policies of intervention and critiques of selfish interests of power can neither grasp the reasons for the shift away from the UN Charter framework of shared international legal norms nor challenge its destabilising consequences.

For many people, critical of the Iraq war and US unilateralism, it is easy to expose the human rights rhetoric and 'value-based' foreign policy claims of major Western powers. The claims to be 'liberating' the Iraqi people rang fairly hollow in the face of a war which sought formal legitimacy on the basis of unfounded allegations of weapons of mass destruction, was waged against legal opinion warning that a second UN Security Council resolution would be necessary, involved high-profile evidence of US and UK torture and mistreatment of prisoners and detainees in open breach of the Geneva Conventions, and was waged without any plans for the post-conflict situation. The Iraq adventure has been widely held to have discredited US claims of international legitimacy as the law-enforcer of the 'international community' as well as UK assertions of new ethical rights of intervention and, in the process, to have taken some of the wind from the sails of the advocates of a new age of liberal internationalism (Clark, 2003; Jacques, 2004).

The Iraq war has put the 'problem of America' at the centre of the concerns of those who would argue for a more internationalist order, where Western power could be projected as a Kantian force for good in the world. As I argue elsewhere (Chandler, 2004a), the Iraq war has seen many advocates of international human rights regimes see their rosy assumptions that 'right' had coincided with 'might' in the post-Cold War order come under question. The points I wish to make below seek to temper the optimism of those who believe that the economic and material aspirations of US-led Western powers have been exposed by opposition to the war in Iraq and that there is little need for critiques of ethical justifications. I will suggest here that the criticism of the US-led war has, in fact, done little to undermine support for new rights of Great Power 'responsibility' and the ethical projection Western power. There has been little critique of the undermining of the international framework of shared legal norms or of the rise of a new destabilising interventionist order.

The consensus of opposition to the Iraq war was not grounded on a critique of underlying claims of Western 'duty' or 'responsibility' to intervene in the cause of ethical universals, but rather on the form that the intervention has taken – US unilateralism. In the words of Mary Kaldor, the US appears to be the 'last nation-state', engaged in a single-handed 'attempt to re-impose international relations' and undermine the shift to Kantian universalism (Kaldor, 2003b:591; see also, Kaldor, 2003a; Sulyok, 2004; Wheeler, 2004). In fact, the central claims of the human rights discourse – of Great Power responsibility, the undermining of sovereign equality and the overturning of the central precepts of international law – have been taken up by academic commentators and international institutions and given even greater urgency since 9/11, not withstanding widespread cynicism and unease over the direction of US foreign policy under President George W. Bush. It is these three core areas which this Afterword will briefly reconsider and update below.

GREAT POWER RESPONSIBILITY

Despite the anti-war protests, the threat of military action is increasingly preferred to diplomacy when it comes to select 'rogue' or 'failed' states. The decision on whether to go to war – in cases where armed intervention is a matter of choice rather than necessity – has become a subject of debate around tactics rather than substance. Military action is no longer a policy of 'last resort'. Without a broader political framework of opposition to the ethical legitimacy of Great Power responsibility, opposition to Western aggression has focused on second order questions – Was there enough evidence? What alternative policies were possible? Was the planning adequate? Was the public consulted?

In the run-up to the UK General Election in May 2005, Prime Minister Tony Blair repeatedly argued that he had a tough tactical decision to make: 'Was it better to leave Saddam in power – or put him in prison?' (BBC, 2005a). There was little questioning of Blair's right to take such a decision regarding the status of another head of state. Leaving aside the fact that the 'regime change' decision was taken by Washington rather than London, Blair was, at least rhetorically, asserting the unilateral right which he claimed in his 1999 Chicago speech, justifying the Kosovo war under the banner of the 'Doctrine of the International Community': 'The most pressing foreign policy problem we face is to identify the circumstances in which we should get actively involved in other people's conflicts.' (UKFCO, 1999)

For Blair, as for George W. Bush, the UN, Nato, the EU, and a host of other agencies and NGOs, 'active involvement in other people's conflicts' is no longer seen as an intervention which undermines their rights, but rather as a duty or responsibility, enabling them to claim their rights. In this context 'intervention' has been normalised and (as discussed in Chapter 6 above) military intervention is no longer seen as undermining the founding principles of the UN framework based on non-intervention, the peaceful resolution of disputes, and sovereign equality. We have come a long way from the days when the UN's primary purpose was held to be ridding humanity of 'the scourge of war', and the Nuremberg trials (retrospectively) put the crime of aggressive war on the statute book.

There has been little challenge to Blair from anti-Iraq war protesters over his argument that he had the right to make such a decision or to treat war as a policy option of choice. As Matrix lawyer Philippe Sands argues, the debate was less about principles than the 'question of integrity and trust' (Sands, 2005:2). The focus was on whether Blair told the truth about the intelligence information or about the legal advice the UK government was given. The lack of challenge to the interventionist rights claimed by the UK Prime Minister was highlighted when the Conservative Party leader Michael Howard argued that, in his view, war for 'regime change' would have been justified. Blair stood accused for lying, and undermining the trust of the government, not for embarking on a war that lacked international support or judging that war was necessary (BBC, 2005b).

It is not just the two major parties in the UK who now argue that 'wars of choice' are a matter for the judgement of the government rather than a question of broader international norms. Many voters appeared to empathise with Blair's presentation of a personal dilemma over his decision whether to send in British troops and risk lives for a cause he, rightly or wrongly, considered to be worthwhile. The dilemmas of intervention or non-intervention; of providing assistance by humanitarian aid or by forceful and coercive measures; of leaving quickly after intervention or staying for the 'long haul', to reconstruct and rebuild, are repeatedly arising over every perceived international trouble-spot. There is little doubt that many people who protested against the Iraq war would be unlikely to take the same position if the decision was taken to send military forces on a human rights mission in the Congo region, or to address the Darfur crisis in the Sudan, or to protect human rights in Zimbabwe; particularly if US-leadership were to be downplayed. If anything, the Iraq debacle has strengthened the broader moral legitimacy of international interventions, military or otherwise, in circumstances where rights are held to be being abused.

As long as the anti-war movement focuses on the problem of America, the underlying consensus resurrecting a new imperial 'duty of care' on the basis of the human rights discourse of victims, abusers and international saviours will go unchallenged. Robert Kagan's 2003 book *Paradise and Power*, which aimed at justifying the US' claims to be above international law, has captured the European sense of a qualitative difference emerging after the end of the Clinton administration (Kagan, 2003). Kagan critiqued Europe's aversion to the use of (US) military power, accusing the Europeans of living in a 'post-modern' idyll – enjoying peace under the protection of US arms and then hypocritically condemning US unilateralism (2003:73). For Kagan, the US was condemned to remain excluded from the European world of Kantian cosmopolitanism and forced to violate Europe's post-modern norms. The US needed to be free of such constraints in order to police the international order and ensure the freedom and post-power tranquillity of Europe (2003:99).

This argument, which started out as a critique of Europe's weakness, has been turned into an asset for those who assert that Europe has a unique role in the promotion of human rights and ethical foreign policy. Robert Cooper, former Blair adviser and currently policy adviser to the EU High Representative for Common Foreign and Security Policy, Javier Solana, has vociferously argued that the European Union does, in fact, possess a Kantian or post-modern identity but that it should enjoy special rights and privileges of intervention specifically for this reason. These arguments for Europe's special privileges are made on the lines that Kagan has articulated and that relate to earlier debates which counterposed Europe's civilian or normative power to US military hegemony (see, for example, Duchêne, 1972; Bull, 1982; Whitman, 1998; Manners, 2002).

For example, Kaldor and Marlies Glasius suggest that the US' use of coercive force and alleged unilateral pursuit of national interest are counterproductive in today's international security context, making Europe's claims to a distinct ethical approach in this area a benefit rather than a weakness (Glasius and Kaldor, 2005:62–3). According to Cooper, members of the EU no longer pursue traditional foreign policies based on security interests or the contestation of national interests: 'foreign policy is the continuation of domestic concerns beyond national boundaries' (Cooper, 2003:53). Foreign policy, for the post-modern state, is about values and ethics and the 'good life', not power and self-interest. For Cooper, Kagan's argument about 'Paradise' is correct but his argument about 'Power' is contested. Europe's post-modern paradise can only be defended by the export of Europe's post-modern values to the 'modern' and 'pre-modern' parts of the world where self-interest or chaos are the dominant features. Because the EU does not pursue the export of order, democracy, human rights and good governance out of narrow, 'modernist' self-interest, and because the abuses of human rights occur in 'pre-modern' states, the rules of international law are no longer held to apply to the EU. Cooper argues:

> For the post-modern state there is, therefore, a difficulty. It needs to get used to the idea of double standards. Among themselves, the post-modern states operate on the basis of laws and open co-operative security. But, when dealing with more old-fashioned kinds of state outside the post-modern limits, Europeans need to revert to the rougher methods of an earlier era – force, pre-emptive attack, deception, whatever is necessary … In the jungle, one must use the laws of the jungle. (Cooper, 2003:61–2)

Here, Europe's alleged post-modernity justifies claims for extra-legal privileges of ethical intervention abroad, little different from the special pleading of the mission of US neo-conservatism. This argument of European uniqueness and the justness of the projection of European power abroad has been made by many liberal intellectuals. Jürgen Habermas famously argued in favour of the Kosovo war in his 1999 essay 'Bestialität und Humanität', published in *Die Zeit*, arguing that:

> Under the premise of human rights policy, this intervention is now to be seen as an armed peace-creating mission, which is authorised by the association of nations (admittedly without a UN mandate). According to this Western interpretation the Kosovo war could turn into a leap from the classical conception of international law for sovereign states towards the cosmopolitan law of a world civil society. (Habermas, 1999)

However, in opposition to US unilateralism, expressed in the National Security Strategy (US, 2002) and the 2003 war against Iraq, Habermas increasingly saw Europe rather than 'the West' as the vehicle for

Kantian cosmopolitanism in international affairs (see Anderson, 2005; Habermas, 2003). While the US neo-conservatives talk in the language of universal mission, Europe's intellectual elites have not been far behind. Zygmunt Bauman in his homage, *Europe: An Unfinished Adventure* (2004), argues that today Europe has 'a planetary mission to perform' and that unlike in the colonial past – when this sense of mission 'was not an unalloyed blessing' for her neighbours – today 'the interests of Europe and of the peoples outside its borders will not just coincide, but overlap' (Bauman, 2004:34–5). Perry Anderson analyses the illiberal consequences of liberal special pleading for rights of intervention in his analysis of the critique of sovereign equality in the work of Habermas, John Rawls and Norberto Bobbio (Anderson, 2005). While sometimes posed as supportive of US intervention and sometimes as hostile to it, European liberal thought has been consistently hostile to the pluralism of the UN Charter framework.

Probably the clearest claim of a unique European mission is one in which the discourse of human rights is clearly at the forefront. The Barcelona Report, *A Human Security Doctrine for Europe* (SGESC, 2004), commissioned by Javier Solana, follows the European Security Strategy agreed by the European Council at the end of 2003, which asserted that Europe has a responsibility for issues of global security because 'the first line of defence will often be abroad' (EU, 2003:7). European 'defence' is alleged to involve engagement and intervention across the world because, in today's globalised world, traditional narrow views of state security are redundant. The primary reason for the adoption of an activist and interventionist security policy is held to be a moral one; that, rather than privileging national interests – as the traditional policy of containment and defensive security practices would – the needs of common humanity should come first (SGESC, 2004:9–10). Apparently, European-led wars of intervention are to be fought primarily under the banner of human rights. Except, of course, as intimated in Chapter 6 above, these wars are no longer 'wars'. They are neither traditional peace-keeping operations, aimed at maintaining the peace, nor are they classic military interventions, aimed at defeating an enemy: 'peace comes before human rights in classic peace-keeping and victory comes before human rights in classic military intervention' (SGESC, 2004:11).

Human rights-led military interventions are held to be a new and unique contribution that the EU can make to 'global security'. The report also suggests that this renewed sense of moral purpose gained through external intervention has additional values in that it 'could turn out to be the most effective way to mobilise political support for the European project at this point' (SGESC, 2004:13). This would tend to reinforce the material (in Chapter 3) above, suggesting that a main dynamic behind value-based foreign policy activism lies in the search for purpose and legitimacy at home (see also a similar conclusion in Laïdi, 1998). According to the Eurobarometer reports in 2004, there was declining support within Europe for the EU, at around 48 percent, but around 65–70 percent European support for a common foreign security policy (Glasius and Kaldor, 2005:80). While disenchantment with Europe at the domestic level looks like stalling the European project, it is in the realm of foreign and security policy that the EU hopes its purpose and cohering values can be articulated.

Kagan amended his 'paradise and power' argument, out of concern that a potential US/Europe split would question the legitimacy of Western power, and made the point in a 2004 article in *Foreign Affairs* that Europe was, in fact, not so different from the US. Here, Kagan argued that European opposition to the US war on Iraq had less to do with any distinct culture or political approach than with European concern over being sidelined from international decision-making in a new US-dominated unipolar world order (Kagan, 2004:72). As he noted, with reference to the Kosovo war:

> [J]ust four years before the Iraq war – they [Europeans] did not seem to believe that international legitimacy resided exclusively with the Security Council, or in the UN Charter, or even in traditional principles of international law ... [Over Iraq] France, Germany, and other European nations were demanding that the United States adhere to an international legal standard they themselves had ignored, for sound moral and humanitarian reasons, a mere four years earlier. (Kagan, 2004:76–7)

In the UK, the same could be said regarding the 'principled' resignations of cabinet members Robin Cook and Clare Short, who were leading advocates of military intervention in 1999. It would be a major mistake to confuse tactical opposition to the Iraq war with any broader challenge to the new ideology of Great Power responsibility or to believe that it could be possible for European states to constrain rather than further encourage this shift away from the UN Charter framework of shared international legal norms.

UNEQUAL SOVEREIGNS

At the same time as the US and European powers claim new rights of intervention and empire-building, under the dispensation of human rights enforcement or the anti-terror war of 'good against evil', they are making the claim that other states – those deemed to be 'pre-modern', 'failed' or at risk of 'failing' – are no longer entitled to the full rights of sovereignty and non-intervention which were the sine qua non of the UN international order. Today, more so than when the first edition of this book came out in 2002, it is even clearer that we have entered an increasingly hierarchical world of stratified forms of sovereignty.

If the twentieth century marked the extension of an inclusive international order based on equal rights of sovereignty, the twenty-first appears to be one in which states are increasingly excluded from the rights and protections of international society. The UN Charter framework was based on pluralism: the acceptance that different political communities were entitled to reach their own agreement on how society should be organised. However, today's international order is increasingly organised on anti-pluralist values; states are being judged according to their protection and enforcement of human rights, their political make-up, and the level of social provision and wealth distribution (Jackson, 2000; Bain, 2003). States which are considered to be suspect or to be on the 'continuum of state failure' are liable to demands that international institutions or external powers intervene to assist and 'capacity-build' them (see, for example, Straw, 2002). Resistance to these demands may well provoke further international pressure and calls for sanctions or more coercive forms of intervention (ICISS, 2001a:23).

The influential International Commission on Intervention and State Sovereignty (ICISS) report, *The Responsibility to Protect*, in its supplementary volume spells out that, in its view, 'sovereignty then means accountability to two separate constituencies: internally, to one's own population; and internationally, to the community of responsible states' (ICISS, 2001b:11). This shift in 'accountability' clearly has major implications for sovereignty because a power which is 'accountable' to another, external, body clearly lacks sovereign authority. As the Commission co-chairs note, this shift changes 'the essence of sovereignty, from control to responsibility' (Evans and

Sahnoun, 2002:101). Sovereign rights to non-intervention are now deemed to be conditional if the state concerned is held not to be acting in a 'responsible' manner by external powers.

While equal rights of sovereignty have been undermined, states themselves have been at the centre of international security concerns. The hostility to sovereignty has rarely been reflected in critiques of the state form as such. This is because sovereignty and statehood are no longer seen to be codeterminous. Though state-building may be at the top of the international agenda, the states which are being capacity-built today have little relationship to the states of the past. Sovereignty has been partially suspended or delegated in states such as Cambodia, Bosnia, Kosovo, East Timor, Afghanistan and Iraq. Law and reality no longer coincide when considering the location of sovereign power and authority (Yannis, 2002:1049). Bosnia is formally a sovereign state and member of the United Nations, but where does sovereignty lie – with the Bosnian government or with the international High Representative? Kosovo is, at the time of writing, formally part of the state of Serbia-Montenegro, but where does sovereignty lie – with Belgrade, with the Kosovan government, or with the United Nations? Did the formal transfer of Iraqi sovereignty from the US-led Coalition Provisional Authority to an Iraqi government in June 2004 reflect any change in the real relations of authority?

While leading Western states are acquiring special privileges of hegemony, other states are losing the basic rights of sovereignty. This transformation, from sovereign equality to a stratified hierarchy of states, is clearly expressed in the enlargement policy practices of the European Union. The 2005 report by the International Commission on the Balkans (ICB), led by former Italian Prime Minister Giuliano Amato, recommends that the EU take over the direct management of the Balkan states rather than pursuing traditional external state-supporting policies and assistance. Integrating these states within the EU would avoid accusations that the EU is acting as a 'neo-colonial' power because, formally, the Balkan states would be equals (ICB, 2005:11). The report underestimates the extent of EU regulation and control in the region (see Chandler, 2003b; 2005) but highlights the development of states without meaningful sovereignty. The separation of statehood and sovereignty reflects the interventionist desire of the EU, in its attempts to regulate its relationship with the states of the region, yet at the same time to avoid responsibility and accountability for its policy prescriptions. For example, the EU's

Special Representative, Paddy Ashdown, who also holds the post of international High Representative, is effectively governing Bosnia. Despite this, the Bosnian representatives and voters are blamed for the fact that there is no political programme to take Bosnian society forward and overcome the legacy of the war (Chandler, 2005; ICB, 2005:37). EU state-building, which undermines the political process linking states with their societies, creates a situation where sovereign responsibility is continually displaced. A similar fate is planned for Kosovo with a suggested transition from the current UN-protectorate status to 'independence without full sovereignty': 'independence' frees the international state-builders from their formal accountability, while reserving to the EU the core regulatory powers of the UNMIK administration. The next stage for Kosovo is that of 'guided sovereignty', where EU leverage, without responsibility, would be directed through the accession negotiations, with the final stage being that of 'shared sovereignty', when Kosovo claims EU membership (ICB, 2005:18–23).

The International Commission report argues that states without full sovereignty are the solution to the failure of the Balkan state-building projects. Rather than state-building, the EU will be doing 'member-state building' in the region – creating states which never have to confront the destabilising difficulties of 'unconditional sovereignty' (see Paris, 2004). The Commission argues that the EU is forced into this role by circumstances and 'has become a reluctant state-builder', having no choice other than state integration if it is to avoid 'allowing a black hole to emerge on the European periphery' (ICB, 2005:30; 38). US liberal theorist Robert Keohane argues that the EU has been the leading experimental force in developing new approaches to post-conflict state management, demonstrating 'that regaining sovereignty need not be one's long-term objective' (Keohane, 2002:756). For Keohane, the EU can help the US avoid accountability for the outcomes of regime change – by blurring the location of sovereign power – suspending sovereignty while maintaining the fiction of state independence (see also Keohane, 2003):

> The European experience suggests that the Afghans should not necessarily seek a sovereign Afghanistan to fight over among themselves. Instead, Afghans and their friends should try to design institutions for Afghanistan that would enable external authorities to maintain order ... (Keohane, 2002:757)

The regulatory discourse of human rights, where democratic political institutions are distrusted and external oversight is facilitated but never held to account, comes across very clearly in the burgeoning literature in this area (see, for example, Zartman, 1995; Rotberg, 2004; Milliken, 2003; Chesterman, 2004; Fukuyama, 2004; Paris, 2004; Chesterman et al., 2005).

INTERNATIONAL LAW?

While US and European leaders may disagree on the grounding of special privileges to act on behalf of international society, there is agreement that the era of sovereign equality has come to an end. Martti Koskenniemi argues that the politicisation of the Security Council – its post-1989 activism on the grounds of 'justice' rather than merely the maintenance of 'order' – has greatly extended the role played by the 'Great Powers' at the expense of the General Assembly and the UN principle of sovereign equality under the law. Rather than policing international society, the Security Council had moved into the realm of law-making or the laying down of international norms, previously reliant upon a much wider state consensus (Koskenniemi, 1995).

In fact, it is now clear that the more the UN shifted its focus to concerns of 'international justice', the more the ethical realm has expanded at the expense of the desire for peace and the maintenance of shared international norms. The emasculation of international law, central to the analysis in the first edition, was not widely apparent at first because the UN Security Council was technically within the law in establishing its own reading of the Charter and in its increasingly *ad hoc* responses to international crises (although see the prescient warnings in Bull, 1966). To many, it appeared that UN activism in the 1990s could usher in a new era of international legal progress which would challenge and constrain, rather than enhance and formally institutionalise, relations of power (see Chapter 5).

Since the end of the Cold War, the US has had a predominant influence over the UN Security Council, leading the shift towards actions of 'coalitions of the willing' with only nominal accountability to the Security Council. The 1991 Gulf War against Iraq may have been formally authorised by the UN, but Resolution 678 gave a 'coalition of the willing', led by the US, a free hand to 'use all necessary means', enabling the 'member states co-operating with the Government of Kuwait' to establish their own terms of military engagement, thereby abandoning the UN principles of striving for the peaceful settlement of international disputes and collective UN oversight (Weston, 1991). This war may have been technically legal but was a clear subversion of the UN's official peace-making role. According to the then UN Secretary-General, Pérez de Cuéllar: 'The [Security] Coucil, which has authorised all this, is informed only after the military actions have taken place' (cited in Weston, 1991:533).

This established the pattern for UN-sanctioned military intervention in the 1990s, where the UN Security Council handed over command and control responsibilities to the member states which were prepared to volunteer their resources. The Pentagon drafted Resolution 794 authorising US command of the UNITAF forces in Somalia the following year and two years later Security Council Resolution 925 gave France operational command over UNAMIR forces in Rwanda, once the US had refused to support an expanded UN-led force. The US led the military invasion of Haiti the same year, again with the blessing of the UN Security Council. Not only was command and control of UN peace operations passed to individual states, but the decisions on whether to intervene or not were taken on the basis of Western states having an interest in volunteering, rather than the gravity of the situation or any equal treatment under international law. Simon Chesterman has cogently argued that the activism of the Security Council in the 1990s undermined rather than strengthened the framework of shared international legal norms:

> [T]he plasticity of the Council's mandate to take enforcement actions appears reducible primary to the political will of those states prepared to act. The danger here is that subjecting such an ostensibly legal process to the fickle winds of the political climate diminishes the normative power of international law. It is precisely the aim of an international rule of law to restrain the arbitrary exercise of power in international society; equally it should prevent the exercise of such power being legitimated by dubious legal processes. (Chesterman, 2001:161)

Adam Branch has highlighted the point that the ambiguous and *ad hoc* extensions of the UN Security Council mandates on the basis of 'unique' or 'exceptional' circumstances meant that 'vague, moral-humanitarian justifications for military interventions ... pre-empted the possibility of legal formalization of the regulation of the use of force'; instead entrenching 'a discourse establishing the sufficiency of such moral-humanitarian claims, to the exclusion of legal claims' (Branch, 2005:121). By the mid-1990s, the UN's role had been transformed from an institutional attempt to provide a collective security system towards one where open-ended resolutions 'authorised' unilateral military interventions which were then retrospectively validated (Chesterman, 2001:164–5). In these readings, the bypassing of the Security Council and formal break with UN Charter law with the 1999 Kosovo war was less a radical break than a logical consequence of the post-1989 shift towards unilateral military action legitimised on ethical or humanitarian grounds.

The developing consensus of Great Power responsibility, at the heart of international human rights frameworks, implicitly equated right with might in arguing that 'with great power went great responsibility' (since popularised by Stan Lee's Spiderman) (Jackson, 1998; ICISS, 2001a). The morality of this position is a highly elitist and inegalitarian one. As Robert Cooper argues, the new ethics of prevention and pre-emption are based on hierarchy rather than consensus:

> If everyone adopted a preventative doctrine the world could degenerate into chaos … A system in which preventive action is required will be stable only under the condition that it is dominated by a single power or a concert of powers. The doctrine of prevention therefore needs to be complemented by a doctrine of enduring strategic superiority – and this is, in fact, the main theme of the [2002] US National Security Strategy. (Cooper, 2003:64–5)

Gerry Simpson astutely argues that the rise of sovereign inequality means that international law can no longer take a universal form (Simpson, 2004:334–9). He argues that the rights of pre-emptive self-defence, claimed by the US, could never be acceded to India or Pakistan (2004:321). Sands supports this view of inequality, stating that it is difficult to imagine international lawyers arguing that Turkey or Iran had the right, claimed by the UK, to decide that Saddam was in breach of his obligations and then to decide unilaterally to use force (Sands, 2005:17). Cooper's insight is apposite: the new rights of intervention – whether cast in terms of a new right of humanitarian intervention or an extended right of self-defence, which includes the right of prevention or pre-emption – cannot be available to any but a select few. These are the rights of Great Power hegemony, not the rights of legal equality. Rights that are the preserve of an elite cannot be cast in the universal form of law but only in the particularist form of customary right or moral 'norms'. There is no more of a universal right of pre-emptive self-defence or of 'regime change', rights claimed by the US and UK over Iraq in 2003 (see Carty, 2005), than there is a universal right of humanitarian intervention, despite the assertions of the International Commission on Intervention and State Sovereignty.

The Iraq war has merely clarified the consequences of the human rights discourse in legitimising the dismantling of the UN Charter framework of shared international legal norms. The framework of the UN Charter principles of equal sovereignty, non-intervention and the peaceful resolution of international disputes are no more than universalist shells. To paraphrase Ken Booth (1991:542), beside the egg-box containing these shells, the global omelette which is cooking is one in which Great Powers have acquired new freedoms of military and regulatory intervention while weaker states have been denied the universal protections of international legal norms.

CONCLUSION

The implications of the discourse of human rights and international intervention, which marked the route from Kosovo to Kabul and beyond, can be seen more broadly as a corrosion of the UN framework. This process has developed through each international crisis since the end of the Cold War, from the first US-led war against Iraq in 1991 to the follow-up in 2003. The divisions and discrediting arising from the recent Iraq adventure will do little to mitigate the dangers of this breakdown of international order or the forces driving it.

This book has attempted to demonstrate that the drive behind human rights activism and international intervention has deeper roots than the needs of particular politicians or administrations and that it is problematic to seek to understand the ethical discourse of human rights as merely the attempt to legitimise acts of national economic interest or geo-political advantage. The discourse of human rights and intervention is not presented here as a mechanism of government rule and ideological control; neither do I focus on foreign policy as a practice of boundary-drawing between the constructed 'Self' and its 'Other' (see Campbell, 1998; Campbell and Dillon, 1993; Walker, 1997). There are no assertions of 'grand strategies' of power hidden behind the universalist rhetoric of intervention and regulation in the cause of human rights, democracy, capacity-building and empowerment. In fact, if anything, the opposite process is in play. It appears to be the lack of grand strategies and clear sense of policy mission which leads institutions, states and individuals to seek meaning through ethical intervention in the international sphere (see Chapter 3 and Chandler, 2004b).

Promoting the interests of the ethical 'Other' – the human rights victim – is a sign of the exhaustion of modern politics; an indication that political elites have given up on the project of taking society forward. The politics of progress was one of self-interest; without self-interest collective interests cannot be formed, as evidenced by the collective struggle for trade unions, for the extension of suffrage, for representation and for self-government. Today the exhaustion of politics is reflected in the difficulties which political elites have of projecting any idea of collective purpose, of a common collective interest of their citizens, encapsulated in an 'idea of the state' or the pursuit of national interests (see further Buzan, 1991). It is this breakdown of social interconnection that explains why the post-modern 'Other' has taken over from the 'Self' as the subject of the political.

For the advocates of post-modern and post-national ethics the displacement of the 'Self' by the 'Other' is seen as a step forward to a new cosmopolitan Kantian order (see, for example, Falk, 1995; Archibugi and Held, 1995; Linklater, 1998; Dillon, 1996; Habermas, 1999; 2001; Ranciere, 2004). This book has attempted to demonstrate that the view of the social at the centre of this ethical and 'Other'-regarding discourse is a degraded one, incapable of overcoming social divisions or inequalities. The discourse of ethical intervention or human security cannot deliver its asserted aim of domesticating the international sphere – of ameliorating injustices or of enhancing international legal frameworks of protection. This is not due to the influence of economic interests or hidden agendas of power, but because there is a corrosive narcissism at the heart of its claims which undermines universal pretensions and institutes division rather than overcoming boundaries.

Just to briefly reinforce this point: ethical foreign policy is neither ethical nor a genuine foreign policy. The linguistic terms of ethical foreign policy or intervention to 'uphold values' speak immediately of a defensiveness and illegitimacy. A genuinely ethical or value-based foreign policy would not need to speak so artificially. Before 'ethical foreign policy' no government believed its policies were 'un-ethical': it was assumed that the promotion of national interests, or geo-strategic interests, or economic aggrandisement, or the balance of power, was not unethical but, in fact, entirely legitimate. There was no division between an ethical understanding of government actions and a political one – the political justification was enough to legitimise the policy practice. Today this is no longer the case, and it appears that ethics are called on to cast political actors in a legitimate light. The outcome can only be the undermining of the coherence of both ethical and political claims. If interventionist foreign policies were really based on the promotion of shared common values, this would be so obvious that there would be no need to justify intervention as value-based. At every turn, the language of the discourse gives off an air of insincerity and inconsistency.

I wish to suggest that, rather than being genuinely 'Other'-regarding, the discourse of ethical or value-based foreign policy refers to policy-making that is, perhaps counter-intuitively, essentially narcissistic or self-regarding. Value-led foreign policy is the area of foreign policy-making where governments have the luxury to really focus upon themselves and their 'narratives' or 'identities' (see Oborne, 2005). This is, in effect, the only area of government activity where it is hoped that a sense of shared values or the sense of purpose and mission, lacking domestically, can be inculcated. This narcissistic drive behind the ethical projection of power means that ethical practice can usually have a freer reign where there are fewer genuine interests and responsibilities at stake; where there is less concern about the consequences on the ground. Far from being a narrow self-interested projection of power, it seems that value-led interventions are often driven by a lack of any clear interests. This makes the projection of power abroad an arbitrary and *ad hoc* one, driven by contingencies rather than grand plans (see further Chapter 3).

Because the drive to place 'Others' at the centre of politics is driven by a collapse of political community, rather than an extension of our sense of common humanity, human rights-based foreign policy is, in fact, an anti-foreign policy. The anti-foreign policy of 'values' tends to sideline regional experts who have worked in foreign office departments for years and know the languages and the context – in the same way as military and intelligence expertise is disregarded (so clearly evidenced over Iraq). While the specialists often warn against moralistic, black and white or good against evil, portrayals of social and political crises, it is central government coteries of advisors and policy-planners which tend to force the issue (see Kampfner, 2004). Human security interventions tend to marginalise traditional foreign policy concerns such as international or regional stability, and pay little regard to the post-conflict consequences of 'ethical' activism (regarding the 'war on terror' see Record, 2003).

The narcissistic nature of the human rights discourse has played a major role in undermining the UN Charter framework of reciprocal relations of sovereignty and the peaceful resolution of international disputes. International relations have, since at least the 1815 Congress of Vienna, been based on shared legal norms that have been founded on relations of formal legal equality tempered by the realities of power inequalities (Simpson, 2004). Today's crisis of international law and of established frameworks of international political processes is not a necessary product of the shift from a bipolar towards a unipolar world. In fact, the inability of the world's remaining superpower to translate military and material superiority into the creation of stable institutions of international political regulation is, as Christian Reus-Smit notes (2004:2), 'a central paradox of our time'.

One of the major factors undermining the creation of a new international consensus has been the prevailing trend for the foreign policy discourse of values to moralise and distort international questions. Responses to international issues are less likely to promote consensual practices, which seek to minimise conflict and promote stability, if leading states are narcissistically engaged in the search for cohering values and domestic meaning (see Laïdi, 1998; and on the meaning of 9/11, Baudrillard, 2003). The narcissistic and inward-looking drive behind value-based policy-making tends to undermine the most basic levels of international co-operation. This is why the rise of 'ethics' in the international sphere has been a profoundly destabilising one; dangerously undermining any shared basis of norms and agreed mechanisms for managing inter-state relations.

References and
Select Bibliography

Addo, M. K. (1998) 'The New Human Rights Law', *Bracton Law Journal*, Vol. 30, pp. 33–42.

AFP (1999) 'Allies Told Peace Dividend is Over, More Defense Spending Needed', 2 December.

AFP (2001) 'NGOs Condemn "Confusion" Between Military and Humanitarian Goals', 8 October.

Aglionby, J. (2000) 'Bungled UN Aid Operation Slows East Timor's Recovery', *Guardian*, 30 August.

Allott, P. (1990) *Eunomia: New Order for a New World* (Oxford: Oxford University Press).

Allott, P. (1999) 'The Concept of International Law', *European Journal of International Law*, Vol. 10, pp. 31–50.

Anderson, P. (2005) 'Arms and Rights: Rawls, Habermas and Bobbio in an Age of War', *New Left Review*, No. 31, pp. 5–40.

Annan, K. (1997a) 'Strengthening United Nations Action in the Field of Human Rights: Prospects and Priorities', *Harvard Human Rights Journal*, Vol. 10, pp. 1–9.

Annan, K. (1997b) 'Advocating for an International Criminal Court', *Fordham International Law Journal*, Vol. 21, No. 2, pp. 363–6.

Annan, K. (1998) 'From the Secretary-General', *UN Chronicle*, Vol. 35, No. 3, pp. 2–3.

Anonymous (1996) 'Human Rights in Peace Negotiations', *Human Rights Quarterly*, Vol. 18, pp. 249–58.

Apodaca, C. and Stohl, M. (1999) 'United States Human Rights Policy and Foreign Assistance', *International Studies Quarterly*, Vol. 43, No. 1, pp. 185–98.

Appleton, J. (2001) 'Lifting the Veil', *Spiked*, 30 October. Available from: <http://www.spiked-online.com/Articles/00000002D2A0.htm>.

Arbour, L. (1997) 'Progress and Challenges in International Criminal Justice', *Fordham International Law Journal*, Vol. 21, No. 2, pp. 531–40.

Archibugi, D. (1998) 'Principles of Cosmopolitan Democracy', in D. Archibugi, D. Held and M. Köhler (eds) *Re-imagining Political Community: Studies in Cosmopolitan Democracy* (Cambridge: Polity Press), pp. 198–228.

Archibugi, D. (2000) 'Cosmopolitical Democracy', *New Left Review*, Vol. 2, No. 4, pp. 137–50.

Archibugi, D. and Held, D. (1995) *Cosmopolitan Democracy: An Agenda for a New World Order* (Cambridge: Polity Press).

Arendt, H. (1979) *The Origins of Totalitarianism* (new edn) (New York: Harvest).

Armstrong, J. D. (1986) 'Non-governmental Organizations', in R. J. Vincent (ed.) *Foreign Policy and Human Rights: Issues and Responses* (Cambridge: Royal Institute of International Affairs/Cambridge University Press), pp. 243–60.

Aspeslagh, R. and Burns, R. J. (1996) 'Approaching Peace Through Education: Background, Concepts and Theoretical Issues', in R. J. Burns and R. Aspeslagh (eds) *Three Decades of Peace Education Around the World: An Anthology* (New York: Garland Publishing), pp. 25–69.

Astier, H. (2000) 'Rights of the Despised: We Ignore the Rights of War Crime Suspects at Our Peril', *American Prospect*, Vol. 11, No. 18, 14 August. Available from: <http://www.americanprospect.com/archives/V11–18/astier-h.html>.

Bain, W. (2003) *Between Anarchy and Society: Trusteeship and the Obligations of Power* (Oxford: Oxford University Press).

Bamforth, M. (1998) 'Parliamentary Sovereignty and the Human Rights Act', *Public Law*, Winter, pp. 572–82.

Barkin, J. S. (1998) 'The Evolution of the Constitution of Sovereignty and the Emergence of Human Rights Norms', *Millennium*, Vol. 27, No. 2, pp. 229–52.

Barrett, D. (2000) '"Rape a Weapon" in Bosnia, Fed Jury Here is Told', *New York Post*, 10 August.

Baudrillard, J. (2003) *The Spirit of Terrorism* (London: Verso).

Bauman, Z. (2004) *Europe: An Unfinished Adventure* (Cambridge: Polity Press).

Baxter, S. (2001) 'Hope Grows Out of the Ash Urns at Ground Zero', *Sunday Times*, 28 October.

BBC (1998) '"Two Cheers" for Ethical Foreign Policy', *BBC Online Network*, 21 December. Available from: <http://news.bbc.co.uk>.

BBC (2005a) 'Blair Tries to Move On from Iraq', *BBC News*, 28 April. Available from: <http://news.bbc.co.uk/1/hi/uk_politics/vote_2005/frontpage/4496029.stm>.

BBC (2005b) 'Howard Stance on Iraq "Unlawful"', *BBC News*, 29 April. Available from: <http://news.bbc.co.uk/1/hi/uk_politics/vote_2005/frontpage/4497777.stm>.

Beaumont, P. (1999) 'Our Global Roll of Dishonour', *Observer*, 24 October.

Beetham, D. (1996) 'Theorising Democracy and Local Government', in D. King and G. Stoker (eds) *Rethinking Local Democracy* (London: Macmillan), pp. 28–49.

Beetham, D. (1999) *Democracy and Human Rights* (Cambridge: Polity Press).

Bellamy, A. (2002) 'What's so Wrong with Human Rights?: Review of *From Kosovo to Kabul*', *International Journal of Human Rights*, Vol. 6, No. 4, pp. 121–33.

Bettati, M. and Kouchner, B. (1987) *Le Devoir d'ingérence* (Paris: Denöel).

Bianchi, A. (1999) 'Immunity Versus Human Rights: The Pinochet Case', *European Journal of International Law*, Vol. 10, pp. 237–77.

Black, C. (1999a) 'An Impartial Tribunal?', June. Available from: <http://www.swans.com/library/art5/zig013.htm>.

Black, C. (1999b) 'An Impartial Tribunal, Really?', November. Available from: <http://www.swans.com/library/art5/zig036.htm>.

Black, C. and Herman, E. (2000) 'Louise Arbour: Unindicted War Criminal'. Available from: <http://emperors-clothes.com/articles/herman/louise.htm>.

Blair, T. (1999a) 'It is Simply the Right Thing to Do', *Guardian*, 27 March.

Blair, T. (1999b) 'A New Generation Draws the Line', *Newsweek*, 19 April.

Blair, T. (1999c) 'I Have No Doubt at All That We Will Win ... This is a Battle Over the Values of Civilisation', interview, *Observer*, 16 May.

Blair, T. (1999d) 'A New Moral Crusade', *Newsweek*, 14 June.

Blair, T. (2001a) 'Full Text of Tony Blair's Speech to the House of Commons, 14 September 2001', *Guardian Unlimited*, 14 September. Available from: <http://www.guardian.co.uk/Archive/Article/0,4273,4257319,00.html>.

Blair, T. (2001b) 'Full Text of Tony Blair's Speech to the Labour Party Conference, 2 October 2001', *Guardian*, 3 October.

Blair, T. (2001c) 'Extracts of Speech Given by Tony Blair to the Welsh Assembly, 30 October', *Guardian*, 31 October.

Bloomer, P. (1999) 'The Chronicle Interview', *UN Chronicle*, Vol. 36, No. 2, pp. 18–21.

Bobbio, N. (1996) *The Age of Rights* (Cambridge: Polity Press).

Boerefijn, I. (1995) 'Towards a Strong System of Supervision: The Human Rights Committee's Role in Reforming the Reporting Procedure under Article 40 of the Covenant on Civil and Political Rights', *Human Rights Quarterly*, Vol. 17, pp. 766–93.

Bolton, J. R. (1999) 'The Global Prosecutors: Hunting War Criminals in the Name of Utopia', *Foreign Affairs*, Vol. 78, No. 1, pp. 157–64.

Bond, M. S. (2000) 'Special Report: The Backlash Against NGOs', *Prospect*, April, pp. 52–5.

Boot, M. (2000a) 'Paving the Road to Hell (Book Review): The Failure of UN Peacekeeping', *Foreign Affairs*, Vol. 79, No. 2, pp. 143–8.

Boot, M. (2000b) 'When "Justice" and "Peace" Don't Mix', *Wall Street Journal*, 2 October.

Booth, K. (1991) 'Security in Anarchy: Utopian Realism in Theory and Practice', *International Affairs*, Vol. 67, No. 3, pp. 527–45.

Booth, K. (1995) 'Human Wrongs and International Relations', *International Affairs*, Vol. 71, No. 1, pp. 103–26.

Booth, K. (1999) 'Three Tyrannies', in T. Dunne and N. J. Wheeler (eds) *Human Rights in Global Politics* (Cambridge: Cambridge University Press), pp. 31–70.

Borger, J., Norton-Taylor, R. and Wintour, P. (2001) 'Air Strikes Delayed as Allies Express Doubts', *Guardian*, 4 October.

Borger, J. (2001) 'Rumsfeld Blames Regime for Civilian Deaths', *Guardian*, 16 October.

Bosco, D. (2000) 'Dictators in the Dock', *American Prospect*, 14 August.

Bowring, B. (1996) 'The War Crimes Tribunals – Legitimate Justice, or a Miscarriage in the Making?', *Socialist Lawyer*, Winter, pp. 18–19.

Boyle, F. A. (1996) 'Negating Human Rights in Peace Negotiations', *Human Rights Quarterly*, Vol. 18, pp. 515–16.

Boyle, F. A. (2001) 'Transcript of Speech Delivered by Prof. Francis A. Boyle at Illinois Disciples Foundation, 18 October 2001'. Available from: <http://listserv.acsu.buffalo.edu/archives/twatch-l.html>.

Boyle, K. (1995) 'Stock-Taking on Human Rights: The World Conference on Human Rights, Vienna 1993', *Political Studies*, Vol. 43, Special Issue, pp. 79–95.

Bradlow, D. and Grossman, C. (1995) 'Limited Mandates and Intertwined Problems: A New Challenge for the World Bank and the IMF', *Human Rights Quarterly*, Vol. 17, pp. 411–42.

Branch, B. (2005) 'American Morality over International Law: Origins in UN Military Interventions, 1991–1995', *Constellations*, Vol. 12, No. 1, pp. 103–27.

Branigan, T. (2001a) 'Murders in Burundi "War Crimes" Says Dead Aid Worker's Family', *Guardian*, 2 January.

Branigan, T. (2001b) 'Al-Qaida is Winning War, Allies Warned', *Guardian*, 31 October.

Brett, R. (1993) 'The Human Dimension of the CSCE and the CSCE Response to Minorities', in M. R. Lucas (ed.) *The CSCE in the 1990s: Constructing European Security and Cooperation* (Baden-Baden: Nomos Verlagsgesellschaft), pp. 143–60.

Brett, R. (1998) 'Non-Governmental Human Rights Organizations and International Humanitarian Law', *International Review of the Red Cross*, No. 324, pp. 531–6.

Bright, M. (2000) 'How Evil Lurks in All Our Minds', *Observer*, 17 December.

Brown, J. (2000) '"Global Justice" May Rewrite US Law Books', *Christian Science Monitor*, 10 August.

Buergenthal, T. (1997) 'The Normative and Institutional Evolution of International Human Rights', *Human Rights Quarterly*, Vol. 19, pp. 703–23.

Bugnion, F. (2000) 'The Geneva Convention of 12 August 1949: From the 1949 Diplomatic Conference to the Dawn of the New Millennium', *International Affairs*, Vol. 76, No. 1, pp. 41–50.

Bull, H. (1966) 'The Grotian Conception of International Society', in H. Butterfield and M. Wight (eds) *Diplomatic Investigations: Essays in the Theory of International Relations* (London: George Allen & Unwin).

Bull, H. (1982) 'Civilian Power Europe: A Contradiction in Terms?', *Journal of Common Market Studies*, Vol. 21, No. 2, pp. 149–64.

Bull, H. (1995) *The Anarchical Society: A Study of Order in World Politics* (2nd edn) (London: Macmillan).

Bunting, M. (2001) 'This is Our Vietnam', *Guardian*, 22 October.

Burgerman, S. D. (1998) 'Mobilizing Principles: The Role of Transnational Activists in Promoting Human Rights Principles', *Human Rights Quarterly*, Vol. 20, pp. 905–23.

Burke, J. (2000) 'England Accused of Ethnic Cleansing … 700 Years Ago', *Observer*, 1 October.

Burke, J. (2001) 'Why This War Will Not Work', *Observer*, 21 October.

Bush, G. (2001a) 'Full Text of George Bush's Speech to the US Congress, 20 September 2001', *Guardian Unlimited*, 21 September. Available from: <http://www.guardian.co.uk/Archive/Article/0,4273,4261868,00.html>.

Bush, G. (2001b) 'Full Text of President George Bush's Address Announcing the Start of "Operation Enduring Freedom", 7 October 2001'. Available from: <http://news.independent.co.uk>.

Buzan, B. (1991) *People, States and Fear* (2nd edn) (Harlow: Pearson).

Buzan, B. and Held, D. (2000) 'Realism vs. Cosmopolitanism'. Available from: <www.polity.co.uk/global/realism.htm>.

Byers, M. (1999) 'Kosovo: An Illegal Intervention', *Counsel*, August, pp. 16–18.

Camilleri, J. and Falk, J. (1992) *The End of Sovereignty?: The Politics of a Shrinking and Fragmenting World* (Cheltenham: Edward Elgar Publishing).

Campbell, D. (1998) *Writing Security: United States Foreign Policy and the Politics of Identity* (2nd edn) (Minneapolis: University of Minnesota Press).

Campbell, D. and Dillon, M. (1993) 'Postface: The Political and the Ethical', in D. Campbell and M. Dillon (eds) *The Political Subject of Violence* (Manchester: Manchester University Press).

Campbell, T. (1999) 'Human Rights: A Culture of Controversy', *Journal of Law and Society*, Vol. 26, No. 1, pp. 6–26.

Carothers, T. (1996) *Assessing Democracy Assistance: The Case of Romania* (Washington, DC: Carnegie Foundation).

Carroll, R. *et al.* (2000) 'West Split on New Push to get Milosevic', *Guardian*, 9 October.

Carty, A. (2005) 'The Iraq Invasion as a Recent United Kingdom "Contribution to International Law"', *European Journal of International Law*, Vol. 16, No. 1, pp. 143–51.

Casey, J. (1999) 'We, Not the Serbs, are of the Middle Ages', *The Times*, 1 April.

Cassese, A. (1998) 'Reflections on International Criminal Justice', *Modern Law Review*, Vol. 61, No. 1, pp. 1–10.

Cassese, A. (1999) '*Ex Iniuria Ius Oritur*: Are We Moving towards International Legitimation of Forcible Humanitarian Countermeasures in the World Community?', *European Journal of International Law*, Vol. 10, pp. 23–30.

CGG (1995) *Our Global Neighbourhood*: The Report of the Commission on Global Governance (Oxford: Oxford University Press).

Chandler, D. (1997) 'Globalisation and Minority Rights: How Ethical Foreign Policy Recreates the East–West Divide', *Labour Focus on Eastern Europe*, No. 58, pp. 15–34.

Chandler, D. (1998) 'Democratization in Bosnia: The Limits of Civil Society Building Strategies', *Democratization*, Vol. 5, No. 4, pp. 78–102.

Chandler, D. (1999) 'The OSCE and the Internationalisation of National Minority Rights', in K. Cordell (ed.) *Ethnicity and Democratisation in the New Europe* (London: Routledge), pp. 61–73.

Chandler, D. (2000a) *Bosnia: Faking Democracy After Dayton* (2nd edn) (London: Pluto Press).

Chandler, D. (2000b) 'Bosnia: Profile of a Nato Protectorate', in T. Ali (ed.) *Masters of the Universe: Nato's Balkan Crusade* (London: Verso), pp. 271–84.

Chandler, D. (2000c) 'Western Intervention and the Disintegration of Yugoslavia, 1989–1999', in P. Hammond and E. S. Herman (eds) *Degraded Capability: The Media and the Kosovo Crisis* (London: Pluto Press), pp. 19–30.

Chandler, D. (2003a) 'Expanding the Research Agenda of Human Rights: Reply to Bellamy', *International Journal of Human Rights*, Vol. 7, No. 1, 2003, pp. 128–40.

Chandler, D. (2003b) 'Governance: The Unequal Partnership' in W. van Meurs (ed.) *South Eastern Europe: Weak States and Strong International Support, Prospects and Risks Beyond EU Enlargement*, Vol. 2 (Opladen: Leske and Budrich/Bertelsmann Foundation), pp. 79–98.

Chandler, D. (2004a) *Constructing Global Civil Society: Morality and Power in International Relations* (Basingstoke: Palgrave).

Chandler, D. (2004b) 'Building Global Civil Society "From Below"?', *Millennium: Journal of International Studies*, Vol. 33, No. 2, pp. 313–39.

Chandler, D. (2005) 'Bosnia: From Dayton to Europe', in D. Chandler (ed.) *Peace without Politics? Ten Years of International State-Building in Bosnia* (London: Taylor & Francis).

Charney, J. I. (1999) 'Anticipatory Humanitarian Action in Kosovo', *American Journal of International Law*, Vol. 93, pp. 834–41.

Charnovitz, S. (1997) 'Two Centuries of Participation: NGOs and International Governance', *Michigan Journal of International Law*, Vol. 18, pp. 183–286.

Charvet, J. (1998) 'The Possibility of a Cosmopolitan Ethical Order Based on the Idea of Universal Human Rights', *Millennium*, Vol. 27, No. 3, pp. 523–41.

Chesterman, S. (1998) 'Human Rights as Subjectivity: The Age of Rights and the Politics of Culture', *Millennium*, Vol. 27, No. 1, pp. 97–118.

Chesterman, S. (2001) *Just War or Just Peace? Humanitarian Intervention and International Law* (Oxford: Oxford University Press).

Chesterman, S. (2004) *You, The People: The United Nations, Transitional Administrations, and State-Building* (Oxford: Oxford University Press).

Chesterman, S., Ignatieff, M. and Thakur, R. (eds) (2005) *Making States Work: State Failure and the Crisis of Governance* (New York: United Nations University).

Chinkin, C. M. (1998) 'International Law and Human Rights', in T. Evans (ed.) *Human Rights Fifty Years On: A Reappraisal* (Manchester: Manchester University Press), pp. 105–29.

Chinkin, C. M. (1999) 'Kosovo: A "Good" or "Bad" War?', *American Journal of International Law*, Vol. 93, pp. 841–7.

Chomsky, N. (1998) 'The United States and the Challenge of Relativity', in T. Evans (ed.) *Human Rights Fifty Years On: A Reappraisal* (Manchester: Manchester University Press), pp. 24–56.

Chomsky, N. (1999) *The New Military Humanism: Lessons From Kosovo* (London: Pluto Press).

Chomsky, N. (2000) 'The Kosovo Peace Accord' in T. Ali (ed.) *Masters of the Universe: Nato's Balkan Crusade* (London: Verso), pp. 387–96.

Chossudovsky, M. (1997) 'Dismantling Former Yugoslavia, Recolonising Bosnia', *Capital & Class*, No. 62, pp. 1–12.

Clapham, C. (1999) 'Sovereignty and the Third World State', *Political Studies*, Vol. 47, No. 3, pp. 522–37.

Clark, D. (2003) 'Iraq has Wrecked our Case for Humanitarian Wars', *Guardian*, 12 August.

Clark, R. *et al.* (1998) *Nato in the Balkans: Voices of Opposition* (New York: International Action Center).

Cobban, A. (1969) *The Nation State and National Self-Determination* (revised edn) (London: Collins).

Cohen, L. J. (1995) *Broken Bonds: Yugoslavia's Disintegration and Balkan Politics in Transition* (2nd edn) (Boulder: Westview Press).

Cohen, N. (2000) 'Murmuring Judges', *Observer*, 16 July.

Cohen, N. (2001) 'Short Measures', *Observer*, 28 October.

Collins, B. (1998) *Obedience in Rwanda: A Critical Question* (Sheffield: Sheffield Hallam University Press).

Cook, R. (1997) 'Human Rights into a New Century', speech by the Foreign Secretary, Mr Robin Cook, Locarno Suite, FCO, London, 17 July. Available from: <http://hrpd.fco.gov.uk/news/speeches.asap>.

Cook, R. and Campbell, M. (2000) 'Revised Role in Humanitarian Tragedies', *Financial Times*, 4 September.

Cooper, R. (2001) 'Dawn Chorus for the New Age of Empire', *Sunday Times*, 28 October.

Cooper, R. (2003) *The Breaking of Nations: Order and Chaos in the Twenty-First Century* (London: Atlantic Books).

Corell, H. (1997) 'The United Nations and the Legal Community in Promotion of Human Rights', *Fordham International Law Journal*, Vol. 21, No. 2, pp. 519–30.

Crawford, G. (1996) 'Promoting Democracy, Human Rights and Good Governance Through Development Aid: A Comparative Study of the Policies of Four Northern Donors', *Working Papers on Democratization*, No. 1, Centre for Democratization Studies, Leeds University.

Crossette, B. (2000) 'Parsing Degrees of Atrocity Within the Logic of the Law: To Punish War Criminals, the World Must Define War Crimes. It Isn't Easy', *New York Times*, 8 July.

Crossley, N. (2000) 'Today's TV', *Guardian*, 19 December.

D'Amato, A. (1994) 'Peace vs. Accountability in Bosnia', *American Journal of International Law*, Vol. 88, No. 3, pp. 500–6.

D'Amato, A. (2000) 'Does the ICTY Unfairly Favor the Prosecution?', comments posted to JustWatch List, 9 July. Available from: <http://listserv.acsu.buffalo.edu/archives/justwatch-l.html>.

Deacon, B. and Stubbs, P. (1998) 'International Actors and Social Policy Development in Bosnia-Herzegovina: Globalism and the "New Feudalism"', *Journal of European Social Policy*, Vol. 8, No. 2, pp. 99–115.

Dempsey, G. T. and Fontaine, R. W. (2001) *Fool's Errands: America's Recent Encounters With Nation Building* (Washington, DC: Cato Institute).

Denitch, B. (1996) *Ethnic Nationalism: The Tragic Death of Yugoslavia* (revised edn) (Minneapolis: University of Minnesota Press).

Dicey, A. V. (1959) *Introduction to the Study of the Law of the Constitution* (London: Macmillan).

Dillon, M. (1996) *Politics of Security: Towards a Political Philosophy of Continental Thought* (London: Routledge).

Dodd, V. and MacAskill, E. (2000) 'Labour Drops "Ethical" Tag', *Guardian*, 4 September.

Donnelly, J. (1998a) 'Human Rights: A New Standard of Civilization?', *International Affairs*, Vol. 74, No. 1, pp. 1–24.

Donnelly, J. (1998b) *International Human Rights* (2nd edn) (Boulder: Westview Press).

Donnelly, J. (1999) 'Ethics and International Human Rights', *Human Rights Working Papers*, No. 1, University of Denver Graduate School of International Studies, December.

Donnelly, J. (2000) *Realism in International Relations* (Cambridge: Cambridge University Press).

Dower, N. (1997) 'Human Rights and International Relations', *The International Journal of Human Rights*, Vol. 1, No. 1, pp. 86–111.

Doyal, L. and Gough, I. (1991) *A Theory of Human Need* (London: Macmillan).

Duchêne, F. (1972) 'Europe's Role in World Peace', in R. Mayne (ed.) *Europe Tomorrow: Sixteen Europeans Look Ahead* (London: Fontana).

Duffield, M. (1996) 'The Symphony of the Damned: Racial Discourse, Complex Emergencies and Humanitarian Aid', *Disasters*, Vol. 20, No. 3, pp. 173–93.

Duffield, M. (2001) *Global Governance and the New Wars: The Merging of Development and Security* (London: Zed Books).

Dunne, T. and Wheeler, N. J. (1999) 'Introduction: Human Rights and the Fifty Years' Crisis', in T. Dunne and N. J. Wheeler (eds) *Human Rights in Global Politics* (Cambridge: Cambridge University Press), pp. 1–28.

Economist (1997) 'Robin Good', 19 July.

Economist (2000a) 'Hopeless Africa', Editorial, 13 May.

Economist (2000b) 'Africa: The Heart of the Matter', 13 May.

Economist (2000c) 'Bringing Rights Home: For 300 Years, Parliament has been Supreme. No Longer', 26 August.

Economist (2001) 'Afghanistan: After the Taliban', 6 October.

Edwards, M. and Hulme, D. (1994) 'NGOs and Development: Performance and Accountability in the New World Order', background paper for international workshop 'NGOs and Development: Performance and Accountability in the New World Order', University of Manchester, 27–29 June.

Egelko, B. (2001) 'International Law: US Campaign in Afghanistan Enters New Legal Territory', *San Francisco Chronicle*, 4 November.

Ellison, M. (2001) 'Number of New York Dead May be 2,000 Less Than Official Tally', *Guardian*, 26 October.

ESEM (2000) *Europa South-East Monitor*, No. 12, Centre for European Policy Studies, Brussels, June.

EU (2003) *A Secure Europe in a Better World*, European Security Strategy, Brussels, 12 December. Available from: <http://ue.eu.int/uedocs/cmsUpload/78367.pdf>.

Evans, G. and Sahnoun, M. (2002) 'The Responsibility to Protect', *Foreign Affairs*, Vol. 81, No. 6, pp. 99–110.

Evans, M. (2001) 'Military Chief Warns of Four-year War, *The Times*, 27 October.

Evans, M. (2005) 'Human Rights, Moral Articulacy and Democratic Dynamism: In Defence of Critical Normative Philosophy', in P. Hayden and C. El-Ojeili (eds) *Confronting Globalization: Humanity, Justice and the Renewal of Politics* (Basingstoke: Palgrave).

Evans, T. (1997) 'Democratization and Human Rights', in A. McGrew (ed.) *The Transformation of Democracy?: Globalization and Territorial Democracy* (Cambridge: Polity Press/Open University), pp. 122–48.

Evans, T. (1998) 'Introduction: Power, Hegemony and the Universalisation of Human Rights', in T. Evans (ed.) *Human Rights Fifty Years On: A Reappraisal* (Manchester: Manchester University Press), pp. 2–23.

Ewing, K. D. (1999) 'The Human Rights Act and Parliamentary Democracy', *Modern Law Review*, Vol. 62, No. 1, pp. 79–99.

Falk, R. A. (1995) *On Humane Governance* (Cambridge: Polity Press).

Falk, R. A. (1999a) 'Kosovo, World Order, and the Future of International Law, *American Journal of International Law*, Vol. 93, pp. 847–57.

Falk, R. A. (1999b) 'The Challenge of Genocide and Genocidal Politics in an Era of Globalisation', in T. Dunne and N. J. Wheeler (eds) *Human Rights in Global Politics* (Cambridge: Cambridge University Press), pp. 177–94.

Falk, R. A. (2000) *Human Rights Horizons: The Pursuit of Justice in a Globalizing World* (London: Routledge).

Farah, D. (2000) 'A Separate Peacekeeping', *Washington Post*, 10 December.

Farrell, S. (2001) '"1,500 Killed in US Raids"', *The Times*, 1 November.

Felice, W. F. (1998) 'Militarism and Human Rights', *International Affairs*, Vol. 74, No. 1, pp. 25–40.

Ferguson, N. (2001) 'Welcome the New Imperialism', *Guardian*, 31 October.

Financial Times (1999) 'Frustration With UN: E. Timor Leaders Feel Cut Off From Administration', News Digest, 12 November.

Fletcher, M. (2001) 'US Jets Also Bombard Afghans With Food Parcels and Radios', *The Times*, 9 October.

Foot, M. (1999) 'Liberty, Fraternity, Statuary', *Observer*, 15 August.

Forsythe, D. P. (1989) *Human Rights and World Politics* (2nd edn) (London: University of Nebraska Press).

Forsythe, D. P. (2000) *Human Rights in International Relations* (Cambridge: Cambridge University Press).

Fox, F. (1999) 'The Politicisation of Humanitarian Aid', draft discussion paper for Caritas Europa.

Franck, T. M. (1999) 'Lessons of Kosovo', *American Journal of International Law*, Vol. 93, pp. 857–60.

Freedland, J. (1999) 'The Left Needs to Wake Up to the Real World. This War is a Just One', *Guardian*, 26 March.

Freeman, M. (1995) 'Are There Collective Human Rights?', *Political Studies*, Vol. 43, Special Issue, pp. 25–40.

Fuchs, P. (1999) *Handling Information in Humanitarian Operations Within Armed Conflicts*. Available from: <http://www.osi.net/Proceedings/ossaaa/aaa4/aaa4ae>.

Fukuyama, F. (2004) *State Building: Governance and World Order in the Twenty-first Century* (London: Profile).

Furedi, F. (1994) *The New Ideology of Imperialism: Renewing the Moral Imperative* (London: Pluto Press).

Furedi, F. (1998) *The Silent War: Imperialism and the Changing Perception of Race* (London: Pluto Press).

Gaer, F. D. (1997) 'UN-Anonymous: Reflections on "Human Rights in Peace Negotiations"', *Human Rights Quarterly*, Vol. 19, pp. 1–8.

Galtung, J. (2000) 'Alternative Models for Global Democracy' in B. Holden (ed.) *Global Democracy: Key Debates* (London: Routledge), pp. 143–61.

Garcelon, M. (1997) 'The Shadow of the Leviathan: Public and Private in Communist and Post-Communist Society', in J. Weintraub and K. Kumar (eds) *Public and Private in Thought and Practice: Perspectives on a Grand Dichotomy* (Chicago: University of Chicago Press), pp. 303–32.

Garten, J. E. (1996) 'The Need for Pragmatism', *Foreign Policy*, No. 105, pp. 103–6.

Garton Ash, T. (1999) 'The Legacy of Appeasement', *Independent*, 31 March.

Gentry, J. A. (1999) 'The Cancer of Human Rights', *Washington Quarterly*, Vol. 22, No. 4, pp. 95–113.

Gerwith, A. (1981) 'The Basis and Content of Human Rights', in J. R. Pennock and J. W. Chapman (eds) *Human Rights* (New York: New York University Press), pp. 119–47.

Gillan, A. (2000) 'The Propaganda War', *Guardian*, 21 August.

Glasius, M. and Kaldor, M. (2005) 'Individuals First: A Human Security Strategy for the European Union', *Internationale Politik und Gesellschaft*, No.1, 2005, pp. 62–82.

Glennon, M. (1999) 'The New Interventionism: The Search for a Just International Law', *Foreign Affairs*, Vol. 78, No. 2, pp. 2–7.

Goldhagen, D. J. (1996) *Hitler's Willing Executioners: Germany and the Holocaust* (New York: Knopf).

Goldhagen, D. J. (1999) 'German Lessons', *Guardian*, 29 April.

Goldstone, R. (2001) 'Terrorists can be Brought to Justice Only by Legal Means', *Independent*, 2 October.

Gordon, J. (1998) 'The Concept of Human Rights: The History and Meaning of its Politicization', *Brooklyn Journal of International Law*, Vol. XXIII, No. 3, pp. 689–791.

Gordon, M. R. (2001) 'A New Kind of War Plan', *New York Times*, 7 October.

Gow, D. (2001) 'Bush Gives Green Light to CIA for Assassination of Named Terrorists', *Guardian*, 29 October.

Gray, J. (2000) 'Crushing Hatreds', *Guardian*, 28 March.

Griffin, M. (2001) *Reaping the Whirlwind: The Taliban Movement in Afghanistan* (London: Pluto Press).

Griffith, J. (1998) 'A Bill of Rights?', *Socialist Lawyer*, Summer, pp. 24–7.

Guardian (1999) 'Nato Errs Again: But Its Cause Remains Valid', Editorial, 15 May.

Guardian (2000a) 'We are Right to be There', Editorial, 13 May.

Guardian (2000b) 'Kosovo One Year On', Editorial, 13 June.

Guardian (2000c) 'Something to Celebrate: A Big Advance for Human Rights in Britain', Editorial, 13 July.

Guardian (2000d) 'New Light on Kosovo: But the Principle of Intervention was Right', Editorial, 18 August.

Guardian (2001) 'In Solemn Recollection: The Holocaust is Part of our History Too', Editorial, 27 January.

Guest, I. (2000) 'Misplaced Charity Undermines Kosovo's Self-Reliance', *Viewpoint*, Overseas Development Council, February.

Gutman, R. (2000a) 'Twenty-five Years of the Helsinki Process: 1975–2000', *Freedom of the Media Yearbook 1999–2000*, Organisation for Security and Co-operation in Europe. Available from: <http://www.osce.org/fom/publications/yearbook9900/III/149>.

Gutman, R. (2000b) 'Ruling Reflects New Global View of Justice', *Newsday*, 11 August.

Gutman, R. and Rieff, D. (1999) Preface in R. Gutman and D. Rieff (eds) *Crimes of War: What the Public Should Know* (New York: W. W. Norton), pp. 8–12.

Habermas, J. (1999) 'Bestialität und Humanität', *Die Zeit*, Vol. 54, No. 18, 29 April, pp. 1–8. Trans. F. Solms-Laubach. Available from: <http://www.theglobalsite.ac.uk/librarytexts/011habermas.htm>.

Habermas, J. (2001) *The Postnational Constellation* (Cambridge: Polity Press).

Habermas, J. (2003) 'February 15, or What Binds Europeans Together: A Plea for a Common Foreign Policy, Beginning in the Core of Europe', *Constellations*, Vol. 10, No. 3, pp. 291–97.

Hain, P. (2001) 'We Must Not be Effete: It's Time to Fight', *Guardian*, 24 September. Available from: <http://www.guardian.co.uk/Archive/Article/0,4273,4263036,00.html>.

Hall, S. (1992) 'The West and the Rest: Discourse and Power', in S. Hall and B. Gieben (eds) *Formations of Modernity* (Cambridge: Polity Press), pp. 275–331.

Halliday, F. (1994) *Rethinking International Relations* (London: Macmillan).

Hammarberg, T. (1998) 'The Human Rights Package', *UN Chronicle*, Vol. 35, No. 4, pp. 18–20.

Hammond, P. and Herman, E. S. (2000) *Degraded Capability: The Media and the Kosovo Crisis* (London: Pluto Press).

Harden, B. (2000) 'Two African Nations Said to Break UN Diamond Embargo', *New York Times*, 1 August.

Harding, L. (2001) 'UN Guards Killed by Stray Missile', *Guardian*, 10 October.

Harnden, T. (2001) 'Building the Case Against Iraq', *Daily Telegraph*, 26 October.

Hartmann, F. (1999) 'Bosnia', in R. Gutman and D. Rieff (eds) *Crimes of War: What the Public Should Know* (New York: W. W. Norton), pp. 50–6.

Hayden, R. M. (2000) *UN War Crimes Tribunal Delivers a Travesty of Justice*, Woodrow Wilson International Centre for Scholars.

Hayes, B. C. and Sands, J. I. (1997) 'Non-Traditional Military Responses to End Wars: Considerations for Policymakers', *Millennium*, Vol. 26, No. 3, pp. 819–44.

Heartfield, J. (1996) 'Rights and the Legal Subject', Freedom and Law discussion paper.

Held, D. (1995) *Democracy and the Global Order: From the Modern State to Cosmopolitan Governance* (Cambridge: Polity Press).

Heller, A. (1993) 'The Limits to Natural Law and the Paradox of Evil', in S. Shute and S. Hurley (eds) *On Human Rights* (New York: Basic Books), pp. 149–74.

Henkin, L. (1981) 'International Human Rights as "Rights"', in J. R. Pennock and J. W. Chapman (eds) *Human Rights*, Nomos XXIII (New York: New York University Press), pp. 257–80.

Henkin, L. (1990) *The Age of Rights* (New York: Columbia University Press).

Henkin, L. (1995) *International Law: Politics and Values* (Dordrecht: Nijhoff).

Henkin, L. (1999a) 'That "S" Word: Sovereignty, and Globalization, and Human Rights, *et Cetera*', *Fordham Law Review*, Vol. 68, No. 1, pp. 1–14.

Henkin, L. (1999b) 'Kosovo and the Law of "Humanitarian Intervention"', *American Journal of International Law*, Vol. 93, pp. 824–8.

Heraclides, A. (1993) *Helsinki II And Its Aftermath: The Making of the CSCE into an International Organization* (London: Pinter Publishers).

Heuer, U. and Schirmer, G. (1998) 'Human Rights Imperialism', *Monthly Review*, March, pp. 5–16.

HMD (2001) 'Lessons for the Future', Official Holocaust Memorial Day website. Available from: <http://www.holocaustmemorialday.gov.uk/>.

Hoagland, J. (2000a) 'More Muscle for the Peacekeepers', *Washington Post*, 4 August.

Hoagland, J. (2000b) 'Justice Under Pressure', *Washington Post*, 10 August.

Holbrook, J. (2000) '"World Court" is a Creature of Politics Rather Than Justice', *The Times*, 26 September.

Holbrook, J. (2001) ' In Defence of Sovereignty', *Spiked*, 2 October. Available from: <http://www.spiked-online.com/Articles/00000002D257.htm>.

Howard, M. (2000) 'Human Rights', Letters, *The Times*, 5 August.

Hume, M. (1997) *Whose War is it Anyway* (London: Informinc).

Hume, M. (1999) 'The War Against the Serbs is about Projecting a Self-Image of the Ethical New Britain Bestriding the World. It is a Crusade', *The Times*, 15 April.

Hume, M. (2001) 'In a Propaganda War, Do You Put Guns Before Peanut Butter?, *The Times*, 22 October.

Hutchinson, J. F. (1996) *Champions of Charity: War and the Rise of the Red Cross* (Boulder: Westview).

Hutton, W. (2001) 'We Have Blood on Our Hands, Too', *Observer*, 21 January.

Ignatieff, M. (1998) *The Warrior's Honor: Ethnic War and the Modern Conscience* (London: Chatto & Windus).

Ignatieff, M. (1999a) 'International Committee of the Red Cross (ICRC)', in R. Gutman and D. Rieff (eds) *Crimes of War: What the Public Should Know* (New York: W. W. Norton), pp. 202–4.

Ignatieff, M. (1999b) 'Human Rights: The Midlife Crisis', *New York Review of Books*, 20 May, pp. 58–62.

Ignatieff, M. (2000a) 'A Bungling UN Undermines Itself', *New York Times*, 15 May.

Ignatieff, M. (2000b) *Virtual War: Kosovo and Beyond* (London: Chatto & Windus).

Ignatieff, M. (2001) 'After September 11: What Will Victory Look Like?', *Guardian*, G2, 19 October.

ICB (2005) *The Balkans in Europe's Future*. Available from: <http://www.beta.co.yu/ftp/Documents/Report1.pdf>.

ICISS (2001a) *The Responsibility to Protect* (Ottawa: International Development Research Centre).

ICISS (2001b) *The Responsibility to Protect: Research, Bibliography, Background* (Ottawa: International Development Research Centre).

IICK (2000) *The Kosovo Report*, Independent International Commisssion on Kosovo (Oxford: Oxford University Press).

Independent (1999) 'We Must Find the Stomach for Years of War Over Kosovo', Editorial, 5 April.

Ischinger, W. (1999) 'Contours of a New German Foreign Policy', *Deutschland*, No. 4, August/September, pp. 18–21.

Jackson, R. H. (1990) *Quasi-States: Sovereignty, International Relations and the Third World* (Cambridge: Cambridge University Press).

Jackson, R. H. (1998) 'Surrogate Sovereignty? Great Power Responsibility and "Failed States"', Working Paper, No. 25, Institute of International Relations, University of Columbia. Available from: <http://www.iir.ubc.ca/pdffiles/webwp25.pdf>.

Jackson, R. H. (1999) 'Sovereignty in World Politics: A Glance at the Conceptual and Historical Landscape', *Political Studies*, Vol. 47, No. 3, pp. 431–56.

Jackson, R. H. (2000) *The Global Covenant: Human Conduct in a World of States* (Oxford: Oxford University Press).

Jacques, M. (2004) 'The Interregnum', *London Review of Books*, 5 February, pp. 8–9.

Jenkins, S. (1999a) 'Bloody Liberals: The Empire has Struck Back, With Greater Force and Left-Wing Sermons', *The Times*, 16 April.

Jenkins, S. (1999b) 'Weep for Poor Orissa: The West Squanders Billions in Kosovo, While a Life in India is Valued at 30 Cents', *The Times*, 26 November.

Jenkins, S. (2000) 'Stuck in the Mire of the White Man's Burden', *The Times*, 10 May.

Jenkins, S. (2001) 'They Opted to Bomb, it had Better Work', *The Times*, 10 October.

Johnstone, D. (1998) 'Seeing Yugoslavia Through a Dark Glass: Politics, Media and the Ideology of Globalization', *Direct Action Quarterly*, Fall, No. 65. Available from: <http://www.caq.com/>.

Judah, T. (2001) 'Reluctant UN Joins the Fray', *Observer*, 21 October.

Kagan, R. (2003) *Paradise and Power* (London: Atlantic Books).

Kagan, R. (2004) 'America's Crisis of Legitimacy', *Foreign Affairs*, Vol. 83, No. 2, pp. 65–87.

Kaldor, M. (1999a) 'Transnational Civil Society', in T. Dunne and N. J. Wheeler (eds) *Human Rights in Global Politics* (Cambridge: Cambridge University Press), pp. 195–213.

Kaldor, M. (1999b) *New and Old Wars: Organized Violence in a Global Era* (Cambridge: Polity Press).

Kaldor, M. (2001) *Analysis*, BBC Radio Four, 29 March.

Kaldor, M. (2003a) *Global Civil Society: An Answer to War* (Cambridge: Polity Press).

Kaldor, M. (2003b) 'The Idea of Global Civil Society', *International Affairs*, Vol. 79, No. 3, pp. 583–93.

Kampfner, J. (2004) *Blair's Wars* (London: Free Press).

Karagiannakis, M. (1998) 'State Immunity and Fundamental Human Rights', *Leiden Journal of International Law*, Vol. 11, No. 1, pp. 9–43.

Keenan, T. (1997) *Fables of Responsibility: Aberrations and Predicaments in Ethics and Politics* (Stanford: Stanford University Press).

Kennedy, H. (2000) Foreword in F. Klug (ed.) *Values for a Godless Age: The Story of the UK's New Bill of Rights* (London: Penguin), pp. xi–xv.

Keohane, R. O. (2002) 'Ironies of Sovereignty: The European Union and the United States', *Journal of Common Market Studies*, Vol. 40, No. 4, pp. 743–65.

Keohane, R. O. (2003) 'Political Authority after Intervention: Gradations in Sovereignty', in J. L. Holzgrefe and R. O. Keohane (eds) *Humanitarian Intervention: Ethical, Legal and Political Dilemmas* (Cambridge: Cambridge University Press).

King, H. T. (1999) 'The Tribute of Power to Reason: The Lessons from Nuremberg', *UN Chronicle*, Vol. 36, No. 2, p. 61.

King, N. and Jaffe, G. (2001) 'US Plans to Use a Bombing Campaign to End Taliban Protection of bin Laden', *Wall Street Journal*, 5 October.

King, T. (1999) 'Human Rights in European Foreign Policy: Success or Failure for Post-modern Diplomacy?', *European Journal of International Law*, Vol. 10, pp. 313–37.

Kite, M. (2001) 'Britain to Have Big Role in Peace Force', *The Times*, 22 October.

Klug, F. (1997) 'Can Human Rights Fill Britain's Morality Gap?', *Political Quarterly*, Vol. 68, No. 2, pp. 143–52.

Klug, F. (2000a) 'Target of the Tabloids', *Guardian*, 14 July.

Klug, F. (2000b) *Values for a Godless Age: The Story of the UK's New Bill of Rights* (London: Penguin).

Klug, F. (2001) 'Now We Really Need Rights', *Observer*, 7 October.

Korey, W. (1999) 'Human Rights NGOs: The Power of Persuasion', *Ethics and International Affairs*, Vol. 13, pp. 151–74.

Korten, D. (1990) *Getting into the 21st Century: Voluntary Action and the Global Agenda* (West Hartford: Kumarian Press).

Koskenniemi, M. (1995) 'The Police in the Temple: Order, Justice and the UN: A Dialectical View', *European Journal of International Law*, Vol. 6, No. 1, pp. 1–25.

Kouchner, B. (1999) 'Perspective on World Politics: Establish a Right to Intervene Against War', *Los Angeles Times*, 18 October.

Krähenbuhl, P. (2000) 'Conflict in the Balkans: Human Tragedies and the Challenge to Independent Humanitarian Action', *International Review of the Red Cross*, No. 837, March, pp. 11–29.

Kundera, M. (1991) *Immortality* (London: Faber).

Laïdi, Z. (1998) *A World without Meaning: Crisis of Meaning in International Politics* (London: Routledge).

Langlois, A. J. (1998) 'Redescribing Human Rights', *Millennium*, Vol. 27, No. 1, pp. 1–22.

Lansing, R. (1921) *The Peace Negotiations: A Personal Narrative* (London: Macmillan).

Lattimer, M. (1999) 'World Must Put its Hangmen in the Dock', *Observer*, 24 October.

Laughland, J. (1999a) 'The Anomalies of the International Criminal Tribunal are Legion. This is not Victors' Justice in the Former Yugoslavia – In Fact, it is no Justice at all', *The Times*, 17 June.

Laughland, J. (1999b) 'Since Law Enforcement is Probably the Single Most Important Sovereign Power, it is Threatened if it is Transferred to Unaccountable Bureaucrats', *The Times*, 10 August.

Lawrence, F. and Wells, M. (2001) 'Lack of Footage Stalls Disaster Appeal', *Guardian*, 5 October.

Leader, N. (1998) 'Proliferating Principles; Or How to Sup With the Devil Without Getting Eaten', *Disasters*, Vol. 22, No. 4, pp. 288–308.

Levin, N. G. (1968) *Woodrow Wilson and World Politics: America's Response to War and Revolution* (Oxford: Oxford University Press).

Lewis, N. (1997) 'Human Rights and Democracy in an Unfree World', paper presented to the 38th Annual Convention of the International Studies Association, Toronto, 18–23 March 1997.

Lewis, N. (1998) 'Human Rights, Law and Democracy in an Unfree World', in T. Evans (ed.) *Human Rights Fifty Years On: A Reappraisal* (Manchester: Manchester University Press), pp. 77–104.

Lijphart, A. (1984) *Democracies* (New Haven: Yale University Press).

Linklater, A. (1998) *The Transformation of Political Community* (Cambridge: Polity Press).

Linklater, A. (2000) 'The Good International Citizen and the Crisis in Kosovo', summary in A. Schnabel and R. Thakur (eds) *Kosovo and the Challenge of Humanitarian Intervention: Selective Indignation, Collective Intervention, and International Citizenship* (forthcoming: United Nations University), pp. 49–50. Summary available: <http://www.unu.edu/p&g/kosovo_full.htm>.

Littman, M. (1999) *Kosovo: Law and Diplomacy* (London: Centre for Policy Studies).

Lloyd, J. (1999) 'Prepare for a Brave New World', *New Statesman*, 19 April, pp. 8–10.

Loescher, G. (1999) 'Refugees: A Global Human Rights and Security Crisis', in T. Dunne and N. J. Wheeler (eds) *Human Rights in Global Politics* (Cambridge: Cambridge University Press), pp. 233–58.

Longworth, R. C. (1999) 'Human Rights Now May Trump Sovereignty', *Chicago Tribune*, 9 December.

Lynch, C. (2000) 'Liberia Warned Again on Support for Sierra Leone Rebels', *Washington Post*, 3 August.

Lyon, P. (2000) 'Perspectives on the Dayton Peace Accords and their Implementation in Bosnia and Herzegovina', paper presented to the Sixth Annual Northwest Regional Conference for Russian, East European and Central Asian Studies, University of Washington, Seattle, 22 April. Available from: <http://depts.washington.edu/reecas/events/conf2000/papers00/Lyon.pdf>.

Lyotard, J. (1993) 'The Other's Rights', in S. Shute and S. Hurley (eds) *On Human Rights* (New York: Basic Books), pp. 135–48.

MacAskill, E. (2001a) 'US Ready to Strike Without UN Mandate', *Guardian*, 22 September.

MacAskill, E. (2001b) 'UN Fears Over Role After Fall of Taliban', *Guardian*, 27 October.

MacAskill, E., O'Kane, M., Gillan, A. and Harding L. (2001) 'America Sees Food Drops as Key to Being Hailed as Saviour, Not Invader', *Guardian*, 5 October.

MacAskill, E. and Traynor, I. (2000) 'Fury as UN Envoy Suggests War Crimes Amnesty for Milosevic', *Guardian*, 5 October.

McCarthy, R. (2001a) 'Call for Aid Operation Before any Missile Hit', *Guardian*, 6 October.

McCarthy, R. (2001b) 'Short Says Ousting Taliban is Best Aid', *Guardian*, 19 October.

Mackinlay, J. and Kent, R. (1997) 'A New Approach to Complex Emergencies', *International Peacekeeping*, Vol. 4, No. 4, pp. 31–49.

MacKinnon, C. A. (1993) 'Crimes of War, Crimes of Peace', in S. Shute and S. Hurley (eds) *On Human Rights* (New York: Basic Books), pp. 83–110.

MacMillan, L. (2000) 'Ascribing Responsibilities for Ensuring Refugee Protection', *Talk Back*, The Newsletter of the International Council of Voluntary Agencies (ICVA), Vol. 2, No. 1, 18 February.

Macrae, J. (1998) 'The Death of Humanitarianism?: An Anatomy of the Attack', *Disasters*, Vol. 22, No. 4, pp. 309–17.

McSmith, A. and Burke, J. (2000) 'Britain Slashes Aid to Ethiopia', *Observer*, 9 April.

Malik, K. (1996) *The Meaning of Race: Race, History and Culture in Western Society* (London: Macmillan).

Mandel, M. (2000) *Text of Michael Mandel's appearance at SCFAIT – Ottawa*, Canadian House of Commons Standing Committee on Foreign Affairs and International Trade, 22 February.

Mandel, M. (2001) 'Say What You Want, But This War is Illegal', *Globe and Mail* (Toronto), 9 October.

Manners, I. (2002) 'Normative Power Europe: A Contradiction in Terms?', *Journal of Common Market Studies*, Vol. 40, No. 2, pp. 235–58.

Maren, M. (1997) *The Road to Hell: The Ravaging Effects of Foreign Aid and International Charity* (New York: Free Press).

Marsden, P. (2001) 'Those That are Not With Us are Against Us, *Guardian*, 22 October.

Mayall, J. (1990) *Nationalism and International Society* (Cambridge: Cambridge University Press).

Mayall, J. (1991) 'Non-intervention, Self-determination and the "New World Order"', *International Affairs*, Vol. 67, No. 3, pp. 421–9.

Mayall, J. (2000) 'Democracy and International Society', *International Affairs*, Vol. 76, No. 1, pp. 61–75.

Meek, J. (2001) 'Northern Alliance Losing Faith in Military Support', *Guardian*, 26 October.

Mendus, S. (1995) 'Human Rights in Political Theory', in D. Beetham (ed.) *Politics and Human Rights* (Oxford: Blackwell), pp. 10–24.

Mészáros, I. (1989) *The Power of Ideology* (London: Harvester Wheatsheaf).

Meyers, M. A. (1997) 'A Defense of Unilateral or Multi-lateral Intervention Where a Violation of International Human Rights Law by a State Constitutes an Implied Waiver of Sovereignty', *ILSA Journal of International and Comparative Law*, Vol. 3, pp. 895–913.

Middleton, N. and O'Keefe, P. (1998) *Disaster and Development: The Politics of Humanitarian Aid* (London: Pluto Press).

Midgley, M. (1999) 'Towards an Ethic of Global Responsibility', in T. Dunne and N. J. Wheeler (eds) *Human Rights in Global Politics* (Cambridge: Cambridge University Press), pp. 160–74.

Mierop, E. S. van (2000) 'The Entanglement of Humanitarians and the Military', *Talk Back*, The Newsletter of the International Council of Voluntary Agencies (ICVA), Vol. 2, No. 1, 18 February.

Miller, B. and Haughney, C. (2000) 'War Crimes Trials Find a US Home', *Washington Post*, 9 August.

Milliken, J. (2003) *State Failure, Collapse and Reconstruction* (Oxford: Blackwell).

Mills, K. (1997) 'Reconstructing Sovereignty: A Human Rights Perspective', *Netherlands Quarterly of Human Rights*, Vol. 15, No. 3, pp. 267–90.

Minear, L. (1999) 'The Theory and Practice of Neutrality: Some Thoughts on the Tensions', *International Review of the Red Cross*, No. 833, pp. 63–71.

Moghalu, K. C. (1999) 'The Indictment of Milosevic: A Revolution in Human Rights', *New Perspectives Quarterly*, Vol. 16, No. 4, pp. 13–16.

Monbiot, G. (2001a) 'Folly of Aid and Bombs', *Guardian*, 9 October.

Monbiot, G. (2001b) 'America's Pipe Dream', *Guardian*, 23 October.

Montgomery, J. D. (1999) 'Fifty Years of Human Rights: An Emergent Global Regime', *Policy Sciences*, Vol. 32, pp. 79–94.

Moorehead, C. (1998) *Dunant's Dream: War, Switzerland and the History of the Red Cross* (New York: St. Martin's Press).

Müllerson, R. (1997) *Human Rights Diplomacy* (London: Routledge).

Murphy, J. and Wastell, D. (2001) 'Desperate Shuttle Before the Storm', *Sunday Telegraph*, 7 October.

Mutua, M. wa (1996) 'The Ideology of Human Rights', *Virginia Journal of International Law*, Vol. 36, pp. 589–657.

Mydans, S. (2000) 'Ruined East Timor Awaits a Miracle', *New York Times*, 22 April.

Nariman, F. (1997) 'International Human Rights and Sovereignty of States: Role and Responsibility of Lawyers', *Fordham International Law Journal*, Vol. 21, No. 2, pp. 541–9.

Neier, A. (1996) 'The New Double Standard', *Foreign Policy*, No. 105, pp. 91–101.

Neumeister, L. (2000) 'Jury Finds Ex-Serbian Leader Owes $745 Million for Wartime Horrors', *Associated Press*, 10 August.

New York Times (1999) 'Then and Now/Reflections on the Millennium: The Powerful Idea of Human Rights', Editorial, 8 December.

Nezick, Z. (2000) 'Encouraging and Supporting Performing Arts Education in the Balkans: A Positive Bond For Youth in Multi-Ethnic Societies', speech given at the Institute for Strengthening Democracy in Bosnia, Third Seminar 'Democracy and Human Rights in Multi-Ethnic Societies', Konjic, Bosnia, 3–7 July.

Nicholls, B. (1987) 'Rubber Band Humanitarianism', *Ethics and International Affairs*, No. 1, pp. 191–210.

Nickel, J. W. (1987) *Making Sense of Human Rights: Philosophical Reflections on the Universal Declaration of Human Rights* (Berkley: University of California Press).

Norton-Taylor, R. (2000a) 'From Killing to Cuddling', *Guardian*, 17 August.

Norton-Taylor, R. (2000b) 'Bombing in Iraq an "Undeclared War"', *Guardian*, 11 November.

Norton-Taylor, R. and Bowcott, O. (1999) 'Deadly Cost of the New Warfare', *Guardian*, 22 October.

Oborne, P. (2005) 'What's Truth Got to Do with It?', *Spectator*, 30 April, pp. 31–3.

Observer (1999a) 'There is No Alternative to This War', Editorial, 28 March.

Observer (1999b) 'Time Now to Raise the Stakes', Editorial, 4 April.

Observer (2000) 'For Our Sake, Don't Cut Third World Aid', Editorial, 9 April.

Observer (2001) 'Fighting for a Better Future: This War Must Save Afghanistan', Editorial, 21 October.

O'Connell, M. E. (2000) 'The UN, Nato, and International Law After Kosovo', *Human Rights Quarterly*, Vol. 22, pp. 57–89.

OHR (1997a) *Report of the High Representative for Implementation of the Bosnian Peace Agreement to the Secretary General of the United Nations*, 11 July. Available from: <http://www.ohr.int/reports/r970711a.htm>.

OHR (1997b) *Office of the High Representative Bulletin*, No. 62, 11 October. Available from: <http://www.ohr.int/bulletins/b971011.htm>.

OHR (1997c) *Bosnia and Herzegovina TV News Summary*, 10 November, Office of the High Representative e-mail service.

OHR (1997d) *Return and Reconstruction Task Force Report*, December. Office of the High Representative. Available from: <http://www.ohr.int/rrtf/r9712.htm>.

Orbinski, J. (1999) 'The Nobel Lecture by the Nobel Peace Prize Laureate 1999: Médecins sans Frontières, 10 December'. Available from <http://www.nobel.no/msf_1999eng.html>.

OSCE (1995) *CSCE/OSCE Provisions Concerning Persons Belonging To National Minorities* (Warsaw: Office for Democratic Institutions and Human Rights (ODIHR)).

Oschlies, W. (1999) 'A Fresh Start: The Stability Pact for the Balkans', *Deutschland*, No. 4, August/September, pp. 22–5.

Parekh, B. (1993) 'Beyond Humanitarian Intervention', in H. Cullen, D. Kritsiotis and N. Wheeler (eds) *Politics and the Law of Former Yugoslavia* (Hull: European Research Unit/University of Hull).

Paris, R. (1997) 'Peacebuilding and the Limits of Liberal Internationalism', *International Security*, Vol. 22, No. 2, pp. 54–89.

Paris, R. (2004) *At War's End: Building Peace after Civil Conflict* (Cambridge: Cambridge University Press).

Pender, J. (2000) 'From "Structural Adjustment" to "Comprehensive Development Framework": Conditionality Transformed?', paper presented to the African Studies Association of the UK Biennial Conference, 'Africa: Past, Present & Future', Trinity College, Cambridge, 12 September.

Pennock, J. R. (1981) 'Rights, Natural Rights, and Human Rights – A General View', in J. R. Pennock and J. W. Chapman (eds) *Human Rights* (New York: New York University Press), pp. 1–28.

Perkins, A. (2001) 'Allies "Will Try to Minimise Suffering"', *Guardian*, 5 October.

Petras, J. and Vieux, S. (1996) 'Bosnia and the Revival of US Hegemony', *New Left Review*, Vol. 1, No. 218, pp. 3–25.

Phillips, J. (2001) 'EU Chief Meets King', *The Times*, 22 October.

Philpott, D. (1999) 'Westphalia, Authority, and International Society', *Political Studies*, Vol. 47, No. 3, pp. 566–89.

Pieterse, J. N. (1997) 'Sociology of Humanitarian Intervention: Bosnia, Rwanda and Somalia Compared', *International Political Science Review*, Vol. 18, No. 1, pp. 71–93.

Pilger, J. (1999) 'Acts of Murder', *Guardian*, 18 May.

Platt, S. (1998) 'Government by Task Force: A Review of the Reviews', *Catalyst Paper*, No. 2, The Catalyst Trust, London.

Posner, M. (1997) 'Foreword: Human Rights and Non-Governmental Organizations on the Eve of the Next Century', *Fordham Law Review*, Vol. 66, No. 2, pp. 627–30.

Pugh, M. (1995) 'Peacebuilding as Developmentalism: Concepts from Disaster Research', *Contemporary Security Policy*, Vol. 16, No. 3, pp. 32–48.

Pugh, M. (1998) 'Military Intervention and Humanitarian Action: Trends and Issues', *Disasters*, Vol. 22, No. 4, pp. 339–51.

Pugh, M. (2000) 'Civil–Military Relations in the Kosovo Crisis: An Emerging Hegemony?', *Security Dialogue*, Vol. 31, No. 2, pp. 229–42.

Pupavac, V. (2000a) 'From Statehood to Childhood: A Study of Self-Determination and Conflict Resolution in Yugoslavia and the Post-Yugoslav States', unpublished PhD thesis, University of Nottingham.

Pupavac, V. (2000b) 'Securing the Community?: An Examination of International Psychosocial Intervention', paper presented at 'Balkan Security: Visions of the Future' Conference, Centre for South-East European Studies, School of Slavonic and East European Studies, University College London, 16–17 June.

Rabkin, J. (1999) 'Nuremberg Misremembered', *Johns Hopkins SAIS Review*, Summer–Fall, pp. 223–39.

Radin, C. A. (2000) 'UN's Peacekeeping a Failure, Report Says', *Boston Globe*, 24 August.

Ramsbotham, O. and Woodhouse, T. (1996) *Humanitarian Intervention in Contemporary Conflict: A Reconceptualization* (Cambridge: Polity Press).

Ranciere, J. (2004) 'Who is the Subject of the Rights of Man?', *South Atlantic Quarterly*, Vol. 103, No. 2/3, pp. 297–310.

RAND (2003) J. Dobbins *et al.*, *America's Role in Nation-Building: From Germany to Iraq* (Santa Monica, CA: RAND Corporation). Available from: <http://www.rand.org/publications/MR/MR1753/>.

Rawls, J. (1993) 'The Law of Peoples', in S. Shute and S. Hurley (eds) *On Human Rights* (New York: Basic Books), pp. 41–82.

Record, G. (2003) 'Bounding the Global War on Terrorism', Strategic Studies Institute, US Army War College, Carlisle, PA, December. Available from: <http://www.carlisle.army.mil/ssi/pdffiles/PUB207.pdf>.

Rees, L. (1997) *The Nazis: A Warning From History* (London: BBC).

Reisman, W. M. (1999) 'Kosovo's Antinomies', *American Journal of International Law*, Vol. 93, pp. 860–2.

Reus-Smit, C. (2004) *American Power and World Order* (Cambridge: Polity Press).

RFE/RL (2000a) *(Un)Civil Societies*, Vol. 1, No. 1, 18 May, Prague, Czech Republic.

RFE/RL (2000b) 'Confronting Evil', *RFE/RL Balkan Report*, Vol. 4, No. 52, 14 July, Prague, Czech Republic.

Rhode, D. (2000) 'Jury in New York Orders Bosnian Serb to Pay Billions', *New York Times*, 26 September.

Ricks, T. E. (2001) 'US Signs Treaty on War Crimes Tribunal', *Washington Post*, 1 January.

Rieff, D. (1999a) 'Humanitarian Intervention', in R. Gutman and D. Rieff (eds) *Crimes of War: What the Public Should Know* (New York: W. W. Norton), pp. 181–4.

Rieff, D. (1999b) 'A New Hierarchy of Values and Interests', *World Policy Journal*, Vol. 16, No. 3, pp. 28–34.

Rieff, D. (2000a) 'Round Three: Concluding Remarks', Roundtable: Picking a Good Fight, *Atlantic*, 14 April. Available from: <http://www.theatlantic.com/unbound/roundtable/goodfight/rieff3.htm>.

Rieff, D. (2000b) 'Humanitarian Intervention: A Forum', *Nation*, 8 May, pp. 21–6.

Rieff, D. (2000c) 'The Necessity of War', Book Reviews, *Los Angeles Times*, 3 September.

Rishworth, P. (1997) 'Human Rights – From the Top', *Political Quarterly*, Vol. 68, No. 2, pp. 171–8.

Roberts, A. (1993) 'Humanitarian War: Military Intervention and Human Rights', *International Affairs*, Vol. 69, No. 3, pp. 429–49.

Roberts, A. (1999) 'The Role of Humanitarian Issues in International Politics in the 1990s', *International Review of the Red Cross*, No. 833, pp. 19–43.

Roberts, A. (2001) 'Intervention: Suggestions for Moving the Debate Forward', Round Table Consultation, London, 3 February 2001, Discussion Paper, International Commission on Intervention and State Sovereignty. Available from: <http://web.gc.cuny.edu/icissresearch/london%20discussion%20paper.htm>.

Robertson, G. (1999) *Crimes Against Humanity: The Struggle for Global Justice* (London: Allen Lane/ Penguin).

Robertson, G. (2000) *Crimes Against Humanity: The Struggle for Global Justice* (revised edn) (London: Penguin).

Robertson, G. (2001a) 'America is Wrong to Shoot First, Then Ask Questions About Guilt Later', *Independent*, 26 September.

Robertson, G. (2001b) 'Lynch Mob Justice or a Proper Trial', *Guardian*, 5 October.

Robertson, George (2000) 'Law, Morality and the Use of Force', speech by Lord Robertson, Nato Secretary-General, at the Institut de Relations Internationales et Stratégiques, Paris, 16 May.

Robinson, F. (1998) 'The Limits of a Rights-Based Approach to International Ethics', in T. Evans (ed.) *Human Rights Fifty Years On: A Reappraisal* (Manchester: Manchester University Press), pp. 58–76.

Robinson, M. (1997) 'Saying What We Mean. Meaning What We Say. Together', *UN Chronicle*, Vol. 34, No. 4, pp. 24–7.

Robinson, M. (1999) 'We Can End This Agony', Saturday Review, *Guardian*, 23 October.

Rorty, R. (1993) 'Human Rights, Rationality, and Sentimentality', in S. Shute and S. Hurley (eds) *On Human Rights* (New York: Basic Books), pp. 111–34.

Rose, G. (1998) 'The Exit Strategy Delusion', *Foreign Affairs*, Vol. 77, No. 1, pp. 56–67.

Rosenberg, J. (1994) *The Empire of Civil Society: A Critique of the Realist Theory of International Relations* (London: Verso).

Rosenberg, J. (1999) 'Just War and Intervention: The Challenge of the International for Social and Political Thought', paper presented at Sussex University International Relations/Social and Political Thought joint seminar series, 'The Kosovo War: Perspectives from Social, Political and International Theory', Summer. Available from: <http://www.sussex.ac.uk/Units/SPT/seminars/kosovo/seminar1>.

Rosemann, N. (2000) 'Lessons from Bosnia and Herzegovina: Human Rights Protection at the National and International Levels', paper presented at the Institute for Strengthening Democracy in Bosnia, Third International Seminar 'Democracy and Human Rights in Multi-Ethnic Societies', Konjic, Bosnia, 3–7 July.

Rotberg, R. I. (ed.) (2004) *When States Fail: Causes and Consequences* (Princeton: Princeton University Press).

Roy, O. (2001) 'Afghanistan After the Taliban', *New York Times*, 7 October.

Rozen, L. K. (2000a) 'Humanitarian Aid', *Boston Globe*, 30 July.

Rozen, L. K. (2000b) 'Bread Instead of Soldiers', *Salon*, 7 August. Available from: <http://www.salon.com/news/feature/2000/08/07/aid/index.html>.

Rozenberg, J. (2001) 'Does Bush Have the Law on his Side?, *Daily Telegraph*, 18 September.

Rumsfeld, D. (2001) 'Text of the Defense Secretary's Briefing on the Military Strikes, the Pentagon, 7 October 2001', *Associated Press*. Available from: <http://www.nytimes.com>.

Ryan, A. (2000) 'My Way', *New York Review of Books*, 10 August, pp. 47–50.

Sampson, A. (2000) 'Mandela Condemns "Policeman" Britain', *Guardian*, 5 April.

Sands, P. (2005) 'Lawless World: International Law after 9/11 and Iraq', Mishcon Lecture, 2005. Available from: <http://www.ucl.ac.uk/laws/mishcon/docs/Mishcon_2005_Sands.pdf>.

Savic, A. (2000) 'Positive Outcomes of the BWI Programme in Terms of Promoting Tolerance, Reconciliation and Dialogue in Multi-Ethnic Societies', speech given at the Institute for Strengthening Democracy in Bosnia, Third Seminar 'Democracy and Human Rights in Multi-Ethnic Societies', Konjic, Bosnia, 3–7 July.

Savic, O. (1999a) 'Introduction: The Global and the Local in Human Rights', in O. Savic (ed.) *The Politics of Human Rights* (London: Verso), pp. 3–15.

Savic, O. (1999b) 'Parallel Worlds', in O. Savic (ed.) *The Politics of Human Rights* (London: Verso), pp. 335–45.

Schachter, O. (1991) *International Law in Theory and Practice* (Dordrecht: Nijhoff).

Scheffer, D. J. (1999) 'Prosecuting War Criminals: Human Rights and International Law', *World Outlook*, No. 27, pp. 82–9.

Schnabel, A. and Thakur, R. (2000) 'Policy Brief: Lessons from the Kosovo Conflict', summary in A. Schnabel and R. Thakur (eds) *Kosovo and the Challenge of Humanitarian Intervention: Selective Indignation, Collective Intervention, and International Citizenship* (forthcoming: United Nations University), pp. 7–12. Summary available from: <http://www.unu.edu/p&g/kosovo_full.htm>.

Schwarz, B. (2000) 'Round Three: Concluding Remarks'. Roundtable: Picking a Good Fight, *Atlantic*, 14 April. Available from: <http://www.theatlantic.com/unbound/roundtable/goodfight/schwarz3>.

Sciolino, E. and Myers, S. L. (2001) 'Bush Says "Time is Running Out" as Forces Move Into Place', *New York Times*, 7 October.

Searls, H. (1995) 'The NGO Revolution', unpublished discussion paper.

Sellars, K. (1999) 'The Tyranny of Human Rights', *Spectator*, 28 August, pp. 11–12.

SGESC (2004) *A Human Security Doctrine for Europe: The Barcelona Report of the Study Group on Europe's Security Capabilities*. Available from: <http://www.lse.ac.uk/Depts/global/Human%20Security%20Report%20Full.pdf>.

Shaw, M. (1994) *Global Society and International Relations: Sociological Concepts and Political Perspectives* (Cambridge: Polity Press).

Shaw, M. (1999) 'Global Voices: Civil Society and the Media in Global Crises', in T. Dunne and N. J. Wheeler (eds) *Human Rights in Global Politics* (Cambridge: Cambridge University Press), pp. 214–32.

Shaw, M. (2000) 'On Slaughter: Mass Killing from War to Genocide', paper presented to Sussex University International Relations and Social and Political Thought joint seminar series 'The New World Order Ten Years On: Norms, Values and Morality in Contemporary Politics'. Available from: <http://www.sussex.ac.uk/Users/hafa3/slaughter>.

Shaw, M. (2001) 'Hard Heads, Soft Liberals', Letters, *Guardian*, 1 November.

Shestack, J. J. (1997) 'Globalization of Human Rights Law', *Fordham International Law Journal*, Vol. 21, No. 2, pp. 558–68.

Shiratori, R. (2000) 'Democratic Government and the Divided Country'. speech given at the Institute for Strengthening Democracy in Bosnia, Third Seminar 'Democracy and Human Rights in Multi-Ethnic Societies', Konjic, Bosnia, 3–7 July.

Shue, H. (1980) *Basic Rights* (Princeton: Princeton University Press).

Shute, S. and Hurley, S. (1993) Introduction, in S. Shute and S. Hurley (eds) *On Human Rights* (New York: Basic Books), pp. 1–18.

Simma, B. (1999) 'Nato, the UN and the Use of Force: Legal Aspects', *European Journal of International Law*, Vol. 10, pp. 1–22.

Simpson, G. (2004) *Great Powers and Outlaw States: Unequal Sovereigns in the International Legal Order* (Cambridge: Cambridge University Press).

Simpson, J. (2001) 'Vicious Taliban Bullies Have no Stomach for the Real Fight Ahead', *Sunday Telegraph*, 7 October.

Skoco, M. and Woodger, W. (2000) 'War Crimes', in P. Hammond and E. S. Herman (eds) *Degraded Capability: The Media and the Kosovo Crisis* (London: Pluto Press), pp. 39–55.

Smillie, I. (1995) *The Alms Bazaar: Altruism under Fire* (London: Intermediate Technology Publications).

Socolovsky, J. (2000) 'Congo Fails to get World Court Order Blocking Arrest Warrant', *Associated Press*, 12 August.

Solomon, N. (2001) 'TV News: A Militarized Zone', 8 October. Available from: <http://www.fair.org/media-beat>.

Sontag, S. (1999) 'An Evil that Makes the Balkan War Just', *Observer*, 16 May.

Stammers, N. (1995) 'A Critique of Social Approaches to Human Rights', *Human Rights Quarterly*, Vol. 17, pp. 488–508.

Stammers, N. (1999) 'Social Movements and the Social Construction of Human Rights', *Human Rights Quarterly*, Vol. 21, pp. 980–1008.

Steele, J. (2000a) 'Serb Killings Exaggerated By West', *Guardian*, 18 August.

Steele, J. (2000b) 'Motivated to Believe the Worst', *Guardian*, 18 August.

Steele, J. (2001) 'Raids Justified by UN Resolutions, US Says', *Guardian*, 9 October.

Steele, J. and Lawrence, F. (2001) 'Aid Agencies Reject "Risky" US Air Drops', *Guardian*, 8 October.

Stockton, N. (1998) 'In Defence of Humanitarianism', *Disasters*, Vol. 22, No. 4, pp. 352–60.

Stoker, G. (1996) 'Introduction: Normative Theories of Local Government and Democracy', in D. King and G. Stoker (eds) *Rethinking Local Democracy* (London: Macmillan), pp. 1–27.

Stone, C. (2000) 'An Insider's View of the International War Crimes Tribunal at The Hague'. Available from: <http://www.bhhrg.org>.

Straw, J. (2001a) 'Speech by the Foreign Secretary, Jack Straw, to the International Institute of Strategic Studies, London, Monday 22 October 2001'. Available from: <http://www.fco.gov.uk/news/speechtext.asp?5448>.

Straw, J. (2001b) 'Building Will Follow the Bombing', *Guardian*, 26 October.

Straw, J. (2002) 'Failed and Failing States: Speech by the Foreign Secretary at the European Research Institute, University of Birmingham', 6 September. Available from: <http://www.eri.bham.ac.uk/events/jstraw060902.pdf>.

Sullivan, A. (2001) 'Victory is an Article of Faith for Bush', *Sunday Times*, 28 October.

Sulyok, G. (2004) 'Review of *From Kosovo to Kabul*', *European Journal of International Law*, Vol. 15, No. 5, pp. 1058–63.

Szafarz, R. (1992) 'CSCE: an International Organization in *Statu Nascendi*?', in A. Bloed and W. de Jonge (eds) *Legal Aspects of a New European Infrastructure* (Utrecht: Europa Instituut/Nederlands Helsinki Comite), pp. 15–22.

Taylor, P. (1999) 'The United Nations in the 1990s: Proactive Cosmopolitanism and the Issue of Sovereignty', *Political Studies*, Vol. 47, No. 3, pp. 538–65.

Taylor, P. M. (1997) *Global Communications, International Affairs and the Media since 1945* (London: Routledge).

Thakur, R. (2001) 'Global Norms and International Humanitarian Law: An Asian Perspective', *International Review of the Red Cross*, March, Vol. 83, No. 841, pp. 19–44.

Thomas, M. (2000) 'Co-ordination in Kosovo: A Failure of Multilateralism', *Talk Back*, The Newsletter of the International Council of Voluntary Agencies (ICVA), Vol. 2, No. 1, 18 February.

Thurer, D. (1999) 'The "Failed State" and International Law', *International Review of the Red Cross*, No. 836, pp. 731–61.

The Times (2001) 'Coverage Under Fire', 1 November.

Toynbee, P. (2001) 'There is Blood on Our Hands but the Taliban are Worse', *Guardian*, 31 October.

Travis, A. and Dyer, C. (2000) 'Power Shifts to the Judges', *Guardian*, 11 September.

UKFAC (1998) *First Report*, Session 1998–1999, United Kingdom House of Commons Foreign Affairs Committee, 21 December. Available from: <http://www.parliament.the-stationary-off...a/cm199899/cmselect/cmfaff/100/10007>.

UKFAC (2000a) 'Annual Report on Human Rights 1999', *First Report*, Session 1999–2000, United Kingdom House of Commons Foreign Affairs Committee, March. Available from: <http://www.publications.parliament.uk/pa/cm/cmselect/cmfaff/ 41/4103>.

UKFAC (2000b) 'Response of the Secretary of State for Foreign and Commonwealth Affairs, Annual Report on Human Rights 1999', *First Report*, Session 1999–2000, United Kingdom House of Commons Foreign Affairs Committee, March (London: Stationary Office).

UKFAC (2000c) *Fourth Report*, Session 1999–2000, United Kingdom House of Commons Foreign Affairs Committee, 23 May. Available from: <http://www.publications.parliament.uk/pa/cm199900/cmselect/cmfaff/ 28/2802>.

UKFCO (1999) 'Doctrine of the International Community, Speech by the UK Prime Minister Tony Blair to the Economic Club of Chicago, Hilton Hotel, Chicago, USA', Foreign and Commonwealth Office, 22 April. Available from: <http://www.globalpolicy.org/globaliz/politics/blair.htm>.

UKJCC (2000) 'United Nations Reform: Peace and Security', Joint Consultative Committee Paper, September. E-mail communication from the Liberal Democrats Whips Office, House of Commons, 5 September.

UKSCD (1998) *Eighth Report*, Session 1997–1998, United Kingdom House of Commons Select Committee on Defence, 10 September. Available from: <http://www.parliament.the-stationary-off...cm199798/cmselect/cmdfence/138/23809>.

Ulbrich, J. (2000) 'In Europe, "Neutrality" is a Concept Whose Time has Passed', *Associated Press*, 29 August.

UN (1992) *An Agenda for Peace: Preventive Diplomacy, Peacemaking and Peacekeeping*, Report of the Secretary-General (A/47/277–S/24111), 17 June.

UN (1994) *An Agenda for Development*, Report of the Secretary-General (A/48/935), 6 May.

UN (1995) *Supplement to an Agenda for Peace*, Position Paper of the Secretary-General on the Occasion of the Fiftieth Anniversary of the United Nations (A/50/60–S/1995/1), 3 January.

UN (1996) 'States Must be Honest About Human Rights, Accept Constructive Criticism, Third Committee Told in Rights Debate', Press Release (GA/SHC/3400), 22 November.

UN (1998) 'Assembly President Stresses "Creative Force" of Universal Declaration', Press Release (GA/SM/4398), 10 December.

UN (1999a) *Promotion of the Right to Democracy*, Commission on Human Rights Resolution 1999/57 (E/CN.4/RES/1999/57), 28 April.

UN (1999b) 'Secretary-General says Global Effort Against Armed Conflict Needs Change from "Culture of Reaction to Culture of Prevention"', Press Release (SC/6759), 29 November.

UN (2000a) *Promoting and Consolidating Democracy*, Commission on Human Rights Resolution 2000/47 (E/CN.4/RES/2000/47), 25 April.

UN (2000b) *'We the Peoples': The Role of the United Nations in the 21st Century*, Millennium Report of the Secretary-General (A/54/2000), (New York: United Nations). Available from: <http://www.un.org/millennium/sg/report>.

UN (2000c) *Report of the Panel on United Nations Peace Operations*, United Nations General Assembly Security Council, 21 August. Available from: <http://www.un.org/peace/reports/peace-operations/>.

UN (2004) *A More Secure World: Our Shared Responsibility, Report of the Secretary-General's High Level Panel on Threats, Challenges and Change*, 15 September. Available from: <http://www.un.org/secureworld/>.

Urquhart, B. (2000) 'In the Name of Humanity', *New York Review of Books*, Vol. XLVII, No. 7, 27 April, pp. 19–22.

US (2002) *The National Security Strategy of the United States of America* (Washington, DC: White House). Available from: <http://www.whitehouse.gov/nsc/nss.pdf>.

USDoS (2000) 'On the Record Briefing Secretary of State Madeleine K. Albright And Assistant Secretary of State for Democracy, Human Rights and Labour Harold Hongju Koh on the Country Reports on Human Rights Practices for 1999', Washington, DC, 25 February.

Verdery, K. (1996) 'Nationalism, Postsocialism, and Space in Eastern Europe', *Social Research*, Vol. 63, No. 1, pp. 7–96.

Vincent, R. J. (1986) Conclusion, in R. J. Vincent (ed.) *Foreign Policy and Human Rights: Issues and Responses* (Cambridge: Royal Institute of International Affairs/Cambridge University Press), pp. 261–65.

Vincent, R. J. (1992) 'The Idea of Rights in International Ethics', in T. Nardin and D. R. Mapel (eds) *Traditions of International Ethics* (Cambridge: Cambridge University Press).

Waal, A. de (1997a) *Famine Crimes: Politics and the Disaster Relief Industry in Africa* (Oxford: James Currey/Indiana University Press).

Waal, A. de (1997b) 'Becoming Shameless: The Failure of Human-Rights Organizations in Rwanda', *Times Literary Supplement*, 21 February, pp. 3–4.

Wadham, J. (2000) 'Human Rights and Judges', speech at 'War Crimes, Litigiousness & Judges: Legal Issues of the 21st Century', University College London, 1 July.

Wadham, J. and Lawrence, I. (2000) 'Will Society Lose Out to the Individual When the European Convention on Human Rights is Introduced?', *Guardian*, 12 August.

Wagenseil, S. (1999) 'Human Rights in US Foreign Policy', *Journal of Intergroup Relations*, Vol. 26, pp. 3–13.

Waldron, J. (ed.) (1987) *Nonsense Upon Stilts: Bentham, Burke and Marx on the Rights of Man* (London: Methuen).

Walker, R. B. J. (1997) 'The Subject of Security', in K. Krause and M. C. Williams (eds) *Critical Security Studies: Concepts and Cases* (Minneapolis: University of Minnesota Press).

Walzer, M. (1997) *Just and Unjust Wars: A Moral Argument with Historical Illustrations* (New York: Basic Books).

Warner, D. (1999) 'The Politics of the Political/Humanitarian Divide', *International Review of the Red Cross*, No. 833, pp. 109–18.

Wartburg, W. von (2000) 'Neutralität ist Universelle Friedenspolitik', *Zeit-Fragen*, No. 65, 20 March.

Washington Post (2000) 'Lawsuits and Foreign Policy', Editorial, 12 August.

Washington Post (2001) 'Return to Nation-Building', Editorial, 14 October.

Watson, R. and Whitworth, D. (2001) 'Bush: "I Gave Them a Fair Chance"', *The Times*, 8 October.

Watt, N. and Denny, C. (2001) 'Allies Step Up the Media War', *Guardian*, 1 November.

WCC (1993) World Council of Churches – Programme on Humanitarian Assistance, *The Mohonk Criteria for Humanitarian Assistance in Complex Emergencies* (Geneva: World Council of Churches).

Webster, P. (2001a) 'Nuclear Safety of World is at Stake, Blair Tells Troops', *The Times*, 27 October.

Webster, P. (2001b) 'Don't Wobble, Warns Blair', *The Times*, 29 October.

Wedgewood, R. (1999) 'Nato's Campaign in Yugoslavia', *American Journal of International Law*, Vol. 93, pp. 828–34.

Weintraub, J. (1997) 'The Theory and Politics of the Public/Private Distinction', in J. Weintraub and K. Kumar (eds) *Public and Private in Thought and Practice: Perspectives on a Grand Dichotomy* (Chicago: University of Chicago Press), pp. 1–42.

Weiss, T. G. (1999) 'Principles, Politics and Humanitarian Action', *Ethics and International Affairs*, Vol. 13, pp. 1–22.

Weiss, T. G. (2000) 'The Politics of Humanitarian Ideas', *Security Dialogue*, Vol. 31, No. 1, pp. 11–23.

Weller, M. (1999a) 'Armed Samaritans', *Counsel*, August, pp. 20–2.

Weller, M. (1999b) 'The US, Iraq and the Use of Force in a Unipolar World', *Survival*, Vol. 41, No. 4, pp. 81–100.

Wells, M. (2001) 'CNN to Carry Hijack Reminders', *Guardian*, 1 November.

Weschler, L. (1999) 'International Humanitarian Law: An Overview', in R. Gutman and D. Rieff (eds) *Crimes of War: What the Public Should Know* (New York: W. W. Norton), pp. 18–22.

Weston, B. H. (1991) 'Security Council Resolution 678 and Persian Gulf War Decision Making: Precarious Legitimacy', *American Journal of International Law*, Vol. 85, No. 3, pp. 516–35.

Wheeler, N. J. (1996) 'Guardian Angel or Global Gangster: A Review of the Ethical Claims of International Society', *Political Studies*, Vol. 44, No. 1, pp. 123–35.

Wheeler, N. J. (1997) 'Agency, Humanitarianism and Intervention', *International Political Science Review*, Vol. 18, No. 1, pp. 9–26.

Wheeler, N. J. (2000) *Saving Strangers: Humanitarian Intervention in International Society* (Oxford: Oxford University Press).

Wheeler, N. J. (2004) 'Humanitarian Intervention after September 11', in T. Lang (ed.) *Humanitarian Intervention: The Moral Dimension* (Washington, DC: Georgetown University Press).

White, M. (2001) 'Uneasy Rebels Plan Campaign to Halt Bombing', *Guardian*, 19 October.

Whitman, R. (1998) *From Civilian Power to Superpower? The International Identity of the European Union* (Basingstoke: Macmillan).

Whitney, C. R. (1999) 'The No Man's Land in the Fight for Human Rights', *New York Times*, 12 December.

Whittaker, B. (1983) *A Bridge of People* (London: Heinemann).

Wintour, P. (2000) 'Memo Leak Reveals Rattled PM', *Guardian*, 17 July.

Wintour, P. (2001a) 'Blair's Vision for Afghan Future', *Guardian*, 10 October.

Wintour, P. (2001b) 'Blair Dismisses Calls to Suspend Bombing', *Guardian*, 18 October.

Wintour, P. and White, M. (2001) 'We're in for the Long Haul – Blair', *Guardian*, 9 October.

Wong, E. (2000) 'Rights Group has Summons Served on Li Peng in New York', *New York Times*, 1 September.

Wood, E. M. (1991) *The Pristine Culture of Capitalism: A Historical Essay on Old Regimes and Modern States* (London: Verso).

Wood, E. M. (1995) *Democracy Against Capitalism: Renewing Historical Materialism* (London; Verso).

Woodger, W. (1997) 'The Letter of Democracy and the Spirit of Censorship: The West Runs the Media in Bosnia', unpublished paper, October.

Woodward, S. L. (1995) *Balkan Tragedy: Chaos and Dissolution after the Cold War* (Washington, DC: Brookings Institution).

Woollacott, M. (2001) 'Blair is Right to Revive the Idea of a "New World Order"', *Guardian*, 5 October.

Worsthorne, P. (1999) 'Good Intentions', *Guardian*, 8 May.

Wren, C. S. and Steinberg, J. (2001) 'US and Britain Clearing Way for "Relentless" Campaign, Bush Says', *New York Times*, 7 October.

Wright, R. (2000) 'Croatia in War Crimes Dilemma', *Financial Times*, 23 August.

Yannis, A. (2002) 'The Concept of Suspended Sovereignty in International Law and its Implications in International Politics', *European Journal of International Law*, Vol. 13, No. 5, pp. 1037–52.

Young, H. (1999a) 'The Free World Does Need a Leader, but Clinton is Not It', *Guardian*, 11 May.

Young, H. (1999b) 'The Time has Come to Send Home the Butcher of Chile', *Guardian*, 21 October.

Zartman, I. W. (1995) *Collapsed States: The Disintegration and Restoration of Legitimate Authority* (Boulder: Lynne Rienner).

Zizek, S. (1999) *The Ticklish Subject* (London: Verso).

Zizek, S. (2000) *The Fragile Absolute or, Why is the Christian Legacy Worth Fighting For?* (London: Verso).

Zweig, S. (1996) *Beware of Pity* (Evanston: Northwestern University Press).

Index